The Impact of the Internet
on Our Moral Lives

THE IMPACT OF THE INTERNET ON OUR MORAL LIVES

ROBERT J. CAVALIER

STATE UNIVERSITY OF NEW YORK PRESS

Published by
STATE UNIVERSITY OF NEW YORK PRESS
ALBANY

© 2005 State University of New York

For information, address State University of New York Press,
194 Washington Avenue, Suite 305, Albany, NY 12210-2384

Production, Laurie Searl
Marketing, Susan Petrie

Library of Congress Cataloging-in-Publication Data

Cavalier, Robert J.
  The impact of the Internet on our moral lives / Robert J. Cavalier.
    p. cm.
  Includes bibliographical references and index.
  ISBN 0-7914-6345-1 (alk. paper) — ISBN 0-7914-6346-X (pbk. : alk. paper)
    1. Internet—Moral and ethical aspects. I. Title.

TK5105.878.C38 2005
303.48'33—dc22

2004045400

10   9   8   7   6   5   4   3   2   1

Dedicated to

Preston K. Covey

a mentor to many of us,

a visionary for all of us

Contents

PART II

Introduction

ROBERT J. CAVALIER

The Cyberpolis we now inhabit poses new challenges to living life success-fully. It also creates new areas for philosophical reflection on these chal-lenges. Many negative aspects of the Internet are simply extensions of the moral life we lead in "real life." But cyberspace also encroaches on us in ways that would never occur to us in regular navigation through our cities, our relations, both personal and professional, and even our states of mind. This collection seeks to explore this impact of the Internet on our moral lives.

While the text is not strictly or exclusively Aristotelian, themes found in Aristotle do appear in various chapters. Aristotle was keen to show the com-plex relation between our cultural and political environment and our ability to live life well or poorly. And he emphasized the role that the virtues play in helping us 'hit the mark' in both our private and public lives. His observa-tions can be relevant to our virtual environment as well. This is most obvi-ous in Part I, in which Aristotle is linked to the work of Norbert Wiener and the impact of the Internet on our inner lives and outward behavior finds expression in such areas as copyright infringement, cheating, and cyber-pornography. Part II contains ontological, cultural, and meta-ethical analyses generated by the very idea of the Internet itself and its impact on who we are and what we can do. This section shows how ethics might help us see these matters more clearly.

The historical emergence of the electronic computer in the 1940s, the Internet in the 1960s, and the World Wide Web in the 1990s converges with and simultaneously creates new types of cases and situations that confront our moral sensibilities and challenge our decision-making capabilities. In so doing, the Information Age (of which the computer is an icon) has given rise to the field of computer ethics. Terrell Bynum's opening chapter traces many of our interests in the ethical and social aspects of the Internet to the writings of mathematician and communication theorist Norbert Wiener. Along with the work of Shannon and Weaver, Wiener applied technical theories of communication to the field of what he called "cybernetics." He also noted the consequence of man–machine communication theory for human flourishing and thus became one of the first to foresee the impact of the "Automatic Age" on our social and moral existence. Bynum finds some fascinating parallels between Aristotle and Wiener here, and uses these parallels to describe Wiener's appropriation of the science of his day to such basic ideas as the nature of humans and the purpose of life. In elucidating Wiener's methodology for what we today call "information ethics," Bynum describes the impact of information technology on human values (such as security and happiness), the social implications of "computerized factories," and the positive contributions of "artificial lungs" and other prosthesis technologies. Wiener even foresaw the creation of a global communications network akin to the Internet and thus anticipated, with his concerns and methods, many of the topics covered in this volume.

Richard Spinello tackles the Napster phenomena in the second chapter. The long philosophical and legal discussion of "property" confronts new challenges in the digital nature of "intellectual property." So, too, do the traditional frameworks for regulating property: more and more social norms seem to sanction the sharing of digital files and, as many college students will attest, the sharing of copyrighted music files is now the way one finds and listens to songs. But a careful analysis of the reasons for copyright law uncovers the role that it can play for the common good. Surely, Spinello argues, some protection of the costs and labor that go into the creation and publication of artistic works is necessary (even Steven Levy was distressed to see his book, *Hackers*, available for free download). But current proposals for software involving digital rights architectures go to extremes. It is important, Spinello says, to return to moral norms and heighten in the minds of users the intensity of the meaning of digital piracy. Using legal arguments that echo Aristotle and Aquinas, we see the need to appreciate the place of law in our lives; with moral arguments from contemporary philosophers like Christine Korsgaard and Bernard Gert, we observe the connection between "illegally copying a software program" and "violating a morally acceptable law to gain some benefit." But a central problem with regard to Napster-like piracy or the casual copying of office software is that for most people this is a moral issue of such "low intensity" that it may not be seen as a moral matter at all. Hence the importance, Spinello argues, of "strengthening the voice of morality." He suggests several ways to achieve this, not the least of which is "to demonstrate that the ramifications of disregarding copyright law for personal satisfaction are not so trivial." A second moral concern relates to the developers of code for the protection of software: awareness of the legitimate needs of users must be built into the software architecture itself. Taken together, the proper understanding of "ethics" and "code" can work in fruitful ways to address the issue of copyright in cyberspace. This chapter should be read alongside Helen Nissenbaum's discussion of hacker culture and her view of the status of property in cyberspace.

The power of search engines and the ease with which people can find materials and copypaste them (unattributed) into term papers, business reports, and even published articles has had a powerful effect on the reliability of original work. In chapter 3, Lawrence Hinman combines philosophical reflection with practical advice regarding what I call "autoplagiarism." Hinman has served on disciplinary boards and crafted documents on academic integrity, and he finds much in Aristotle's ethics relevant to the discussion of cheating. Following Donald McCabe's pre-Web empirical research in this area, he divides students into those who "never cheat," "cheat occasionally," and "habitually cheat." Those roughly 20 percent of the students who never cheat need a campus culture that, he argues, is as "supportive as possible of their commitment to academic integrity." The middle group, roughly 60 percent in the McCabe study, are the ones most tempted by the Internet to engage in intermittent and spontaneous cheating (often caused by deadlines and panicked desires to get a higher grade). The last 20 percent fall into the hard-core group, those who cheat habitually and without scruple. Hinman uses Aristotle's famous discussion of performing right and wrong actions to analyze these types of noncheaters and cheaters. For those who don't cheat, they seem either to desire to do the right thing for its own sake (the "temperate") or because they know it is the right thing to do, even though they might desire to do otherwise (the "continent"). In both cases, these students exercise a degree of "self-restraint." Of those who do cheat, there are some who exhibit what was once called "weakness of the will." The temptation to copy sections of another's Web page into their paper, for example, just seemed too easy to do given the pressure of the due date, the difficulty of the topic, and so on. By far, most students who cheat fall into either this group or the "continent" group and they are the ones most tempted use the Internet to do something they would regret on reflection (or on being caught). The last group chooses to cheat and is not bothered by it. They fall into the category of the "incontinent" for Aristotle; they are the bad apples and can only be dissuaded by strict monitoring. For all the others, some discussion of the virtues of academic integrity might be of use. It is to these fundamental virtues of honesty, trust, fairness, respect, and responsibility that Hinman turns in the second part of his chapter. Following this rich discussion, he addresses the issues of distance learning and digital file sharing and their effects on online academic integrity.

One of the most hotly debated topics concerning the Internet is pornography. Susan Dwyer reviews the common arguments revolving around the moral (and legal) status of pornography and finds that the issue can be approached somewhat differently, given the unique power of the Internet. Chapter 4 revives an ancient concern with the inner self and suggests that the practice of consuming pornography online carries risks of doing harm (though not of the kind that would involve state censorship). Surely there are Internet sites that will cause even the most jaded some cause for concern: "Hanging Bitches" is devoted to images of women being hung from rafters and so forth; certain sites specialize in images of forced rape and torture; illegal sites contain prepubescent child pornography. What the Internet enables, indeed encourages through the use of Java scripts and cookies, is an ever-cascading progress from 'regular' porn to its most extreme forms. And the cultivation of such fantasizing made possible by the Web is not without consequences for our sense of moral agency. Dwyer argues that these kinds of sexual fantasizing are *actions* that affect one's self (creating an ugliness of one's soul, as Plato might say). A thought experiment seeks to reveal this phenomenon: imagine two worlds, A and B, and imagine that in World A people have the most violent sexual fantasies (though they never act them out) and in World B people do not have these kinds of fantasies. The *Gedanken* asks: Which is the morally preferable world?

John Weckert discusses a central moral issue confronting the Information Age: online trust. He seeks to link the concept of trust to the very human dimensions of goodwill and friendship. But he also attempts to analyze the concept following the tradition of analytic philosophy: What does it really *mean* to say that A trusts B? For Weckert, trust (online or offline) is not solely a cognitive matter (as if "Jones trusts Smith" translates into a set of expectations that a rational actor applies when placing a bet). Trust is best construed in terms of "Seeing as": "Jones's seeing Smith as trustworthy is reasonable to the extent that Jones's seeing Smith in this way gives a coherent account of Smith's behavior." Adopting a position going back to the American pragmatist William James, he argues that genuine trust online emerges when those online *see* others online *as* trustworthy (the U.S. stock market crisis of 2002 demonstrates what happens when people stop seeing X as trustworthy). There are daunting obstacles to achieving online trust, but Weckert points to empirical studies of "virtual teams" in which such trust plays an important part in successful projects. And while we might not trust the e-mail that entices us to "open the attached files," many people now buy the bulk of their books online. Weckert's analysis may help us to understand that better.

Aristotle's definition of "man" as a "rational animal" has survived through the centuries. Formally, human beings are part of the genus "animal" and we are bipeds like apes. But the specific difference between an ape and a human being is that the latter has "reason." This is the essential nature of man as expressed in the Aristotelian definition. With the computational turn taking place in fields as diverse as psychology, robotics, philosophy, and cognitive science, this fundamental notion of what it means to be human is undergoing a profound transformation. What if "information processor" became a new genus? Would it not be possible to speak of "man," "whale," and "computer" as a species of information processors (the first two being carbon based, the latter silicon based)? The potential for a radical transformation of what it means to be human marks the transition to Part II when James Moor poses the question: "Should we let computers get under our skin?"

Moor's chapter focuses on the use of computer implants to create cyborgs. He points out that many of us are already cyborgs to the extent that we use cardiac pacemakers and a whole range of transplant products coming out of the field of biotechnology. So it is not a question of whether we should become cyborgs, but how we should do so in light of potential ethical problems. He reviews the debate over the use of computer implants for therapy and/or enhancement. As the controversy over cochlear implants has shown, it is not always easy to draw the line between therapy and enhancement. (Is hearing really such a disability that it requires therapeutic use of implants in all cases?) From another perspective, should people be free to avail themselves of computer-based enhancements as long as they do no harm to others? Moor is sympathetic to this Millian argument, but he is also aware of the slippery slope toward the Borg world of *Star Trek* fame. One can imagine a "Web/human system" that begins to take on a life of its own, where control of our actions becomes ambiguous at best. There are practical moral consequences and policy vacuums awaiting us in this brave new world. Moor looks at these from the perspectives of privacy, control, and fairness.

Today the term "hacker" has become associated with the world of malcontent adolescents, hactivist true believers, and high-tech terrorists. But Helen Nissenbaum reminds us that this was not always so and that the term "hacker" has itself been highjacked by the media to stand for something it did not originally mean. Chapter 7 seeks to find a framework for the shifting interpretation of the hacker, from the hero of Steve Levy's book on the heyday of programming in the 1980s to the criminal vandals of today. At least a part of this shift can be understood as a change in the ontological meaning of cyberspace: from the new frontier envisioned by John Perry Barlow to the current marketplace with its property rights and economic infrastructure. The latter can be seen in property metaphors and norms of behavior that constitute what some have called a "second enclosure movement." The results of this shift in the meaning of cyberspace are best understood, argues Nissembaum, by following John Searle's work on the construction of social reality. In this new environment, hackers (in the traditional sense) are seen as the bad actors (breakers of the rules and norms of the newly institutionalized world of cyberspace). Worse still, they become residual elements of a fervent programming ethic that are subsumed under the prototypical category of

criminal behavior (the latter actually referring to "crackers" for those favor-
ing a more nuanced terminology).

The once utopian vision of the Internet as a global village has in fact created a cyberworld that embeds (for better or worse) much of the Western,
indeed American, values of commerce (including the free market of pornography) carried out in the language of English. It is not surprising that this cultural flavor of the Internet has evoked strong reaction. Benjamin Barber's
rhetorical disjunction, Jihad or McWorld, points to a crisis within cultures
seeking to sustain their identities in the face of global homogenization.
Charles Ess's chapter seeks a way to retrieve cultural identity (both for the
person and the society) within the thoughtful use of computer-mediated
communication (CMC) technologies. After a survey of various cultural adap-
tations of CMC (including examples from South Korea and Kuwait), Ess suggests a Habermasian interpretation of the global village, one informed by a
"culture of dialogue" aimed, in part, at preserving and enhancing diverse cultural identities. Here, CMC users will be enmeshed in their "thick cultures"
as "embodied users" interwoven with a specific history and community. Ess
discusses feminist and postmodern perspectives on these matters and concludes with an "Educational Imperative" that sketches out a possible synthesis of Eastern and Western traditions with regard to thoughtful use of the
Internet. Integral to this education is the Medieval and Renaissance experience of "cultural flows" that were once obtained by personal travel but can
now become part of our practical wisdom through a Web that sees others as
others (and not just consumers for our products, etc.). The Socratic passage
out of Plato's cave can be viewed as a perspective-taking on our own culture
and an appreciation of other cultures (the ignorance overcome here is that of
ethnocentrism). In this regard, Aristotle's *phroneisis* is not only an ethical
virtue, but a wisdom filled with cultural experiences and dialogues. These
Western conceptions of virtue and wisdom, finally, cohere with the Confucian goal of becoming a truly "exemplary person."

Charles Ess's tantalizing speculations about the potential of the World
Wide Web are continued in chapter 9 by Luciano Floridi and J. W. Sanders.
Just as Aristotle's *Poetics* focused on our human ability to *create* and *produce*
drama and epic poetry, the authors here emphasize our ability to use the Web
in a "poetical way." Indeed, they argue that viewing the Web as a "poetically
enabling environment" entails a certain kind of "constructionist ethics" well
positioned to reflect on the meaning and use of the Web itself. Constructionist ethics can be seen in the idea that persons "construct their lives" and,
assuming that they want to be the best they can be, they do so by cultivating
certain virtues and eradicating certain vices. From this perspective, a virtue
ethics is a kind of existentialist ethics. It focuses on a subject-oriented
approach and its concomitant philosophical anthropology. But, the authors
argue, a change in the *direction* of constructionism is required to move from

"individual virtues" to "global values." This move recognizes the agent's responsibility toward the digital environment that it creates. It forms the theoretical ground for a future cyberethics.

Using Hans Jonas's classic work on the impact of modern technology on our moral condition as a point of departure, Herman Tavani's chapter reviews the current debate about whether the Internet creates novel circumstances that supercede our previous conceptual apparatus for analyzing and understanding our "moral condition." Along the way he discusses "expansionist and traditionalist" responses to the types of cases that seem to arise through the Internet (e.g., "cyberstalking"). Expansionists argue that the Internet alters the *scope* and *scale* of our behavior to such an extent that our traditional categories of ethics need to be expanded as well (in order to account for behaviors such as cyberstalking, online rape, digital child pornography, etc.). Traditionalists deny that entirely new ethical theories are necessary. They also deny that the Internet poses any truly new challenges. Tavani agrees with first part of the part of the traditionalist theory, but disagrees with the second. To support his position, he discusses Brey's "disclosive method" and Moor's concept of "policy vacuum" and concludes that, until there are new kinds of "objects" that warrant special consideration (like the robots in the movie *AI*), Brey and Moor's insights provide us with an adequate methodological framework. The "meta-ethical" nature of this chapter can be compared to the reflections of Floridi and Sanders in their discussion of *homo poieticus*.

Many of the scholars represented in this collection gave presentations on their topics through the University Lecture Series at Carnegie Mellon, special sessions at the American Philosophical Association (sponsored by the APA Committee on Philosophy and Computers), and panels at the Computing and Philosophy (CAP) conferences. The editor would like to thank those groups that made these presentations possible.

PART I

ONE

Norbert Wiener's Vision

The Impact of the "Automatic Age" on Our Moral Lives

TERRELL WARD BYNUM

FORESEEING THE INFORMATION AGE

DURING THE SECOND WORLD WAR, while working to design a new kind of antiaircraft cannon, mathematician Norbert Wiener and several of his colleagues developed a new branch of applied science—the science of information feedback systems—that Wiener named "cybernetics." With impressive foresight, Wiener realized that this new science, when combined with the electronic digital computers that were being developed to support the war effort, had enormous social and ethical implications. Soon after the Second World War, therefore, Wiener began to write and lecture about the social and ethical challenges of the coming "automatic age," which he also called "the second industrial revolution." As early as 1948, in his book *Cybernetics: or Control and Communication in the Animal and the Machine*, Wiener published the following comments:

> It has long been clear to me that the modern ultra-rapid computing machine was in principle an ideal central nervous system to an apparatus for automatic control; and that its input and output need not be in the form of numbers or diagrams but might very well be, respectively, the readings of artificial sense organs, such as photoelectric cells or thermometers, and the

11

performance of motors or solenoids. . . . Long before Nagasaki and the public awareness of the atomic bomb, it had occurred to me that we were here in the presence of another social potentiality of unheard-of importance for good and for evil. (Wiener, 1948, p. 36)

Perhaps I may clarify the historical background of the present situation if I say that the first industrial revolution, the revolution of the "dark satanic mills," was the devaluation of the human arm by the competition of machinery. . . . The modern industrial revolution [i.e., the computer revolution] is similarly bound to devalue the human brain. . . . The answer, of course, is to have a society based on human values other than buying and selling. To arrive at this society, we need a good deal of planning and a good deal of struggle. (pp. 37–38, bracketed words added)

In his writings on the social and ethical impact of this "automatic age," Wiener examined ways in which information and communication technology could affect—both positively and negatively—*fundamental human values*, such as life and health, work and wealth, knowledge and ability, creativity and happiness, democracy and freedom, peace and security.

Wiener's groundbreaking research on the ethical implications of "the modern ultra-rapid computing machine" and related technologies established him as a seminal figure in the applied ethics field that, today, is variously called "computer ethics," "information ethics," or "ICT ethics" (information and communication technology ethics). *Information ethics* is perhaps the most appropriate name for Wiener's field of ethical research, because it concerned all means of storing, transmitting, and processing information, including, for example, perception, memory, printing, phonographs, telephones, telegraph, radio, television, computers, and so on. (Henceforth, in this chapter, the term "information ethics"[1] will be used to refer to the applied ethics field that Wiener founded.)

The central importance of information in a human life, from Wiener's point of view, is revealed in the following quotation from his book *The Human Use of Human Beings: Cybernetics and Society:*[2]

Information is a name for the content of what is exchanged with the outer world as we adjust to it, and make our adjustment felt upon it. The process of receiving and of using information is the process of our adjusting to the contingencies of the outer environment, and of our living effectively within that environment. The needs and the complexity of modern life make greater demands on this process of information than ever before. . . . To live effectively is to live with adequate information. Thus, communication and control belong to the essence of man's inner life, even as they belong to his life in society. (Wiener, 1954, pp. 17–18)

AN ARISTOTELIAN FOUNDATION
FOR INFORMATION ETHICS

In creating the field of information ethics, Wiener laid down a foundation that is very Aristotelian.[3] Although there is no evidence that he explicitly based himself on Aristotle, the similarities are striking between Aristotle's accounts of animal behavior and human action on the one hand, and Wiener's explanations of animal behavior, human action, and machine agency on the other. (See Bynum, 1986, for the Aristotelian details.) Both Aristotle and Wiener described animals, including humans, as information-processing beings that take in information from the outside world through their sense organs, process and store that information in ways dependent on the specific structure of their bodies, and adjust their behavior to take account of past experiences and new information. And like Aristotle before him, Wiener saw an intimate relationship between the *information-processing* nature of human beings and the *purpose* of a human life. For Wiener as for Aristotle, the overall purpose of a human life is to *flourish* as a creating, adapting, perceiving, learning, thinking, reasoning being empowered by sophisticated internal information processing. (Aristotle called it "theoretical and practical reasoning.")

The ability of human beings to flourish in this way, according to Wiener, is dependent on human physiology. To emphasize this point, Wiener often compared the bodies of humans with those of other animals like insects:

> I wish to show that the human individual, capable of vast learning and study, which may occupy about half of his life, is physically equipped, as the ant is not, for this capacity. Variety and possibility are inherent in the human sensorium—and indeed are the key to man's most noble flights—because variety and possibility belong to the very structure of the human organism. (Wiener, 1954, pp. 51–52)

> *Cybernetics takes the view that the structure of the machine or of the organism is an index of the performance that may be expected from it.* The fact that the mechanical rigidity of the insect is such as to limit its intelligence while the mechanical fluidity of the human being provides for his almost indefinite intellectual expansion is highly relevant to the point of view of this book. (p. 57, italics in original)

ENTROPY AND PURPOSE IN A HUMAN LIFE

Like Aristotle, Wiener used the science of his day to help understand human nature and derive an account of purpose in a human life. Of course, the science in Aristotle's time was his own biology and physics,[4] while that of

Wiener included late nineteenth and early twentieth-century sciences like thermodynamics, statistical mechanics, and Darwinian biology. Of special interest to Wiener was the second law of thermodynamics and the associated concept of *entropy* because these are closely related to information. As Wiener explained:

> Messages are themselves a form of pattern and organization. Indeed it is possible to treat sets of messages as having an entropy like sets of states of the external world. Just as entropy is a measure of disorganization, the information carried by a set of messages is a measure of organization. In fact, it is possible to interpret the information carried by a message as essentially the negative of its entropy. . . . That is, the more probable the message, the less information it gives. (Wiener, 1954, p. 21)

The negative relationship between information and entropy presented Wiener with a challenge that Aristotle did not face because Aristotle's biology and physics were fully consistent with his assumption of purpose and value in a human life. For Wiener, however, entropy appeared to be the "enemy" of information, organization and purpose. Thus, because of increasing entropy, "it is highly probable that the whole universe around us will die the heat death, in which the world shall be reduced to one vast temperature equilibrium in which nothing really new ever happens. There will be nothing left but a drab uniformity" (Wiener, 1954, p. 31). How can there be purpose and value in a human life, if entropy is constantly increasing and thereby destroying anything of value?

Wiener's answer was that our tiny corner of the universe is *an enclave of decreasing entropy* brought about by living things and machines. The universe as a whole may be running down, but on earth (and possibly in other little corners of the universe) entropy is *decreasing* because of living things and machines. The final "heat-death" of the world is millions, perhaps billions, of years in the future; and humans have every reason to believe that their values and purposes will be important for a very long time to come:

> In a very real sense we are shipwrecked passengers on a doomed planet. Yet even in a shipwreck, human decencies and human values do not necessarily vanish. . . . [Thus] the theory of entropy, and the considerations of the ultimate heat death of the universe, need not have such profoundly depressing moral consequences as they seem to have at first glance. (Wiener, 1954, pp. 40–41)

FROM HUMAN PURPOSE TO PRINCIPLES OF JUSTICE

Having established the continuing importance of human purpose and human values, Wiener was in a position to derive an account of ethics and justice from his definition of human flourishing. To live a good life, as Wiener saw it, is to realize "the great human values which man possesses" through creative and flexible adaptation to the environment, made possible by sophisticated learning, reasoning, and thinking. This is human information processing at its best—"the key to man's most noble flights." Of course, one person's achievements will differ from those of others, because humans have different levels of talent and potential. It is possible, therefore, to lead a good human life in a variety of ways—as a statesman, scholar, scientist, musician, artist, tradesperson, farmer, and so on.

To enable human beings to reach their full potential and live a good life, according to Wiener, society must uphold three "great principles of justice" and minimize the state's interference in human freedom. To highlight Wiener's "great principles of justice," let us refer to them as "the principle of freedom," "the principle of equality," and "the principle of benevolence." (Wiener himself did not assign them names.) Using Wiener's own statement of these ethical principles produces the following set of definitions (Wiener, 1954, pp. 105–106):

- *The Principle of Freedom*—Justice requires "the liberty of each human being to develop in his freedom the full measure of the human possibilities embodied in him."
- *The Principle of Equality*—Justice requires "the equality by which what is just for A and B remains just when the positions of A and B are interchanged."
- *The Principle of Benevolence*—Justice requires "a good will between man and man that knows no limits short of those of humanity itself."

Like Aristotle, Wiener viewed humans as fundamentally *social* beings who can reach their full potential only by active participation in a community. Society, therefore, is indispensable for a good human life. Society, however, also can be oppressive and despotic in ways that limit or even stifle individual freedom; so Wiener added a fourth principle, which could appropriately be called "the principle of minimum infringement of freedom" (Wiener himself did not give it a name):

- *The Principle of Minimum Infringement of Freedom*—"What compulsion the very existence of the community and the state may demand must be exercised in such a way as to produce no unnecessary infringement of freedom" (Wiener, 1954, p. 106).

Given Wiener's account of the purpose of a human life—to realize one's full human potential in variety and possibility of action—it is not surprising that the principle of freedom is first on his list. [His desire to minimize society's interference in personal freedom seems very similar to the "libertarian" attitude of later Internet "hackers" (in the positive sense of that term) who passionately argued for maximum freedom on "the electronic frontier" of cyberspace. (See, e.g., Barlow, 1991.)] And since, for Wiener, the purpose of a human life is the same for everyone, the principle of equality follows nicely from his account of human nature. The third principle of justice expresses Wiener's belief that human freedom is best served when people sympathetically and helpfully look out for the well-being of all.

WIENER'S INFORMATION ETHICS METHODOLOGIES

Given his account of human flourishing and his principles of justice, Wiener was keen to ask questions about "what we do and how we should react to the new world that confronts us" (Wiener, 1954, p. 12). He employed several methods or strategies for analyzing, understanding, and dealing with social and ethical issues in the coming Information Age. His book *The Human Use of Human Beings* (especially the 1954 Doubleday Anchor revised second edition) is the richest source of examples, though many passages are disappointingly sketchy—even if inspiring and suggestive. Often, Wiener's discussions are casual and incomplete in exactly the places we want him to be rigorous and thorough. For these reasons, we must examine what he *does* as well as what he *says* in order to understand his methodology. Wiener used at least three strategies for dealing with topics in information ethics. These include:

1. Exploring or envisioning the impacts of information technology upon fundamental human values with an eye toward advancing and defending those values.
2. Identifying ethical problems generated by information technology, and then suggesting ways to resolve those problems.
3. Proactively seeking ways to use information technology to create a better world.

Let us consider each of these strategies, one at a time, examining some examples from Wiener's writings, and then briefly discussing ways in which later thinkers employed similar methods.

EXPLORING THE IMPACT OF INFORMATION TECHNOLOGY ON HUMAN VALUES

It is already clear from what has been said that Wiener regularly discussed ways to *defend* human values from damaging uses of information technology, as well as ways to *advance* those values with beneficial uses of such technol-

ogy. He had much to say, for example, about the impacts of information technology on human *happiness* and *survival*. Thus, in chapter X of *The Human
Use of Human Beings*, he warned about grave harm to *human security* that
could result if game-playing computers are used to set military strategy. And
in chapter III, he examined the central role of information feedback mechanisms in *learning*, both in humans and machines.

In that same book, Wiener described communications within a society
as "the cement which binds its fabric together" (p. 27), and he noted the
crucial importance of open communications in a *democracy*, where "blocks
to communication among individuals and classes are not too great" and
freedom is thereby strengthened. He pointed out that, in fascist and despotic
societies, communication among individuals and groups is severely
restricted and censored, and freedom is thereby diminished. He also
expressed worries about the communication infrastructure of America in
the 1950s because growing costs and complexities of communication technology were weakening the democracy-enhancing benefits of such technology. A number of later scholars have discussed the impact of information
technology on democracy, including, for example, Deborah Johnson in her
article "Is the Global Information Infrastructure a Democratic Technology?" (Johnson, 1997).

During the five decades after Wiener founded information ethics, a variety of other thinkers have used the strategy of examining the effects of information technology on human values. For example, in 1991, a major scholarly
conference, the National Conference on Computing and Values,[5] was explicitly organized around this approach. In a keynote address to the attendees of
that conference, the following challenge was given:

> Too often, new technology develops with little attention to its impact upon
> human values. . . . Let us do better! In particular, let us do what we can in
> this era of "the computer revolution" to see that computer technology
> *advances* human values. True enough, we could argue endlessly over the
> meanings of terms like "privacy," "health," "security," "fairness" or "owner-
> ship." Philosophers do it all the time—and *ought* to. But people understand
> such values well enough to desire and even to treasure them. We do not
> need absolute clarity or unattainable unanimity before we do anything to
> advance them. (Bynum, 1991, p. 1)

The fruitfulness of the "human-values approach" to information ethics can be
seen in several recent developments, including the emergence of a new field
of research called "value-sensitive computer design." (Example articles
include Friedman, 1997; Friedman and Nissenbaum, 1996; Introna and Nissenbaum, 2000; and Johnson, 1997.) The most sophisticated and carefully
developed version of this approach, to date, is presented in Philip Brey's
important article "Disclosive Computer Ethics" (Brey, 2000).

RESOLVING ETHICAL PROBLEMS GENERATED
BY INFORMATION TECHNOLOGY

The second strategy or methodology that Wiener used for information ethics was to *identify or envision ethical problems that information technology has generated or is likely to generate in the future, and then suggest ways to eliminate or minimize those problems.* The clearest and most fully worked out example is Wiener's analysis of the ethical implications of computerized factories. (See especially chapter IX of *The Human Use of Human Beings.*) In the early 1950s, Wiener predicted that the world would soon see the creation of "the automatic factory," with an "ultra-rapid computing machine" functioning like a "brain" to control the production processes and monitor the quality of the factory's output. The computer would be hooked up to "artificial sense organs," like thermometers and gauges, enabling it to keep track of environmental conditions in the factory as well as the progress of production runs. There would also be hardware "effectors" that would "act on the outer world," functioning like the arms, legs, and tools that human workers would have used on the assembly line. In the "automatic factory," therefore, computer-driven hardware would replace the muscles and sense organs of human blue-collar workers, while the reasoning and calculating components of the computer would replace "low-level judgments" and actions of white-collar employees such as accountants, clerical workers, and factory librarians. The end result, said Wiener, might be unscrupulous factory owners getting very rich at the expense of laid-off workers and society in general.

To forestall such disastrous consequences, Wiener suggested that union leaders, business managers, and public policymakers should plan ahead and develop ways to deal with these problems before they happen. Thus, Wiener said, "instead of decreasing the responsibility of planners and organizers, we shall greatly increase them, for we shall make it possible for them to do things which they would not have thought of doing before" (Wiener, 1959, p. 39). As a socially active thinker, Wiener himself met with union leaders, business managers, and public policymakers to discuss new rules and laws that should be put in place to minimize possible harm from automatic factories.

A number of later scholars in information ethics have developed similar methodologies. For example, in the mid-1970s Walter Maner discovered, in his Medical Ethics classes at Old Dominion University, that ethical problems are often exacerbated or significantly altered when computers get involved. In response to this realization, Maner created a new university course, which he called "Computer Ethics." Students in that course were to identify ethical problems "created, aggravated, or transformed by computer technology" and then ethically analyze those problems with an eye to resolving or eliminating them. (See Maner, 1980, and Pecorino and Maner, 1985.)

The most influential and carefully developed methodology that is, in some ways, like Wiener's second strategy is that of James Moor in his classic article "What Is Computer Ethics?" (Moor, 1985). According to Moor, computer technology is so flexible and so "logically malleable" that it functions almost like a "universal tool." Because of this, computer technology enables us to do things that were never done before, and we are then faced with "policy vacuums"—*should* we do the many new things that computer technology makes possible? To answer this question, said Moor, we must formulate "new policies for the ethical use of computer technology."

Today, the field of computer ethics is replete with cases that illustrate the usefulness of Moor's "policy vacuum" approach. The Internet, for example, makes it very easy for college students to "construct" their term papers with plagiarized materials downloaded from the World Wide Web. As a result, teachers, librarians, and school administrators must now scramble to fill many "policy vacuums" with new rules and practices to minimize plagiarism. Another example is "hard-core" pornography that lurks just a click away on the family computer. Parents and law enforcement officials are faced with the challenge of quickly developing policies to protect children from hard-core porn, even in the "sanctuary" of their own homes and playrooms.

CREATING A BETTER WORLD WITH INFORMATION TECHNOLOGY

Wiener's third information ethics methodology was *to proactively use information technology to create a better world.* He regularly noted in his writings that such technology can be used for good as well as for evil; his principle of benevolence implies that people should advance the interests of others as well as themselves.

Wiener took his own advice and participated in a variety of projects to develop prostheses and other devices to solve medical problems. Some of his projects included, for example, machines to help patients overcome tremors, an "artificial lung" controlled by the patient's own central nervous system, and a "hearing glove" to enable those who are deaf to "hear" spoken words by converting sounds into tactile sensations. In his discussion of such prostheses, Wiener raised some important ethical and philosophical questions:

> Render unto man the things which are man's and unto the computer the things which are the computer's. This would seem the intelligent policy to adopt when we employ men and computers together in common undertakings. . . . What we now need is an independent study of systems involving both human and mechanical elements. (Wiener, 1964, p. 75)

> Thus there is a new engineering of prostheses possible, and it will involve the construction of systems of a mixed nature, involving both human and

mechanical parts. However, this type of engineering need not be confined
to the replacement of parts that we have lost. There is a prosthesis of parts
which we do not have and which we never have had. (p. 76)

Wiener pointed out that the propeller of a ship functions much like prostheses for humans, which are similar to "artificial flukes" on the tail of a dolphin.
And what is the automatic pilot of an airplane but a "nervous system" for a
man–machine that can fly? Beings that consist of human and mechanical
parts working together can be powerful agents capable of doing much good in
the world—but also much evil as well. These concerns about man–machine
combinations, which Wiener raised in the 1950s and early 1960s, are similar
in many ways to contemporary worries about cyborgs.

WIENER AND THE INTERNET

Norbert Wiener died in 1964, five years before the US government launched
the ARPANET—a military computer network that would evolve into the
Internet by the mid-1970s. Wiener, therefore, did not live to see even the
earliest stages of the Internet or today's globally extended World Wide Web.
Yet it is clear from his writings that he anticipated many of the ethical issues
and philosophical questions associated with the Internet; if he were to return
to earth today, he would not be surprised to find the Internet here. Indeed, by
the mid-1950s, Wiener already assumed that communications technologies
had effectively created a global information network:

> The invention of the telephone, the telegraph, and other similar means of
> communication have shown that this capacity [i.e., the ability to carry on
> conversations between individuals] is not intrinsically restricted to the
> immediate presence of the individual, for we have many means to carry this
> tool of communication to the ends of the earth. (Wiener, 1954, p. 91, brack-
> eted words added for clarification)

But Wiener envisioned a much more sophisticated network in the future—a
network that would include machines communicating with humans and with
each other:

> It is the thesis of this book that society can only be understood through a
> study of the messages and the communication facilities which belong to it;
> and that in the future development of these messages and communication
> facilities, messages between man and machines, between machines and
> man, and between machine and machine, are destined to play an ever-
> increasing part. (Wiener, 1954, p. 16)

Wiener also noted that the ability to send and receive messages over networks empowers a person to act at a distance and, in a sense, "be everywhere":

> Where a man's word goes, and where his power of perception goes, to that
> point his control and in a sense his physical existence is extended. To see
> and to give commands to the whole world is almost the same as being every-
> where. . . . Even now the transportation of messages serves to forward an
> extension of man's senses and his capabilities of action from one end of the
> world to another. (Wiener, 1954, pp. 97–98)

To illustrate this point, Wiener described an imaginary case in which an archi-
tect in Europe supervises the construction of a building in the United States
without ever leaving Europe by sending and receiving plans, photos, and
instructions over telephone lines using an early version of the fax machine.

Wiener's vision of the automatic age included the possibility of a communications network with humans and machines interacting—a network
that bestows the power of action "from one end of the world to another"—a
network that enables one to "be everywhere." Given this vision of the future,
plus Wiener's view that communications constitute the "cement" that binds
society together, it is an easy step to speculate about the possibility of a future
world community or a world government. Indeed, even without a powerful
global network like the Internet to pique his imagination, Wiener made comments like this:

> With the airplane and the radio the word of the rulers extends to the ends
> of the earth, and very many of the factors which previously precluded a
> World State have been abrogated. It is even possible to maintain that mod-
> ern communication, which forces us to adjudicate the international claims
> of different broadcasting systems and different airplane nets, has made the
> World State inevitable. (Wiener, 1954, p. 92)

Information ethics scholars who came after Wiener also speculated about
world government; others have explored less comprehensive global consequences like the possible emergence of a "global ethics." For example, in her
article, "The Computer Revolution and the Problem of Global Ethics,"
Krystyna Gorniak-Kocikowska (1996) predicted that the computer revolution will lead to the emergence of a new worldwide ethics that will supercede
"local" ethical theories, like Europe's Benthamite and Kantian systems and
ethical systems in other regions of the world; and Charles Ess, in his "Cultures
in Collision: Philosophical Lessons from Computer-Mediated Communication" (Ess, 2002) envisions a "genuinely *global* ethics," which nevertheless
respects and encourages a rich diversity of cultures and values.

ETHICS AND NONHUMAN AGENTS

Wiener's predictions about the coming automatic age included his view that
there will be many machines with "brains of brass and thews of iron"—

machines that will learn and reason and make decisions on their own. Such predictions were very controversial at the time, and many people simply did not believe him. Wiener offered examples of decision-making machines that already existed, including (1) a checkers-playing machine that quickly learned from its "experiences" and then regularly defeated the man who made it, (2) a chess-playing machine that could play chess at the level of an amateur, and (3) a war-games machine used by the U.S. government to teach military planning and tactics. Such machines, he explained, can learn in two different senses:

1. They can record information from their past activities, and then use this information to adjust their future activities.
2. They can save information about how successfully their programming guided their behavior, then use this information to *reprogram* themselves to alter their future behavior.

Wiener believed that it was at least theoretically possible for machines to someday duplicate the intellectual abilities of a human being: "Theoretically, if we could build a machine whose mechanical structure duplicated human physiology, then we could have a machine whose intellectual capacities would duplicate those of human beings" (Wiener, 1954, p. 57). He was skeptical, however, that we would ever succeed in building such a machine because he thought the requisite parts of a mechanical brain would be too numerous and too large to duplicate the functions of billions of neurons in a human being, yet he was unwilling to completely rule out this possibility. (See Wiener, 1954, p. 159, and Wiener, 1959, pp. 36–41.) He *did* rule out, however, the idea that a human should ever trust machines to make critical decisions in place of human beings: "[A person should] not leap in where angels fear to tread, unless he is prepared to accept the punishment of the fallen angels. Neither will he calmly transfer to the machine made in his own image the responsibility for his choice of good and evil, without continuing to accept a full responsibility for that choice (Wiener, 1954, p. 184).

For decision-making machines, we seem to need something like a code of ethics that can be programmed into them:

> Any machine constructed for the purpose of making decisions, if it does not possess the power of learning, will be completely literal-minded. Woe to us if we let it decide our conduct, unless we have previously examined the laws of its action, and know fully that its conduct will be carried out on principles acceptable to us! (Wiener, 1954, p. 185)

But if our machine can learn, it might alter the code of ethics that we placed into it when we built it:

On the other hand, the machine . . . which can learn and can make decisions on the basis of its learning, will in no way be obliged to make such decisions as we should have made, or will be acceptable to us. For the man who is not aware of this, to throw the problem of his responsibility on the machine, whether it can learn or not, is to cast his responsibility to the winds, and to find it coming back seated on the whirlwind. (Wiener, 1954, p. 185)

In recent years, decades after Wiener first raised such troubling issues, information ethics scholars have been hard at work trying to cope with them. [See, e.g., Eichmann's seminal article, "Ethical Web Agents" (Eichmann, 1994) and Floridi and Sanders, "On the Morality of Artificial Agents" (Floridi and Sanders, 2001b).]

WIENER'S LEGACY

Norbert Wiener was a great scientist who helped to create the Information Age. In addition, he was also one of those very rare scientists who could see the social and ethical importance of his own great achievements and those of his fellow scientists. Many of the ethical issues he struggled with are the same ones we struggle with today; the light that he shed on them will brighten many corners of our research in the coming years. Furthermore, the philosophical foundation that Wiener laid for the field of information ethics is deep and profound, and it remains a valuable resource for research and practical action.

NOTES

1. For several contemporary works on information ethics, see the recent writings of Luciano Floridi listed in the References.

2. First published in 1950 by Houghton Mifflin. In 1954, Doubleday Anchor published a significantly revised version. In the present chapter, all quotations from *The Human Use of Human Beings* are from the 1954 version.

3. For a detailed comparison of Aristotle and Wiener on animal behavior and human action, see Bynum, 2000.

4. An extensive discussion of the relationship between Aristotle's science and his account of human action and purpose can be found in Bynum, 1986.

5. Sponsored by the Research Center on Computing & Society at Southern Connecticut State University and funded by grants from the National Science Foundation.

REFERENCES

Barlow, J. P. 1991, March. Coming into the Country, *Communications of the ACM* 34.3: 19–21.

Brey, P. 2000. Disclosive Computer Ethics, *Computers and Society* 30.4: 10–16.

Bynum, T. W. 1986. *Aristotle's Theory of Human Action,* doctoral dissertation at the Graduate Center of the City University of New York, University Microfilms.

———. 1991. Human Values and the Computer Science Curriculum, keynote address at the National Conference on Computing and Values, New Haven. Published as "Computer Ethics in the Computer Science Curriculum" in Bynum, T. W., W. Maner, and J. L. Fodor (Eds.). 1993. *Teaching Computer Ethics.* New Haven: Research Center on Computing & Society. (Also available at http://www.computerethics.org.)

———. 2000. The Foundation of Computer Ethics, *Computers and Society* June 2000: 6–13.

Eichmann, D. 1994. Ethical Web Agents available at http://archive.ncsa.uiuc.edu/SDG/IT94/Proceedings/Agents/eichmann.ethical/eichmann.html.

Ess, C. 2002. "Cultures in Collision: Philosophical Lessons from Computer-Mediated Communication," in Moor, J. H., and T. W. Bynum (Eds.), *Cyberphilosophy: The Intersection of Philosophy and Computing.* London: Blackwell.

Floridi, L. 1999. Information Ethics: On the Theoretical Foundations of Computer Ethics, *Ethics and Information Technology* 1.1: 37–56, http://www.wolfson.ox.ac.uk/~floridi/pdf/ieotfce.pdf.

———. 2002. Information Ethics: An Environmental Approach to the Digital Divide, *Philosophy in the Contemporary World* 9.1: 39–45.

———, and J. W. Sanders. 1999. Entropy as Evil in Information Ethics, *Etica & Politica,* special issue 1.2, http://www.univ.trieste.it/~dipfilo/etica_e_politica/1999_2/homepage.html.

———, and J. W. Sanders. 2001a. Artificial Evil and the Foundation of Computer Ethics, *Ethics and Information Technology* 3.1: 55–66, http://www.wolfson.ox.ac.uk/~floridi/pdf/ae.pdf.

———, and J. W. Sanders. (2001b) "On the Morality of Artificial Agents," CEPE *2001, Computer Ethics: Philosophical Enquiry* (Lancaster University, 14–16 December, 2001), http://www.wolfson.ox.ac.uk/~floridi/pdf/maa.pdf.

Friedman, B. (Ed.). 1997. *Human Values and the Design of Computer Technology.* Cambridge: Cambridge University Press.

———, and H. Nissenbaum. 1996. Bias in Computer Systems, *ACM Transactions on Information Systems* 14.3: 330–347.

Gorniak-Kocikowska, K. 1996. The Computer Revolution and the Problem of Global Ethics, in Bynum, T. W., and S. Rogerson (Eds.), *Global Information Ethics,* a special issue of *Science and Engineering Ethics* 2.2: 177–190.

Introna, L. D., and H. Nissenbaum. 2000. Shaping the Web: Why the Politics of Search Engines Matters, *The Information Society* 16.3: 1–17.

Johnson, D. G. 1997, September. Is the Global Information Infrastructure a Democratic Technology? *Computers and Society* September: 20–26.

Maner, W. 1980. *Starter Kit in Computer Ethics*. Hyde Park, NY: Helvetia Press (published in cooperation with the National Information and Resource Center for Teaching Philosophy). (Originally self-published by Maner in 1978.)

Moor, J. 1985. What Is Computer Ethics?, in Bynum, T. W. (Ed.), *Computers & Ethics*. Blackwell, pp. 266–275. (Published as a special issue of *Metaphilosophy* 16.4: 266–275.)

Pecorino, P. A., and W. Maner. 1985. A Proposal for a Course on Computer Ethics, in Bynum, T. W. (Ed.), *Computers & Ethics*. London: Blackwell, pp. 327–337.

Wiener, N. 1948. *Cybernetics: or Control and Communication in the Animal and the Machine*. Boston: Technology Press.

———. 1950/1954. *The Human Use of Human Beings: Cybernetics and Society*. Boston: Houghton Mifflin. (Second rev. ed. New York: Doubleday Anchor, 1954.)

———. 1959. Man and the Machine. An interview with Norbert Wiener. *Challenge* June: 36–41.

———. 1964. *God & Golem, Inc.—A Comment on Certain Points Where Cybernetics Impinges on Religion*. Cambridge: MIT Press.

TWO

Beyond Copyright

A Moral Investigation of Intellectual
Property Protection in Cyberspace

RICHARD A. SPINELLO

THE IDEALISTIC VISION of the Internet as a "celestial jukebox" in which diverse content would be available at the push of a button is overshadowed by an unfortunate reality: the illicit and ubiquitous copying of copyrighted content. The music industry, for example, has been fighting an uphill battle to protect its content and has been hesitant to embrace digital distribution for fear of piracy. At least one U.S. senator has referred to the Internet as a "haven for thievery."

As we struggle to understand the impact of the Internet on our moral sensibility and social awareness, one thing seems certain: we have not yet come to terms with the moral and legal status of intangible property. The vast majority of citizens respect tangible property rights; they do not steal cars or help themselves to new clothes at the local Wal-Mart. Yet people who would not go into a record store and walk out with a few CDs of their favorite rock group think that it's perfectly acceptable to download pirated music on the Web, perhaps with the assistance of a peer-to-peer network such as KaZaA. What accounts for such a divergence in their moral assessment of these situations?

The ultimate source of the problem is, of course, the nature of digital information. We are now able to efficiently digitize more and more types of information, including audio and video. By reducing information into a compressed digital format, a stream of 1s and 0s, it has become possible to make limitless, perfect copies of books, videos, and music, and to distribute those products quickly, easily, and at zero marginal cost. The ease with which these digital media can be shared is of great concern to many copyright holders who fear that they will have to sacrifice revenues as they lose control over the distribution of their works.

This new digital reality also invites a certain conceptual confusion. Are intangible products with digital properties really equivalent to "things" that can be stolen? What bearing does the ontological status of digital information have on the moral propriety of copying software? There seems to be something morally ambiguous about downloading a copy of a software application or digital music while leaving the original intact. When I take a physical product, the rightful owner is deprived of this property, but, when I make a digital copy, the owner retains the original. So where is the harm if the owner is not being deprived of anything?

Thus, the nature of digital property along with the capabilities of the Internet seem to desensitize us to the worth of intellectual property and the need to respect copyright laws as a matter of justice. The ease of replicating and transferring the Internet's content, digital information, appears to foster a cavalier attitude among many users, who do not perceive this as a serious moral issue. Does technology change the normative and social context for making moral judgments about property rights? Or are the justifications put forth by those making illicit copies simply thin rationalizations for their questionable activities?

More important, are these even the proper questions we should be asking? Maybe copyright traditionalists have it wrong and it's time to seriously reexamine our moral presuppositions about intellectual property. Should digital works even be entitled to copyright protection? Perhaps the counterculture is right, and those students who claim that art and digital music should be "free goods" are on to something. Can an ethical case be made that content should not be controlled for money and that it is meant to be free when the Internet is involved? Is the capitalist model the right one for creating and disseminating works of art? These are all valid questions and none of them suggest simple or straightforward answers.

This chapter will probe several of these controversial questions from a moral perspective in order to suggest a few answers. In the first part we will explore the problematic of intellectual property in more depth by looking at the Napster case. We will rely here on Larry Lessig's framework and demonstrate how the traditional constraints or modalities of regulation have been unable to deter software piracy. We highlight in particular the failure of social norms and the growing tendency to regard the sharing of copyrighted music files as socially acceptable. In the second portion of the chapter we will review questions about the need to revise and revamp the copyright system.

We argue that, while some changes might be economically feasible, it would be impractical and imprudent to abandon copyright laws entirely and make cyberspace a copyright-free zone. Copyright laws still serve a useful purpose that advances the common good. In the third part we will examine some possible solutions to the problem of piracy, given the need to preserve the essentials of the current copyright system. The most popular solution being advocated by those in the music industry is the use of software such as digital rights architectures. But this remedy, which tends to give copyright holders almost perfect control over their content, may lead to certain excesses. And finally, in the fourth part, we turn to a discussion of moral norms and argue that they represent a more viable constraint than social norms, provided that moralists can increase the intensity of the digital piracy issue. Community standards send mixed signals about the social acceptability of duplicating copyrighted material, but the application of moral norms is much less equivocal. We also argue that the moral authority of copyright law cannot be casually dismissed. Copyright laws are certainly imperfect and unnecessarily complicated, and there may be other ways of achieving the same end. But none of this implies that these laws are unjust. And as Aristotle consistently reminds us in the *Nicomachean Ethics*, the virtuous person is one who manifests the highest regard for the just laws of society. Finally, a heightened moral awareness can also diminish the need for more coercive solutions relying on software code.

I

COPYRIGHT LAW: A BRIEF OVERVIEW

Copyright law in the United States can be traced back to the Constitution. The Founding Fathers recognized that such protection was necessary for commercial and artistic advancement. As a result, Article I of the Constitution confers on Congress the power "to promote the Progress of Science and the useful Arts, by securing for limited Times to Authors and Inventors the exclusive Right to their respective Writings and Discoveries."[1] Congress has chosen to fulfill this obligation by establishing a comprehensive regime of patent and copyright laws that assures producers the right to profit from their innovative or creative works.

In 1790, copyright protection extended only to publishers of maps, charts, and books with a term of fourteen years. But copyright laws have changed dramatically, and the scope of protection has been greatly expanded. The Copyright Act of 1976 carefully delineates the rights and restrictions of copyright holders. Copyright now protects any original literary, musical, dramatic, artistic, architectural, audio, or audiovisual work as long as it is fixed in some tangible medium of expression. Copyright laws give authors exclusive rights to their works, especially the rights to reproduction and distribution. Copyright law also gives copyright holders the right to prepare derivative works based upon their copyrighted material. Finally, copyright holders have the right to control the public performance and display of their works. Direct copyright infringement occurs when any of these rights is violated.

Copyright protection has certain limitations considered to be in the public interest. According to Goldstein, one such limitation or "safety valve" is the fair use provision.[2] For example, copyrighted literary works can be quoted and a small segment of a video work can be displayed for limited purposes, including criticism, research, classroom instruction, or news reporting. Another restriction is the first sale provision, which allows the purchaser of a copyrighted work to sell or lend that work to someone else without the copyright holder's permission. Copyright protection also has a limited term; when that term expires, the work enters the public domain or "intellectual commons." For individuals, the current term of a copyright is the life of the author plus seventy years and for a company the term is ninety-five years. These limits on copyright law are designed to balance the rights of the copyright holder with the public's interest in the broad dissemination and availability of literary and artistic works.

THE RISE AND FALL OF NAPSTER

The repudiation of copyright law in cyberspace seems beyond dispute. There has been rampant copying of music, video, and software applications especially on college campuses. To comprehend the full scope and ramifications of the problem let us turn to a brief case study. Consider the problems associated with digital music and the case of Napster, which has received widespread publicity. The rise of digital music has been made possible by a standard known as MP3, an audio compression format that creates near-CD-quality files that are as much as twenty times smaller than the files on a standard music CD. Thanks to MP3, digital music can now be accessed and transmitted over the Web without the need of a physical container such as a compact disk.

The downside of this system, of course, is the potential for piracy. Because MP3 files are unsecured they can be easily copied and redistributed in cyberspace. The music industry's response to this problem has been predictable—they have doggedly pursued the parties responsible for programs that facilitate digital music file sharing, including companies like Napster. Napster functioned as an intermediary in this process. The Napster software enabled users to search the directories on the hard drives of other Napster users and locate MP3 files. Once a particular piece of music was found on another Napster user's computer system (with help of the central Napster server), it could be downloaded directly from that system in MP3 format and stored on the recipient's hard drive. Napster did not store or "cache" any digital music files on its own servers, and it was not directly involved in any copying of music files. Napster did, however, maintain a central directory of the music available among all Napster users.

Napster became an overnight sensation, particularly among college students, who quickly seized the opportunity to download their favorite songs, free of charge. Within days of going online, Napster software was downloaded by several thousand people. By early 2001, Napster had over thirty-eight million users. At its zenith in the month of February 2001, the estimated number of songs downloaded from Napster peaked at over 2.5 billion.

The Recording Industry Association of America (RIAA), which represents the interests of the major record labels in the United States, was incensed by Napster's flagrant violation of copyright law. As a result, it sued the company for vicarious and contributory copyright infringement—that is, for facilitating and "inducing" the infringement of copyrights for financial benefit. Of course, to prove these allegations the RIAA had to demonstrate that Napster users were engaged in direct copyright infringement. The RIAA was worried not only about Napster but also about the proliferation of other Web sites from which users could download MP3 music files. In its main brief, the RIAA summed up the problem quite clearly: "If the perception of music as a free good becomes pervasive, it may be difficult to reverse."[3]

Napster was also sued by the rock band Metallica for contributory copyright infringement and racketeering. This group (and others such as Eminem, Dr. Dre, Busta Rhymes) felt betrayed by Napster. According to Dr. Dre, "I'm in business to make money, and Napster is [screwing] that up."[4] Even the rapper Ice-T was moved to defend the copyright system in light of Napster's activities: "If you create something, you're entitled to some kind of money or reward or something if somebody else wants it; ain't nothing wrong with that."[5]

Beyond the confines of the entertainment industry, there was little social outrage about Napster's popularity. Several universities such as Brown and Hofstra prevented student use of Napster, but only because the downloading of music files was consuming too much bandwidth. Other institutions such as Stanford and the Massachusetts Institute of Technology refused to ban Napster, even after Metallica named several universities in its lawsuit. Very few universities voiced opposition to Napster purely on moral grounds.

The RIAA had requested a preliminary injunction to stop the Napster service before more harm was done to copyright holders. The hearing took place in the summer of 2000 at the Federal District Court of San Francisco. Judge Patel quickly ruled against Napster, agreeing to grant the injunction. Napster's lawyers immediately filed a motion to stay that injunction. Two days later the Ninth Circuit Court of Appeals granted that motion and overruled Judge Patel, arguing that no decision should be made until there was a full hearing. That hearing in front of the Ninth Circuit Court took place in October 2000. The plaintiffs argued that a majority of Napster users were downloading and uploading copyrighted music. They estimated that 87 percent of the music downloaded by Napster users was copyrighted by one of the recording labels that were a party to this lawsuit. These actions constituted direct infringement of the musical recordings owned by the plaintiffs. And since Napster users were culpable of direct copyright infringement, Napster itself was liable for contributory copyright infringement.

In defense of Napster, its attorney, David Boies, argued that the granting of a permanent injunction would be unprecedented. According to Boies, "The plaintiffs in this case ask the court to do several things that no appellate court has done in the history of copyright: First, they ask this court to hold a company liable for contributory or vicarious infringement, when the direct infringer is not engaged in commercial activity, and does not have a commercial relationship with the contributory infringement."[6] Boies was alluding here to the fair use exception to copyright law: when one Napster user copies a song from another user for his or her own personal use and not for commercial gain, that copying constitutes fair use of the copyrighted song.

Napster argued that its users often downloaded MP3 files to sample their contents before making a decision about whether to make a purchase. Hence, according to this line of reasoning, Napster's service could even help promote sales of audio CDs. Napster users were also engaged in space shifting, which occurs when one downloads MP3 files to listen to music one already owns on an audio CD. Throughout the trial, Napster compared its technology to that of the videocassette recorder. In the 1984 case of *Sony v. Universal City Studios*, the U.S. Supreme Court had exonerated Sony from liability for the copying that could occur by means of its VCR technology. It also held that, in general, VCRs did not infringe copyright since viewers were engaged in time shifting, that is, recording a television show for viewing at a later time. According to Greene, "Relying on the Sony decision, Napster attempted to establish that its service has substantial non-infringing uses and that Napster users who download copyrighted music, like VCR users who record copyrighted television programming, are entitled to a fair use defense."[7]

Despite the cleverness of Napster's defense, these arguments did not persuade the skeptical Ninth Circuit judges. They ruled unanimously that "the district court did not err; Napster, by its conduct, knowingly encourages and assists the infringement of plaintiffs' copyrights."[8] They rejected these fair use claims, concluding that Napster had an adverse effect on the market for audio CDs, especially among college students. The scale of file sharing enabled by Napster meant that this sharing could not be considered a private affair. While file sharing is certainly not always infringing, by making music on their hard drives accessible to many other individuals over the Internet, Napster users were functioning as distributors of protected material. And although Napster itself was not yet reaping profits from this file sharing, its users were achieving an economic gain. According to the court, the fact that "Napster users get for free something they would ordinarily have to buy suggests that they reap economic advantages from Napster use."[9]

In June 2002, Napster declared bankruptcy and its ultimate fate remains in doubt. But the free circulation of music is unlikely to cease anytime soon. Libertarians were outraged by the Napster decision and they vowed continued defiance. At the conclusion of the trial, John Perry Barlow proclaimed, "I think the only way to deal with law on the Internet is to ignore it flagrantly. I want everyone in this room to consider themselves revolutionaries and go out and develop whatever they damn well please."[10]

In addition, new file-sharing architectures have emerged that are far more difficult to contain than the Napster technology. For the most part, the architectures facilitating this new mode of music distribution are purer versions of peer-to-peer (P2P) computing. Unlike the server-based technology, in which distribution to clients emanates from a central server, with peer-to-peer any computer in the network can function as the distribution point. In this way the server is not inundated with requests from multiple clients. P2P systems enable efficient file sharing among individual personal computers. For example, personal computer X may ask other PCs in a peer-to-peer network if they have a certain digital file. That request is passed along from computer to computer until the file is located and a copy is sent along to the requester's system.

Napster was not a true peer-to-peer system since it relied on a central directory. But its successors, Morpheus, KaZaA, and Gnutella, operate without any central server. Unlike Napster, on the P2P network known as Gnutella, requests are sent to other peers on the network in order to search and download content. Gnutella has no central server that maintains any listing of available music. The actual downloading of music does not take place over the Gnutella network but is performed by means of the http protocol. But, as with Napster, so with Gnutella: any individual on the Gnutella network can make a piece of copyrighted music available for thousands of other users to download. From both a technical and legal standpoint, however, shutting down Gnutella will be much more difficult than disabling Napster since it is a distributed network with no central node to attack.

Many observers now claim that efforts to undermine these rogue networks will be an exercise in futility. File sharing will persist in new and different formats. Moreover, the challenge of protecting digital music foreshadows similar challenges for other forms of digital content such as DVD files. The Napster case underscores how the traditional constraints against piracy have not worked well on the digital frontier. Is there no recourse for content providers? To address that question we must consider more precisely why it is so difficult to protect digital content in cyberspace.

CONSTRAINTS AGAINST COPYING

In his book *Code and Other Laws of Cyberspace*, Larry Lessig describes four constraints on our behavior in real space. In answering the question about the regulability of cyberspace, Lessig argues that in the physical world we are regulated by four distinct forces: law, norms, the market, and architecture. The most obvious constraints are laws set by the government and the informal social norms imposed by the communities in which we participate. If we violate these laws or norms, we are subject to ex post sanctions. Less obvious are the constraints imposed by the marketplace and "architecture." The market constrains by the prices it sets for goods and services (including labor). Finally, architecture (i.e., the physical characteristics of the world) imposes many physical constraints on our behavior—some are natural (such as the mountains and caves of Afghanistan), while others are human constructs (such as buildings and bridges).

As in real space, so in cyberspace, these same four modalities of regulation apply. There are laws that restrict our behavior such as the copyright laws that control access to content like digital music and videos. Cyberspace also has its own set of norms; spam is not illegal but spammers are usually shunned and vilified by the cyberspace community. The market, too, plays a role in influencing behavior. The more advertising revenues a Web site generates, the greater its ability to attract more users and develop a sustainable competitive advantage.

But arguably the most powerful regulative force in cyberspace is the analogue for architecture that Lessig calls "code." According to Lessig, "the software and hardware that makes cyberspace what it is constitute a set of constraints on how you can behave. The substance of these constraints may vary, but they are experienced as conditions on your access to cyberspace."[11] In the United States, laws to forbid access to pornographic material for children have been declared unconstitutional, but code in the form of software filters installed by parents, schools, and libraries has been a far more efficacious solution.

One problem with Lessig's general argument is the inclusion of ethical standards in the broad category he calls "norms." In our view, however, cultural norms should be segregated from ethical ideals and principles. Cultural norms are nothing more than variable social action guides, completely relative and dependent on a given social or cultural environment. Their validity is to some extent dependent on custom, prevalent attitudes, public opinion, and a myriad of other factors. Just as customs differ from country to country, the social customs of cyberspace could be quite different from the customs found in real space. Also, these customs will likely undergo some transformation over time as the Internet continues to evolve.

The fundamental principles of ethics, however, are meta-norms, since they have universal instead of local validity. They remain the same whether we are doing business in Brazil or interacting in cyberspace. Like cultural norms, they are prescriptive, but, unlike these norms, they have lasting and durable value because they transcend space and time. Ethics is about (or should be about) intelligible human goods intrinsic to our humanity and the chosen acts that realize those goods—hence the continuity of general ethical principles despite the diversity of cultures.

If we look at the problem of copyright protection in cyberspace through this filter of constraints proposed by Lessig, we can gain a more nuanced comprehension of why copying of copyrighted material has become so rampant. Copyright laws apply to digital works as well as nondigital ones, but those laws have been ineffectual for digital works since they are so difficult to enforce. It's not feasible to chase down and punish every college student who uses Napster or KaZaA. As a result, law has not been a stabilizing force for the safeguarding of digital content.

Social norms send off ambivalent signals about downloading pirated material. Content providers and others have attempted to foster respect for property rights. But attitudes about piracy are still heavily influenced by software liberationists and digital libertarians (like Barlow) who make the case that software and information should be free. Even if copying is wrong, it's not seen as a serious offense, but as a minor and victimless crime. Major universities did not ban Napster even when some of them were threatened with a lawsuit; such inaction seems to implicitly condone students' behavior. It's also difficult for most users to feel any sympathy for the music and movie industries. Furthermore, in the real world people are inhibited from taking music in a physical container, but those inhibitions seem to dissolve when it comes to copying a containerless MP3 music file. When one takes a physical object, it's a zero-sum game since the owner no longer possesses that object, but that is not the case with digital content. As a result, there is a tendency to regard the downloading of copyrighted digital music as a socially acceptable activity.

Market forces are also not much of a constraint because the economics of digital technology make copies readily available and suggest that copyright is an archaic artifact from the pre-digital era. The economics of digital content distribution differ substantially from the costly distribution structure associated with the physical realm of bricks and mortar. Illicit file sharing on a massive scale can be accomplished without a physical distribution network or manufacturing facilities. Moreover, ceteris paribus, there is little willingness to pay for music that one can easily get for free.

Finally, the current architectures of the Internet support piracy. In the real world it would be time consuming and cumbersome to make illicit copies of the latest Moby CD and sell them on the street. Also, as Ku observes, "an analog recording of a CD or a photocopy of a book is not the same as the original, and subsequent recordings continue to degrade."[12] On the other hand, digital copies are perfect replicas, all identical to the original digital master, and the underlying architecture of the Internet enables anyone to make an unlimited number of perfect copies of that CD. Thanks to the basic TCP/IP protocol, music like any digital data is treated as a stream of bits that can be sent anywhere on the Internet with the usual alacrity of Internet transmissions. And architectures such as peer-to-peer technology provide an opportunity to locate music on the systems of other music lovers, thereby making possible an unprecedented level of file sharing.

Thus, a system of constraints that worked reasonably well in the physical world fails abysmally in the virtual world. Law is ineffective and hard to enforce; economics and code favor free, unfettered distribution; and ambivalent social norms suggest that this activity is socially acceptable and not equivalent to the pilfering of tangible goods. Perhaps now we can appreciate the deep concerns of the RIAA along with some individual copyright holders like Metallica.

II

RETHINKING THE INTELLECTUAL PROPERTY SYSTEM

Napster may have lost its battle in court and in the marketplace, but it has surely won the hearts and minds of many college students and music lovers who see nothing wrong with this service. Along with civil libertarians, these students have embraced technologies like Napster and declared that cyberspace should be a "copyright-free zone," where the restrictive laws of the physical world will not apply. These laws do not appear to fit with the dominant information technologies of this new millennium. It is difficult for copyright law to coexist with the digitization of information and other architectures such as peer-to-peer file sharing. We have repeatedly heard that content on the Internet wants to be free—isn't that in fact the nature and the magic of this medium? Digital information, including music and video, costs nothing to copy, and it cannot be easily confined in cyberspace. Thus, at a minimum, the technological revolution that has given us cultural phenomena like Napster and KaZaA, should prompt us to reconsider the institutional framework that supports copyright protections for intellectual property.

What are we to make of such arguments? Is it time to overthrow the old intellectual property regime? Is Negroponte right when he proclaims that copyright is "totally out of date" and a "Gutenberg artifact?"[13] This outdated law seems to needlessly encumber architectures designed to move and propagate information. In this virtual world of digital products that can be duplicated and redistributed at no cost, traditional distribution structures that depend on ownership of content and an exclusive right to distribute seem anachronistic.

In addition, strong intellectual property rights have certain negative consequences for society. They tend to commercialize creativity and concentrate it in the hands of the major entertainment companies such as Disney. Proprietary rights could also impair the vitality of the public domain. The more we enclose intellectual property, the less robust our collection of publicly accessible works will be. The end result could be diminished creative expression. As Cohen observes, "creativity requires the freedom to use and reuse inputs that are basic building blocks of communication and 'meaning-making' within society."[14]

Although these arguments have merit and we concede that new legal models loosening property controls are perfectly appropriate, it seems premature to declare that cyberspace should be a copyright-free zone. We maintain that there is still a place for copyright protection, even on the digital frontier of cyberspace. Consider first the grounds for protecting intellectual property in real space. The presumption that ownership of intellectual property is a natural right is a matter of some debate. Proponents of this view often cite Locke's famous labor-desert theory to justify such a claim. Whether that theory can withstand critical scrutiny is a question for another day.

An equally plausible but more widely accepted justification for an appropriate level of intellectual property protection derives from pragmatic, utilitarian reasoning: society must provide the level of intellectual property protection necessary to promote future innovation and creativity. This implies that the higher the cost to create something, the more critical the need for incentives such as intellectual property protection. Without such protection it would be impossible for innovators to recover their initial investment. If society wants drugs that cure cancer and AIDS, it will need to protect aspiring innovators from free riders. If it wants expensive movies and well-crafted artworks, it will have to protect those items as well.

On the other hand, the costs of creating some forms of music are fairly low. If artists will continue to create popular music without strong intellectual property protection, perhaps that music shouldn't be eligible for a copyright. Musicians can now produce their own music and distribute it on the Web and thereby bypass the infrastructure of the major record labels. If there are enough incentives for these musicians to develop new works, copyright protection may no longer be necessary. At some point the U.S. Congress should probably revisit copyright law to make some adjustments in the wake of digital technology. Nonetheless, while copyright and patent law may require some revision and rethinking, they still serve a useful purpose as long as they are balanced and measured. The system is not corrupt or otiose.

CYBERSPACE AS A COPYRIGHT-FREE ZONE

However, even if intellectual property in the real world must be protected for purely utilitarian reasons, why not allow cyberspace to remain a copyright-free zone? Many skeptics may concede that moderate intellectual property protection is needed in real space, but, they might argue, it does not necessarily follow that this protection is necessary in cyberspace. Maybe copyright laws simply do not belong on the Internet where they do not seem to work very well anyway.

Although this viewpoint has become commonplace, it is rather naïve. The fundamental problem is that the borders between real space and cyberspace are permeable—whatever information gets created in the real world will quickly become digitized and migrate to cyberspace. Lack of copyright protection in cyberspace will have a negative economic impact on sales of these goods in the real world. Many will not pay for a book or piece of music if they can wait a while and acquire this object in cyberspace at no charge. For example, Steven Levy described how both his popular books *Hackers* and *Crypto* were scanned and posted at different Web sites for anyone to download without his knowledge or permission. Levy expresses his dismay over this misappropriation of this work: "[I] think I'm entitled to some payment for my work and wonder what will happen when electronic reading devices become more convivial, and downloaders of these files won't pay a penalty in eyestrain."[15] Once objects like Levy's books or the latest Disney movie make their way into the maze of hyperlinked Web sites by some clever subterfuge, there is no way to forestall their anarchic distribution. The copyright holder would have little legal recourse, even against intermediaries that unwittingly facilitated such distribution.

The fate of online content and offline content are closely linked and this will remain so as long as the boundaries between the physical and virtual realms are so porous. Most reasonable people, who accept the premise that intellectual property rights are morally justified, would acknowledge that there is something unfair about Mr. Levy's plight, especially if he is trying to earn a living from his writings. They might even sympathize with media companies like Disney that might not recover an investment for a movie if it found its way into the copyright-free zone of cyberspace. At the present time, therefore, we have little alternative but to retain the current system in which digital works are entitled to the same copyright protection as their physical counterparts.

III

THE DIGITAL DILEMMA

If we assume that the sovereignty of intellectual property law must be sustained even in cyberspace, how do we fix this broken system that fails to protect digital content? How do we impede the diffusion of P2P networks such as KaZaA that facilitate file sharing on such a massive scale? Which of the constraints cited by Lessig should take priority?

One possibility is to do a better job enforcing the law. In the past, music companies were quite hesitant to go after the direct infringers because these people are their customers. They preferred to pursue universities and other organizations whose servers enabled the illicit copying. But in the summer of 2003 the recording industry decided to initiate a legal assault on consumers who swap large amounts of music on the Web, threatening to impose big fines if they did not desist these illegal activities. The success of this bold tactic, which generated substantial negative publicity, remains in doubt. Moreover, technology continues to adapt, and now many file sharers have turned to elusive "darknets," private networks for trading music that can be put up and removed quickly before they can be detected by law enforcement officials.

The recording industry has also given up its resistance to an online music business model. This suggests the possibility of a market-based solution. If users can purchase music online cheaply and conveniently, perhaps they may refrain from resorting to file-sharing networks. Apple has led the way with its iTunes Music Store that sells online music for $.99 a song. That music can be downloaded and played on its popular iPod device. But the industry must still compete with free music readily available on darknets or more conventional peer-to-peer networks.

Third, attempts can be initiated to influence social norms. It will be difficult, however, to change unreflective opinions about software piracy or to inspire the Internet and academic communities to put social pressure on students to eschew peer-to-peer technologies like Morpheus or KaZaA. The more that piracy becomes socially acceptable, the more likely that it will threaten to undermine the music industry. Law and social norms, at least on their own, will probably not succeed in changing behavior in cyberspace.

The most promising possibility is certainly code, and this brings us to the so-called digital dilemma. On the one hand, it is easy to make and distribute digital copies, but, on the other hand, technology can allow creators and producers to exercise an unprecedented level of control over their work. It is no surprise therefore that the RIAA has been advocating the Secure Digital Music Initiative (SDMI). The goal of SDMI is to "require manufacturers of consumer electronics to adopt trusted system technology if they want their devices to play commercially recorded music."[16] A trusted system consists of hardware and software programmed to follow certain rules or usage rights that express how and when a digital work can be used. According to Stefik, "trusted systems can take different forms, such as trusted readers for viewing digital books, trusted players for playing audio and video recordings, trusted printers for making copies that contain labels (watermarks) that denote copyright status, and trusted servers that sell digital works on the Internet."[17] Content providers would distribute their work in cyberspace in encrypted form in such a manner that they would be accessible only by users with trusted machines. Trusted systems also rely on digital rights management that determines what "rights" a user has for a piece of content (e.g., a right to read only, make copies, etc.). Thanks to this technology, which envelops the content in an encrypted enclosure and probably anchors it to a specific machine, content providers can charge every time a copy is made or each time a song is listened to, depending on the terms of the arrangement with the purchaser.

We are now in a position to appreciate the full import of the digital dilemma: digital technology can liberate content or enclose it. Given that other solutions appear to be so ineffectual, tighter enclosure seems to have the force of inevitability. And code becomes a more potent constraint when it is buttressed by laws such as the Digital Millennium Copyright Act, which makes it illegal to circumvent technology protection mechanisms such as encryption programs.

Even those who are sympathetic with content providers and appreciate the value of limited copyright protection in cyberspace realize that the solution of tight enclosure has its drawbacks. There are technical obstacles associated with anchoring content to a single machine—for example, what happens when a user wants to replace his or her personal computer? In addition, as noted, copyright law is not absolute—there are limits such as the provision for fair use, first sale, and limited term. But will trusted systems accommodate these "safety valves"? Will these values be preserved with such pay-for-use systems? The problem is that nothing requires content providers to respect these values. According to Lessig,

> What happens when code protects the interests now protected by copyright law? . . . Should we expect that any of the limits [now provided by copyright law] will remain? Should we expect code to mirror the limits that the law imposes? Fair use? Limited term? . . . The point should be obvious: when intellectual property is protected by code, nothing requires that the same balance be struck. Nothing requires the owner to grant the right of fair use.[18]

As we struggle to find solutions to the problem of Napster and its successors, we are left with some stark choices. Law and norms do not seem to work at all and code seems to work too well, giving the content provider more control than the law itself. Are we condemned to making a painful Hobson's choice between a free-wheeling cyberspace with no restraints on copying versus one in which all content is tightly enclosed by its owner? Can we find a more moderate and measured solution that prevents illicit copying but still preserves limitations on copyright such as fair use and first sale?

IV

THE VIABILITY OF A MORAL CONSTRAINT

This analysis seems to have taken us to a difficult place. Is there any way to transcend the digital dilemma and overcome the unpalatable alternatives of uncontested file sharing on darknets or tightly enclosed digital content?

As one searches for a more viable and measured solution to this problem, the role of ethics, ignored by lawyers and policymakers, deserves more serious attention. As noted, Lessig lumps together ethical standards and social conventions under the constraint he calls "norms." This is misguided since real ethical standards are fixed and not variable, as are social norms. Nor are they contingent on the subjective opinions and whims of the community. In the case of copying digital content, social conventions send a mixed signal, but, if we look at this issue through the lens of general ethical principles, that signal is much clearer. The application of ethical standards generally tends to confirm that taking another's property is wrong, regardless of whether that property is tangible or intangible. Similarly, the principles of common morality and natural law reinforce the critical importance of obedience to the law.

Perhaps an ethical perspective based on Kant's moral philosophy can shed some light on why downloading copyrighted files is an immoral activity. For Kant, the fundamental ethical law is articulated in the Categorical Imperative: act so that your subjective maxim (or implied principle) could become universal law. This standard of universalizability is the sole criterion for the validity of specific moral imperatives.[19]

If we assume that the theories justifying intellectual property (such as utilitarianism) have some validity, we must conclude that common ownership of intangible property is impractical and inconsistent with the public good. According to one account, "In the real, dynamic world, producers of ideas respond to incentives; if they are granted no rights in their creations, they will create less or not at all."[20] As Korsgaard observes, "property is a practice,"[21] and we have argued that from a purely utilitarian standpoint this practice makes sense for both physical and intellectual property. For example, if we want to see blockbuster movies from Disney that cost $150 million to produce, it will be essential to give Disney some limited copyright protection over its property. While some libertarians resist this way of thinking, most individuals would admit that collective ownership of intellectual property, in which *all* creative works belong to the intellectual commons immediately, is not conducive for stimulating creative expression, especially when a large investment of labor or capital is required. Thus, given the pragmatic necessity of private intellectual property, a universalized maxim that permitted stealing of such property as a standard procedure would be self-defeating. That maxim would say, "It's acceptable for everyone to steal anyone else's privately owned intellectual property." Such a universalized maxim is self-defeating precisely because it would lead to the destruction of the entire practice of proprietary intellectual property rights; without those rights as an incentive, the quality and quantity of creative works would be greatly diminished. Since the maxim allowing an individual to freely appropriate another's intellectual property does not pass the test of normative universalization, a moral agent is acting immorally when he or she engages in acts such as the unauthorized copying of digital movie or digital music files.

In addition, copyright infringement represents a violation of law, and law has moral authority unless it is unjust. Copyright laws in the United States are rooted in the Constitution and designed to promote the common good by stimulating creative and innovative works. There may be other reasonable ways to "promote the progress of Science and the useful Arts" but lawmakers have chosen *this* way. Aquinas argues persuasively that lawmakers have the prerogative to choose among many options when they craft laws in a process he calls *determinatio*.[22] They have wide latitude to delineate specific laws in advancing a general idea as long as no option "is in itself repugnant to natural justice."[23]

Aquinas, following Aristotle, further insists that laws should presumptively determine one's moral obligations, unless those laws are truly unjust, that is, inconsistent with the common good and basic human rights or promulgated by a legislative body that has exceeded its authority. Just laws enunciate standards of fairness and protect rights, and most individuals in society base their projects and investments on the premise that the law will be respected by others. Although copyright law may have certain deficiencies and excesses, it is difficult to make the case that those laws are intrinsically unjust. Most casual users do not see themselves engaged in civil disobedience when they download an MP3 or DVD file. They copy these files simply because they want free music, not because they have made a moral judgment about the injustice of copyright law. Furthermore, one cannot capriciously decide that copyright law should not apply to certain content or media. For example, one cannot elect to abide by copyright protection for books and videos but reject such protection for music by concluding that the Internet makes such protection outdated. According to Finnis, "picking and choosing amongst the law's requirements will inevitably undermine the law's protections of rights and interests."[24] He derives this insight from Aquinas, who argues that "by usurping and ignoring the legal process," we act against "common justice" and also give a "corrupting example."[25] Defiance of just, albeit imperfect, laws is a source of disorder for society because it sets an example that could entice others to follow the same path.

One can rationalize that breaking copyright laws is inconsequential, but this act of breaking the law puts the perpetrator on a slippery slope. And it's not all together clear where one finds the principled breaking point. Lower down on that incline are other laws violated such as the federal tax code or traffic rules that protect public safety, or worse. Just laws therefore must be obeyed for the sake of the common good and what Aristotle calls "general justice."

Advocacy of these arguments surely does not preclude other legitimate moral perspectives on the issue. It *might* be possible for a strict utilitarian to reason that such copying is acceptable under certain circumstances when all costs and benefits are calculated. Nissenbaum has argued that some cases of copying software do not constitute a moral violation, though she does not "completely reject the constraints of software copyright protection."[26] Other ethicists, however, take sharp exception to her conclusions. Gert, for example, argues that when we carefully examine the activity of "illegally copying a software program," we recognize that the proper description of this act is "violating a morally acceptable law to gain some benefit." According to Gert's framework of common morality, one cannot justify breaking a morally acceptable law unless "one would be willing to publicly allow any morally acceptable law to be violated," but no rational impartial person could possibly allow this.[27]

Unless one is ready to reject the whole system of intellectual property law, the case against willfully breaking copyright laws, as many Napster users did, seems pretty formidable. But where does that get us? Does this issue have any moral saliency outside the rarefied world of academics?

In a study on software piracy conducted some years ago, Logsdon, Thompson, and Reid surveyed college students about their attitudes regarding the unauthorized copying of microcomputer software.[28] Their hypothesis was that the higher one's level of moral judgment, the less likely one will engage in activities such as unauthorized copying of software. But the study did not confirm this hypothesis. The reason, according to the authors, is the low moral intensity of this issue. This seems quite plausible and, without the benefit of a survey, one could conclude that the rampant copying of music and video files can also be partly attributable to the low moral intensity of the issue. According to Jones, the following characteristics of an issue tend to make it more intense and thereby connected to higher levels of moral decision making: magnitude of consequences; social consensus; probability of effect; temporal immediacy; proximity; and concentration of effect.[29]

In the Logsdon study it became evident that the issue of unauthorized software copying had a low intensity level. Most individuals reasoned that this activity was inconsequential; they regarded the social consensus as mixed; they perceived the probability of causing harm as low; there was some length of time between the act of copying and any unfavorable consequences; the victims (i.e., software companies) were distant from the copier; and the negative consequences, if any, would be confined to a few companies or individuals.

Although there are no parallel studies for the unauthorized copying of digital music, it is safe to infer that this too is a low intensity issue for the same fundamental reasons. For example, there was a general attitude among Napster users that the only ones being hurt by file sharing were the "big five" music companies. Also, as we observed, while society may not have viewed this copying with approbation, it certainly did not regard the activity as particularly perfidious.

According to Jones, a moral issue of low intensity may not be perceived as a moral issue at all and will most likely not "elicit moral behavior as frequently" as high intensity issues.[30] As long as the copying of software, music, or video files remains a moral issue of low intensity, it seems likely that appeals to Kantian morality or the imperative of "general justice" will fall on deaf ears. Moral norms seem to be no more effective than social norms in curtailing the spread of piracy.

STRENGTHENING THE VOICE OF MORALITY

In our view, however, this issue's current lack of moral gravity does not imply that the constraint of morality has no viability. Morality should have a decisive role to play in addressing the problem of software piracy and resolving the digital dilemma. Without the influence of morality, it is likely that inhibitions about copying will continue to decline. As noted, social norms send an ambiguous message—many members of the Internet community argue for the toleration of piracy based on ideology or some revolutionary impulse. But moral norms send a much clearer signal that must be heard.

Morality's persuasive pedagogy needs to play a more prominent role in helping to check the spread of piracy. Moralists and educators must work harder to increase the intensity of this issue by making persistent reference to the moral arguments cited in this chapter. The music industry, for example, "embraces education as a way to get students to adopt a respectful attitude towards copyrights."[31] As long as the issue of unauthorized copying is perceived as a trivial matter, ethical arguments, however sound, will not resonate. Hence the need to demonstrate that the ramifications of disregarding copyright law for personal satisfaction are not so trivial. This means emphasizing the harms that come to copyright holders and society in general when protected material is copied. The cases of Steve Levy's misappropriated books or those musicians distraught by Napster's complicity in infringement of their copyrighted materials are striking examples of how artists can be hurt by this practice. Also, students must be made mindful that copyright protection serves the public good. Companies will not invest in major projects without a guarantee of a return and the more that this arrangement is jeopardized by copying, the lower the incentive to make an investment. This will mean a diminished level of innovative content.

Most important, emphasis must be placed on the corrosive effects of breaking the law. Violating laws that are not obviously unjust is imprudent, potentially subversive, and a source of disorder. It also yields collateral damage by leading others into wrongdoing—law breaking sets a bad example that can reverberate through society. It is important to impress on all individuals that just laws have moral authority and that breaking those laws is not socially or morally acceptable.

It is difficult but not impossible for moral education to make the issue of piracy more compelling by appealing to such arguments. Consider the problematic area of digital music. Most of the piracy has taken place on college campuses. Yet most universities did little to discourage this activity by exhorting their students to act responsibly or intervening to stop this rampant downloading of MP3 files by disabling Napster technology. A more proactive and principled approach from university administrators along with a greater emphasis on piracy in ethics courses and symposia could go a long way to elevate the visibility of this issue.

There is also some consensus emerging about the need to assert these arguments with young people who are novice Internet users. There has been little effort made to prepare students for using the Internet in a responsible fashion, and this lack of preparation undoubtedly contributes to the problem. According to Schwartz, experts "compare the situation with giving every student a car without providing drivers' education classes."[32] If high school and middle school students are taught to respect intellectual property law and that message is reinforced in college, there may be some opportunity to reverse the trend of illicit copying of digital goods. In the long run, ethical preparation and awareness seem to be far more effective than reliance on ambivalent social norms and unenforceable laws. The cultivation of moral restraint will diminish the need to rely on more restrictive code-based solutions.

However, we must recognize that these moral arguments will not be embraced by everyone. As a result, it is inevitable that code will play a critical part in the solution to online piracy. But, as we have argued, code is not an acceptable solution unless it is tempered by moral awareness, and herein lies another role for the constraint of morality. Those individuals who develop software code that will protect content must do so in a way that is respectful of moral values. Developers can build this code so that it is sensitive to moral concerns and respects long-established values such as fair use and limited term, or they can choose to ignore those values. While some dispute whether it's possible to incorporate fair use into digital rights management, the consensus is that this can be done, although with considerable effort. It would be irresponsible to design these rights management systems without somehow allowing for fair use and taking account of other safety values enshrined in the legal tradition. If digital rights architectures can be built with moral competence and sensitivity to the consumer's rights, we will begin to make progress in achieving an equitable resolution of the digital dilemma.

CONCLUSIONS

Morality provides an important but neglected point of control to ensure that digital content can be disseminated without anarchy. Moral principles offer a clear sense of direction that is lacking in social conventions. Educators must reinforce the immorality of digital piracy because it damages the common good and breaks the law. By asserting this normative claim with more vigor, they might be able to increase the intensity level of this issue. Not everyone will be persuaded by these moral arguments, so code-based solutions will most likely be deployed to protect vulnerable content. Moral norms must discipline and guide those solutions so they avoid excess and do not trample on consumer rights of fair use and first sale. Unless the constraint of morality begins to exert this kind of influence, the epidemic of unauthorized copying will continue, only to be countered by more Draconian and coercive solutions that lack balance and nuance.

NOTES

1. U.S. Constitution, Article I, §8, Clause 8.

2. Paul Goldstein, *Copyright's Highway* (New York: Hill & Wang, 1994), p. 20.

3. Plaintiff's Complaint, *A&M Records v. Napster*, Inc. 2000 WL 573136 (N.D. Cal. [2000]).

4. Amy Kover, "Napster: The Hot Idea of the Year," *Fortune*, June 26, 2000: 149.

5. John Alderman, *Sonic Boom: Napster, MP3 and the New Pioneers of Music* (Cambridge: Perseus Books, 2001), p. 125.

6. Ibid., p. 158.

7. Stephanie Greene, "Reconciling Napster with the Sony Decision and Recent Amendments to Copyright Law," 39 *American Business Law Journal* 57, 2001.

8. *A&M Records, Inc. v. Napster* 239 F. 3d, 9th Cir., 2001.

9. Ibid.

10. Alderman, op cit., p. 180.

11. Larry Lessig. *Code and other Laws of Cyberspace* (New York: Basic Books, 1999), p.77.

12. Raymond Ku, "The Creative Destruction of Copyright," 49 *University of Chicago Law Review* 108, 2002.

13. Nicholas Negroponte, *Being Digital* (New York: Knopf, 1995), p. 58.

14. Julie Cohen, "Information Rights and Intellectual Freedom," *Ethics and the Internet*. Ed. A. Vedder (Antwerp: Intersentia, 2001).

15. Steven Levy, "The Day I Got Napsterized," *Newsweek*, May 28, 2001: 44.

16. Ku, op cit., p. 108.

17. Mark Stefik, "Trusted Systems," *Scientific American*, March 1997: 87.

18. Lessig, op cit., p. 135.

19. Immanuel Kant, *Foundation of the Metaphysics of Morals* (New York: Macmillan, 1990).

20. "Market for Ideas," *The Economist*, April 14, 2001: 72.

21. Christine Korsgaard, *Creating the Kingdom of Ends* (Cambridge: Cambridge University Press, 1996), p. 97.

22. John Finnis, *Aquinas* (Oxford: Oxford University Press, 1998), pp. 266–267.

23. Ibid., p. 268.

24. Ibid., p. 272.

25. St. Thomas Aquinas, *Summa Theologiae* (New York: Benziger Brothers, 1947), II–II, q. 66 a. 5 ad. 3.

26. Helen Nissenbaum, "Should I Copy My Neighbor's Software?," *Computers, Ethics, and Social Values*. Eds. D. Johnson and H. Nissenbaum (Englewood Cliffs, NJ: Prentice-Hall, 1995), p. 201.

27. Bernard Gert, "Common Morality and Computing," conference paper delivered at Computer Ethics: A Philosophical Enquiry (CEPE98), London School of Economics, December 14–15, 1998.

28. Jeanne Logsdon, Judith Thompson, and Richard Reid, "Software Piracy: Is It Related to Level of Moral Judgement?," *Journal of Business Ethics* (vol. 13, 1994), pp. 849–857.

29. Thomas Jones, "Ethical Decision Making by Individuals in Organizations: An Issue-Contingent Model," *Academy of Management Review* (vol. 16, 1991): 366–395.

30. Ibid.

31. Alderman, op cit., p. 170.

32. John Schwartz, "Trying to Keep Young Internet Users from a Life of Piracy," *The New York Times*, December 25, 2001, p. C1.

REFERENCES

Alderman, John. 2001. *Sonic Boom: Napster, MP3 and the New Pioneers of Music*. Cambridge: Perseus Books.

Aquinas, St. Thomas. 1947. *Summa Theologiae*. 3 Volumes. New York: Benziger Brothers.

Aristotle. 1985. *Nicomachean Ethics*. Trans. T. Irwin. Indianapolis: Hackett Publishing.

A&M Records, Inc. v. Napster. 2001. 239 F. 3d 1004 (9th Cir.).

Cohen, Julie. 2001. Information Rights and Intellectual Freedom, in A. Vedder (Ed.). *Ethics and the Internet*. Antwerp: Intersentia, pp. 11–32.

Gert, Bernard. 1998. Common Morality and Computing. *Computer Ethics: A Philosophical Enquiry (CEPE98)*. London School of Economics, December 14–15.

Goldstein, Paul. 1994. *Copyright's Highway*. New York: Hill & Wang.

Greene, Stephanie. 2001. Reconciling Napster with the Sony Decision and Recent Amendments to Copyright Law, *American Business Law Journal* 39: 57.

Jones, Thomas. 1991. Ethical Decision Making by Individuals in Organizations: An Issue-Contingent Model, *Academy of Management Review* 16: 366–395.

Kant, Immanuel. 1990. *Foundation of the Metaphysics of Morals*. New York: Macmillan.

Korsgaard, Christine. 1996. *Creating the Kingdom of Ends*. Cambridge: Cambridge University Press.

Kover, Amy. 2000. Napster: The Hot Idea of the Year, *Fortune* June 26: 149.

Ku, R. 2002. The Creative Destruction of Copyright, *University of Chicago Law Review* 49: 108.

Lessig, Larry. 1999. *Code and other Laws of Cyberspace*. New York: Basic Books.

Levy, Steven. 2001. The Day I Got Napsterized, *Newsweek* May 28: 44.

Logsdon, Jeanne, Judith Thompson, and Richard Reid. 1994. Software Piracy: Is It Related to Level of Moral Judgement? *Journal of Business Ethics* 13: 849–857.

Market for Ideas. 2001. *The Economist* April 14: 72.

Negroponte, Nicholas. 1995. *Being Digital*. New York: Knopf.

Nissenbaum, Helen. 1995. Should I Copy My Neighbor's Software, in D. Johnson and H. Nissenbaum (Eds.), *Computers, Ethics, and Social Values*. Englewood Cliffs, NJ: Prentice-Hall, pp. 201–213.

Plaintiff's Complaint, *A&M Records v. Napster*, Inc. 2000. WL 573136 (N.D. Cal.).

Schwartz, John. 2001. Trying to Keep Internet Users from a Life of Piracy. *The New York Times* December 25: C1 and C4.

Stefik, Mark. 1997. Trusted Systems, *Scientific American* March: 73–97.

THREE

Virtual Virtues

Reflections on Academic Integrity
in the Age of the Internet

LAWRENCE M. HINMAN

WHEN I WAS AN undergraduate in the 1960s, many things were different. Vacuum tubes were still common, even in computers not associated with air traffic control. Xeroxing was possible, but still considered extravagant. And plagiarism was different as well. We would hear rumors that certain fraternities had files of term papers that members could access. Occasionally we learned of someone who used a book or journal in the library and typed portions of it into a term paper. Once in a while a friend would write or rewrite a paper for someone else, usually a girlfriend for a boyfriend. But that was about it. Plagiarism was tedious, time consuming, and required some forethought in most cases.

The academic community in which we lived was also different then. In many ways, this community for many of us was akin to Aristotle's description of the polis in Book III of *The Politics*:

> This is obvious; for suppose distinct places, such as Corinth and Megara, to be brought together so that their walls touched, still they would not be one city, not even if the citizens had the right to intermarry, which is one of the rights peculiarly characteristic of states. Again, if men dwelt at a distance from one another, but not so far off as to have no intercourse, and there were laws among them that they should not wrong each other in their exchanges, neither would this be a state. Let us suppose that one man is a

49

carpenter, another a husbandman, another a shoemaker, and so on, and that
their number is ten thousand: nevertheless, if they have nothing in common
but exchange, alliance, and the like, that would not constitute a state. Why
is this? Surely not because they are at a distance from one another: for even
supposing that such a community were to meet in one place, but that each
man had a house of his own, which was in a manner his state, and that they
made alliance with one another, but only against evil-doers; still an accurate thinker would not deem this to be a state, if their intercourse with one
another was of the same character after as before their union. It is clear then
that a state is not a mere society, having a common place, established for the
prevention of mutual crime and for the sake of exchange. These are conditions without which a state cannot exist; but all of them together do not
constitute a state, which is a community of families and aggregations of families in well-being, for the sake of a perfect and self-sufficing life. Such a
community can only be established among those who live in the same place
and intermarry. Hence arise in cities family connections, brotherhoods,
common sacrifices, amusements which draw men together. But these are
created by friendship, for the will to live together is friendship. The end of
the state is the good life, and these are the means towards it. And the state
is the union of families and villages in a perfect and self-sufficing life, by
which we mean a happy and honorable life.

Our conclusion, then, is that political society exists for the sake of
noble actions, and not of mere companionship.[1]

The academic community, while not a city-state in all the ways Aristotle
describes, nonetheless possesses the distinguishing characteristic of the academic community at its best: the coming together of individuals for noble
actions—in this case for the advancement of knowledge through research
and scholarship, the transmission of knowledge through undergraduate education, and the formation of future scholars and researchers through graduate education.

The situation today is very different. Although the life of the academic
community remains, this life now intersects with the lives we lead on the
Internet. If the traditional academic community is akin to the Aristotelian
polis, the world of the Internet is closer to Hobbes's state of nature. While it
would be an exaggeration to say, following Hobbes's description of the state
of nature, that "the notions of right and wrong, justice and injustice . . . have
no place," this description fits life on the Internet more closely than the Aristotelian one does. Pockets of genuine community do exist on the Internet,
and it has made distance much less relevant than was the case in Aristotle's
view. Genuine scholarly communities thrive on the Web, often around mod-
erated listservers that are based on some specific noble goals. However, the
Web as a whole has an anarchical structure much closer to Hobbes's state of

nature than Aristotle's polis, a structure (or perhaps, more precisely, the absence of a structure) in which right and wrong, justice and injustice, have little or no place.

This tension between the Internet as an Aristotelian polis and a Hobbesian state of nature can be seen in the ongoing controversy over spam and its regulation. The full consequences of a Hobbesian worldview are beginning to emerge with the proliferation of spam reaching the level at which many of our mailboxes are clogged to overflowing because of unsolicited commercial e-mail. The Aristotelian model of the polis presents a much more powerful alternative to the Hobbsian schema, one in which some awareness of the common good plays a significant role in individual decisions.

We may also have seen a devolution of this world from an Aristotelian polis in its early stages to a much more Hobbsian world more recently—or at least the appearance of a devolution. As Helen Nissenbaum has noted, we have observed a distinct shift in the kind of people who are publicly *recognized* as hackers. Our earlier image of the hacker was a person who was, in a quirky way, committed to the Aristotelian polis, one for whom excellence— usually to be found in writing elegant code—was of central importance, and one for whom the good of the (cyber) community was a principal concern. Such people still exist, but, as Nissenbaum points out, are not recognized as being among the group known as hackers. In effect, we now acknowledge only Hobbesian hackers as being hackers.

The world of the Web has not supplanted the academic world, but each has changed the other in important ways. They exist, not in identity or opposition, but like overlapping circles in a Venn diagram, partially sharing the same space but each in itself a larger world.

In this new world plagiarism is fast and easy—just a few clicks away on the Web—although it is often costly. A Google search on "term papers" yields over 1.7 million results. A few are free; many are recycled papers that have been turned in before in other classes, and these seem to sell from $25 and up to $15 per page. Browsing through the ethics section of a typical site, I found papers on common topics such as "Kant's Moral Law and Mill's Utilitarianism" and much more obscure themes such as "Air Traffic Controllers Dismissal and Its Relation the Works of Kant." You can also have custom papers written just for you, although there is something ironic about a site guaranteeing that it is a newly written paper for your plagiaristic pleasure. Some sites even offer to write masters theses and doctoral dissertations, and presumably the price for that would be quite high. It is also hard to imagine what kind of relationship would exist between a student and a thesis or dissertation director that this would even be possible. Some sites even advertise for writers, requiring at least a master's degree and claiming that writers can earn as much as $2,000 per week writing full-time. Plagiarism has not become big business, but it has certainly become at least small business.

The rise of term-paper mills is not the only factor that influences the increased ease with which assignments can be plagiarized from the Web. Newspapers, magazines, and organizations of all kinds put materials on the Web, and students can sometimes use these as sources from which to plagiarize. (They can also, of course, use them to do research, and in many cases they offer excellent resources for the serious student.) Professors often put their own papers online, some journals are now online, and in some cases students put their own assignments online as part of a course requirement. In many cases, these resources are not in a password-protected area and thus they become additional free resources for students intent on plagiarizing.

Just as plagiarism has become a business, so too has its detection. A Google search on "plagiarism" returns 462,000 entries, and we can easily see that there has been an expansive attempt to fight technological fire with more technological fire. Some sites offer tips on how to spot plagiarism.[2] Others offer plagiarism-detection software programs.[3] Still other sites provide plagiarism-detection services. The best known of these is TurnItIn.com, which began as Plagiarism.org.[4] This service works by matching submitted papers against its database of available papers and then producing a color-coded report showing what percentage of the paper appears to be taken from other sources. The submitted paper is then added to the database for future reference.

Technological responses to the challenge of plagiarism often elicit technological countermeasures. Recognizing that antiplagiarism software relies on matching word patterns, students turn to Microsoft Word's AutoSummarize function in the hope of fooling the detection software. My suspicion is that there is other software out there that is dedicated to changing papers sufficiently to avoid being flagged by plagiarism-detection software. We've come a long way from vacuum tubes!

In the following remarks, I want to explore some of the ways in which we can respond to the moral challenges posed by the ease of plagiarism on the Web. We will see that this is an interesting and complex moral terrain, shaped in part by technological innovations and in part by nontechnological considerations. As I map out this terrain, a single figure—Aristotle—will hover in the background, providing guidance and insight. In particular, Aristotle's account of virtues as excellences of character will offer us the philosophical framework within which we can most fruitfully examine the full issue of academic integrity. In order to show this, I would first like to sketch out some background information about who cheats, and then turn to a framework for understanding academic integrity, and then look in depth at the issue of intellectual property rights and academic integrity, offering some practical suggestions for reducing the lack of clarity in this area.

WHO PLAGIARIZES?

One of the pioneers in empirical research in this area, Donald McCabe,[5] a Professor of Management at the Business School at Rutgers University, has suggested a very useful typology for grouping students in regard to the issue of academic integrity.[6] He suggests that students can be divided into three groups: those who never cheat, at one end of the spectrum; those who routinely cheat as their preferred choice, at the other end of the spectrum; and, in the middle, those who cheat occasionally. He found that these groups reflect a 20:60:20 division, that is, about 20 percent of the students never cheated, about 60 percent cheated occasionally, and about 20 percent habitually tried to cheat. In recent years, that has changed somewhat, with the "never cheat" category shrinking in size while the "habitually cheat" category has grown. These numbers vary, depending on the type of school, selectivity of the admissions process, school culture, and so on. Schools with honor codes typically have the lowest overall rates of cheating.[7]

If we wished to minimize plagiarism, each of these three groups must be approached differently. The first group, the one that never cheats, obviously does not need to be deterred from cheating. The most important factor in regard to this group is providing a campus culture that is as supportive as possible of their commitment to academic integrity. They will not be influenced by the ready accessibility of term papers on the Internet, but they may well falter in their commitment if they find widespread plagiarism around them going unpunished.

The third group, the habitual cheaters, certainly find that their life is made easier by the ready accessibility of Web-based resources for plagiarism, but, generally speaking, they do not plagiarize *because* these resources are available. If they were not, they would find some other way of plagiarizing. It is here that antiplagiarism software can be very helpful, for these are students whose papers ought to be checked regularly. It should be noted, furthermore, that these students are often the best at cheating and plagiarizing. They have done it before. They are not usually encumbered by guilt. Among those who cheat, these are the pros.

The middle group, those who occasionally cheat or plagiarize, are the most interesting and the most likely to be affected by the easy availability of Web-based resources. McCabe has suggested that the challenge of academic integrity today is to figure out how best to work with this group. The first group will take care of itself, at least in a minimally supportive environment. The third group can only be detected and caught, and in some cases might be deterred by very aggressive monitoring. The middle group, however, is most influenced by the easy availability of Web resources, since their plagiarism is more likely to be a spur-of-the-moment decision. Let me give two examples.

First, I have sat on a number of hearing committees as a faculty representative. This is the accused student's "day in court." The professor presents the complaint. The student presents his or her side of the case separately. Each is questioned by committee members. Typical scenarios in such
hearings involve students who have failed to manage their time well. They
have a paper due, realize they cannot complete the assignment on time, and
turn the night before to the Web to get a paper or portions of a paper that
they then turn in as their own work the next day. (I also realize, sitting on
these committees, that I am often looking at the students who do not cheat
well, in part because they do not cheat often; the hard-core cheaters, the
third group, are often more skilled and consequently harder to catch.) Had
the Web resources not been available, some of these students would probably have not handed in a paper or turned in some very minimal assignment.
The Web offers them another possibility, not previously available at that
late date.

Let me share a second example, changing a few incidental details to
ensure that the actual student is not recognizable. I was teaching an ethics
course, and one of the assignments was for students to do a weekly journal of
personal reflections on the readings. In one class, when I was away at a conference, my grad assistant showed the movie *Mississippi Burning* at my request,
since we were covering moral issues about racism that week. During the last
week of class, a student asked if they were required to write a journal entry on
the movie. I said they were not, but if they wanted to write about it, I would
give them extra credit. One of the students, who was rarely present in class,
turned in his journal with an entry on the movie—and it turned out to be a
movie review from a well-known American movie critic. It took me about
thirty seconds to track it down (the second entry on an MSN search), and my
guess is that it took the student approximately the same amount of time to
find it as well. (There are in fact a number of good, critical resources available on the Web about this movie, even if this review did not happen to be
one of them.) I am not sure if this student belonged in the second or third
category, but my assumption is that this student would never have bothered
to plagiarize this extra-credit assignment if it had not been so easy—and, in
this case, free.

The data on whether this assumption is justified are inconclusive. In
McCabe's most recent research with high school students and cheating, he
found that "90% of the students using the Internet to plagiarize have also plagiarized from written sources . . . [in other words,] The Web has 'created' few
new cheaters—6% of all students."[8] As more data become available, we
should get a clearer empirical picture of the extent to which the Web is
encouraging students who cheat occasionally to do so more often.

This issue is similar to that addressed by Richard Spinello in the previous chapter. Spinello says that "the nature of digital property along with the

capabilities of the Internet seems to desensitize us to the worth of intellectual property." Spinello notes the way in which copyright infringement seems to many to be less significant because the original is left instact (in contrast, say, to stealing a CD from Borders), but in the case of Internet plagiarism this plays a much less significant role than the fact that such plagiarism is both private and fast.

It is also helpful to note within this context that Internet plagiarism is now a centralized business, relying on centralized servers and a clear system of payment. Interestingly, a Gnutella-like network for term papers does not seem to have arisen. On some level, this would seem to have been a "natural," since we find both the motivation for such an enterprise and also the people (students are deeply involved in these issues). Nor, to my surprise, has there be an eBay-like term paper service that has come to dominate the market. I got only eight hits on an eBay search for "term papers." A comparable Google search yields over 2.3 million entries. There are a few such services, like Directessays.com, that exist, but they do not seem to have the major market share that something like SchoolSucks.com does. (Interestingly, Directessays.com also offers college application essays. One of them begins "Throughout the last four years of high school, I have learned so much about myself and the reality of life. High school prepares a person for the rest of his/her life, and going by the last few years, I feel that I am ready to make my mark on the world. I have always tried to involve myself in a. . . ." What more needs to be said?)

We can place these three groups of students within the context of Aristotle's discussion of the virtues and vices.[9] Aristotle draws a helpful distinction between two kinds of goodness: the temperate person and the continent person. Let me illustrate this first in terms of food (one of my favorite subjects), and then apply this distinction to academic integrity issues.

A temperate person is one who not only does the good, but also desires it for its own sake. I know people, although I do not count myself as a member of this group, who not only eat foods that are good for them, but do so because they *like* those foods. These are *temperate* people in regard to food. They have, in Aristotle's phrase, rightly ordered desires. Others, and on my good days I count myself a member of this group, eat foods that are good for them, but they do not enjoy doing so. They do it because they know they should, but it is not enjoyable for them. These are *continent* people, individuals who do the right thing ever though on some level they do not *desire* the right thing.

Individuals who fail to do good may also be divided into two groups, although this has been a much more contentious issue in moral theory. On the one hand, we have those who want to do the right thing, but are weak and thus fall to temptation. How one explains weakness of will (*akrasia* was Aristotle's term) is a matter of dispute, but we all recognize the phenomenon.

On the other hand, there are those who seem consciously to choose the bad or the evil. (There is a debate about whether one can really know the good and not choose it, but we do not need to settle that debate here.) Unfortunately, we probably all recognize this phenomenon as well.

We can apply this set of distinctions to McCabe's research. The third group of students, those who habitually cheat, belong in this final category, those who choose the bad. The first group, those who never cheat, are in all likelihood temperate individuals who are honest because they find that rewarding in itself; they desire the good. The middle group, the one for whom we are battling, is the group of individuals who are either continent or weak-willed. It is this group that we must support and educate in the virtues of the academic life.

Within this context of this discussion, it is also helpful to note what the appeal of plagiarism is to a significant number of students. One sometimes hears the claim "Cheaters only hurt themselves." This makes plagiarism into something akin to a "victimless crime," not unlike prostitution and pornography. However, this is misleading, at least in regard to plagiarism. Just as we have to acknowledge that people are drawn to Internet pornography because, on some level, they *like* it, so too with plagiarism. (In regard to Internet-based pornography, see chapter 4.) Students plagiarize, whether using the Internet or in the old-fashioned ways, because doing so generally benefits them. As much as we want to maintain the fantasy that the student benefits immeasurably more from writing that paper on the construction of gender roles in *The Canterbury Tales*, realisitically we have to admit that some students might benefit more from the combination of additional sleep and an "A" on a plagiarized paper.

I stress this point because it is important to realize that the principal harm that results from Internet plagiarism is that it hurts *other* students, not necessarily the cheater. Not only is it important to change the moral perceptions of the plagiarizer, but it is also necessary to change the perceptions of the honest students who often fail to recognize the damage that cheating does to the fabric of the academic polis.

THE FUNDAMENTAL VIRTUES OF ACADEMIC INTEGRITY

In 1998, at the request of my dean, I became involved in revising the document that eventually was named "The Fundamental Values of Academic Integrity"[10] and is now available from the Center for Academic Integrity, which is affiliated with the Kenan Institute for Ethics at Duke University. The process of working with faculty and administrators on this issue was enlightening in several ways and I gradually came to have a much richer notion of academic integrity than I originally had.

A MINIMALIST CONCEPT OF ACADEMIC INTEGRITY

Before I became involved in the Fundamental Values project, I had what one might call a minimalist conception of academic integrity: don't cheat and don't copy. It was simple, and easy for everyone to remember.

A RICH CONCEPT OF ACADEMIC INTEGRITY

As I began working with the Fundamental Values project, I encountered a different, far richer concept of academic integrity. Basically, the question the original authors of this document asked was this: what values are necessary to a flourishing academic life? Their answer was that there were five such fundamental values:

- Honesty
- Trust
- Fairness
- Respect
- Responsibility

Taken together, these five values constitute what I would call the rich definition of academic integrity.

FROM VALUES TO VIRTUES

The Fundamental Values project framed the issue of academic integrity in terms of values, but I would like to recast it in a more Aristotelian light by considering these values as the fundamental *virtues* of academic life.

ARISTOTLE ON THE VIRTUES

Aristotle's virtues approach is particularly helpful here because of its strong focus on the importance of flourishing. Aristotle's general question about the virtues was straightforward: what are the strengths of character necessary to human flourishing? The focus is a positive one, since for Aristotle the payoff of the virtues, to put the matter more crudely than Aristotle did, is that the individual's life is better because of them. So, too, about the vices: they are weakness of character that diminish our lives. Vices are not only objectionable because they harm other people, but our vices are also harmful to ourselves. Our lives are diminished because of our vices.

Aristotle also sees the ways in which specific virtues are responses to particular challenges in life. Courage, for example, is the strength of character that we need to face danger and the possibility of death. Similarly, we can ask the question: what strengths of character do we need to flourish in the academic life, both as students and as professors? The virtues of honesty, trust, fairness, respect, and responsibility, when taken together, provide the foundation of a flourishing academic life. Let me comment on each of these virtues.

HONESTY

Honesty is the bedrock virtue on which the academic life rests. Consider research in the sciences. If researchers are not honest in reporting their findings, there is little chance that science can make any progress. Either scientists will be forced to reinvent the wheel every time they design an experiment or they will find themselves relying on data that proves to be inaccurate. To be sure, sometimes mistakes happen; no one is infallible. Being honest is not equivalent to being right. However, as long as researchers report their results accurately and honestly, we can assume that in most cases the results are at least as accurate as they can make them.

Honesty is a strength of character, and it does not begin just with honesty toward others. It is also honesty with oneself. Whether scientist or philosopher, whether student or professor, in order to have a flourishing intellectual life, each of us must be rigorously honest with ourselves, always trying to ensure that we see in our work what is actually there, not what we either hope or fear to see. Such honesty is akin to a spiritual discipline, requiring precisely the kind of strength of character that Aristotle describes as "virtue."

Of course, we have to be honest with students as well as with ourselves. We have to exhibit honesty to them by telling the truth, even when the truth contradicts our own cherished beliefs. The professor who is an ideologue falls short of this ideal, and is likely to be surrounded by people who are either true believers or vociferous atheists. Professors who hold themselves to a standard of intellectual honesty and rigor provide a model for students and other faculty alike.

We as teachers need to be honest with our students in other ways as well. We need to share our mistakes as well as our insights. The college environment is all too often dominated by textbooks, which give the impression of timeless truths. Students often feel a pressure to look like they always know the answer—even if the only way they can accomplish this is by being quiet—and rarely do we value mistakes for what they can teach us. My experience is that students are often very interested in hearing about situations in which I have changed my views on an issue, and this often gives them permission to see their own intellectual journey in developmental terms.

Similarly, we need to be honest with students, faculty, and administrators in difficult areas such as evaluations and recommendations. We live in an era of inflation, including inflation of grades and recommendations. One of the ways in which professors can model the virtue of honesty for their students is to provide them with honest feedback and evaluation.

The Web is having an impact on honesty in several ways, some positive, some negative. We have already discussed the impact on plagiarism, which is the area in which its impact is most visible. However, the Web has had an influence on honesty issues in other ways as well. Let me mention two of them here.

First, some students find it easier to be honest in Web-based communications (online class forums, etc.) than they do in face-to-face classroom situations. This sounds paradoxical, since one thinks of honesty as a paradigmatically face-to-face virtue, but in fact those students who find direct communication uncomfortable sometimes flourish in online chat rooms and in other virtual venues.

Second, as we will see in more detail later in this chapter, students are increasingly likely to be placed in learning situations in which there is in fact no teacher as computer-based teaching becomes more common. It is precisely here that Aristotle's emphasis on the importance of virtues *for the self* becomes so important. Students engaged in computer-based learning often have no one else to be honest *to*; after all, they are responding primarily to a computer program. The incentive for being honest in these contexts must be primarily self-referential: without honesty, the student simply will not benefit from that particular educational experience. Dishonesty, in this context, harms the student first and foremost.

TRUST

If honesty is the foundation of the academic life, trust is the natural result of such honesty. Just as professors may trust students, so too students must be able to trust their professors. The virtue of trust is the glue that holds the academic life together.

The paradigm case of trust is found in a relationship between two people, in which one (A) trusts the other (B) to do or be a certain thing (x). Thus, there are three elements in trust: the one who is doing the trusting, the one who is being trusted, and the trusted matter that is at stake. Typically, this trusted matter must be important and there must be an objective element of uncertainty about it. I can trust a good friend to watch out for my children if anything suddenly happened to me, but I cannot trust that friend to know that 2 + 2 = 4. That is something that I can know on my own, and there is no element of uncertainty attached to it.

One of the most interesting implications of the Web for academic integrity issues turns on the issue of trust. As was mentioned in the beginning of this chapter, antiplagiarism software can be used to automatically screen all incoming assignments and rate them for possible plagiarism. But what is the impact of doing this on the relationship of trust between student and professor, especially when all incoming papers are automatically tested this way? It seems that this is an indication of a lack of trust, and no different in principle from, say, urine testing for Olympic athletes. We test precisely because we do not trust.

Chapter 5 contains some important insights into this issue. Weckert discusses the way in which trusting someone involves a particular kind of "seeing as," and it is helpful to understand the way in which such continual electronic monitoring may adversely affect the "seeing as" relationship on both sides of the podium. Teachers begin by seeing students as potential cheaters rather than as potential learners, and students come to see teachers as monitors and enforcers rather than as sources of intellectual leadership.

Let me contrast two ways of responding to the possibility of Web-based plagiarism. The first way is to fight fire with more technological fire. Here the example of TurnItIn.com is most relevant. Individual instructors can purchase these services on a per-course basis, but they typically sell their services to larger groups—departments, colleges and universities—as a package. (Since the papers that are submitted for screening are also added to the database, there is a double incentive to sign up entire departments or institutions.) If a university subscribes to this service, then individual professors can send all papers in a given course to TurnItIn.com for screening.

Let me suggest an alternative approach to Web-based plagiarism, both low tech and old-fashioned: better teaching. Typically, it is easiest to plagiarize a term paper from the Web when you simply have an assignment to turn the paper in at the end of the semester. If, on the other hand, professors meet with students to discuss topics and encourage them to choose highly individualized subjects, then plagiarism becomes more difficult. If professors require that, at regular intervals, students submit a topic, an initial outline, a preliminary bibliography, a short rough draft, and then the final paper, the possibility of plagiarism plummets; it is simply too much trouble to take a plagiarized paper and work back to each of the preceding steps. Moreover, if professors require that students respond to comments at each stage and incorporate that response into the next stage, then plagiarism becomes even less possible. If students present their work in class, this further reduces the odds.

Web-based plagiarism often arises in a vacuum, when students feel that they are not really seen or respected. There is much to be said for resisting the tendency to respond to this by additional technological means. We are much more likely, I think, to be able to reduce this by trusting our students and engaging them directly in the challenges of the material we are teaching.

There is, however, a good technological fix for what sometimes appears to be "inadvertent" plagiarism, that is, cases in which people lose track of the sources for their data.[11] This is particularly easy to have happen in a drag-and-drop environment, and I am sure faculty are often plagued by this problem as well. The fix is straightforward: an option (yes, one more checkbox under Tools/Options) that would enable your word processing program and your browser to work together, so that every time you drag and drop something from the Web into a document, the reference is automatically created with it.

There is yet another aspect to the issue of trust and the Web. One of the skills we have to teach our students is how to determine which sources of information are trustworthy. The virtue of trust has a element of *phronesis* in it, what Aristotle called practical wisdom. In the case of trust, we find that this has both cognitive and volitional elements to it, which again is characteristic of Aristotle's account of the virtues. We have to be willing to trust (that's the volitional element), and we have to know what is worth trusting (the cognitive element).

This is particularly a problem on the Web, where peer review is rare. Students are often *too* willing to trust, and lack the discrimination necessary to distinguish sources worth trusting from those that ought not to be trusted. Aristotle tells us that vices can be excesses or deficiencies. Here too much trust is a vice, making students overcredulous and gullible. In my experience, the other end of the spectrum, the overly skeptical student, is much less common. Typically, students know that they can trust articles they find in mainstream journals and books published by major university presses, but they have much less sense about what they can trust in Web sites.

FAIRNESS

Fairness is an intellectual virtue, akin to justice in many ways. It is certainly crucial to the academic life. For the academic life to flourish, we need to be fair to people and fair to ideas as well. This latter kind of fairness is an intellectual virtue, consisting of giving each idea its due, being open to the implications of an argument, judging claims on the basis of their merit rather than on the basis of their source, being—in Martha Nussbaum's beautiful phrase— "finely aware and richly responsible."

Fairness in this sense is akin to what Aristotle called justice, and just as justice is the fundamental virtue of the well-functioning polis, so too fairness is one of the most important virtues in the interactions of the academic community. Fairness is a virtue of interaction, of relationship regarding the way in which we assess one another and also apportion the goods and burdens of the academic life.

The impact of the Web in regard to fairness is primarily found in the way in which certain groups will typically have less access to the Web. Increasingly, professors make Web access a mandatory part of their courses, but some students simply do not have the financial resources to have their own computers and high speed Internet access. This "digital divide" disadvantages some students and gives an unfair boost to others who have had long familiarity with the Web. But this is not just an economic issue. There is certainly a percentage of students—rich, poor, and in between—who are just not comfortable with computers and computer-mediated instruction. The fairness issue extends to them as well, for they may be students who in many other ways are quite talented.

Teachers often feel caught between the proverbial rock and a hard place in regard to this issue. Until two years ago, I made sure that everything in my course was accessible to those without computers, but I gradually found my policy changing on this. I became increasingly concerned that those who did not use computers in fact needed to be helped (and perhaps pushed) in this direction, and now my courses regularly require Web access. However, one of the things that made this possible is that our university provides very good computer lab facilities, so students without their own computers can get online for as long as they want and do so without a wait. In addition, I found myself conducting mini-courses for those who were not yet comfortable with using computers, to try to reduce ways in which they might otherwise have been disadvantaged because of this requirement.

RESPECT

Respect manifests itself in many different guises. One of the most important ways in academic life that we can show respect for other people is to take their ideas seriously. Lack of respect will often undermine trust and the other fundamental values.

The impact of the Web on respect seems, at best, indirect. Respect is an interpersonal virtue, so it appears that insofar as the Web establishes contexts in which individuals are less likely to recognize one another as persons, there may be some undermining of respect, but this typically only occurs in situations of high anonymity (online groups, flaming, etc.), but in educational contexts these are exceptions.

The other context in which issues of respect arise is respect for property, and here the Web has had an impact. All too often, we just fail to respect copyright restrictions and the like, even when this is not a matter of plagiarism. I will discuss this in more detail.

RESPONSIBILITY

The final fundamental value of academic integrity is responsibility. In its most basic sense here, to show responsibility means to take control of one's own educational career and make it one's own—to say, in effect, "This is me," rather than "This is a G.E. requirement" or "This is something my parents want me to take."

The impact of the Web in this area is less easy to discern. The relevant variable here is anonymity. Insofar as some Web-based structures increase anonymity, they may diminish responsibility. This is particularly an issue in courses that are taught without an instructor. We will discuss this issue next.

Thus, the five fundamental virtues are the strengths of character necessary to a flourishing academic community. While the impact of the Web on some of them (especially respect and responsibility) is minimal, its impact on others (honesty and trust, most notably) is much greater. Let's now turn to another area in which the Web is increasingly influential: distance education.

VIRTUE AT A DISTANCE

Much of the preceding discussion has been confined to the impact of the Web on academic integrity within the traditional classroom. Interesting though that may be, the most interesting changes are going to occur as the Web transforms the traditional classroom into new and challenging configurations.

WHAT THE FUTURE HOLDS

There are several ways in which the traditional classroom will be transformed by the Web. These are not mutually exclusive, alternative futures but rather parallel developments, and they have important implications for academic integrity in the rich sense previously discussed. Let's examine several of these.

The Hybrid Course. Increasingly, many traditional courses will be taught as a combination of the traditional face-to-face classroom and the virtual classroom. This can occur in many configurations. Consider three. First, online discussions may simply be added to the regular class meetings. However, this quickly gives rise to the question: if we are spending more and more time online together, then can't we reduce the amount of actual classroom time? Second, following the model of lecture/lab in the sciences, some courses may have the main presentation of material on the Web and then schedule small-group face-to-face interactions that deal with applications of the lecture. This is particularly useful when a single professor is offering a course that meets on several campuses simultaneously. The lecture occurs online, and then grad assistants conduct the discussion at the various campuses. Third, in some cases the main presentation may actually be a live lecture, followed by online meetings that function like discussion sections.

The hybrid character of such courses will not of itself have a significant impact on academic integrity.

The "Rent-a-Course" Option. Consider the following scenario. A university is doing well. Enrollments are increasing every year, and are now constrained only by the capacity of the current campus. But administrators are cautious; they know that if they begin building additional facilities, they could open themselves to long-term liabilities that would be difficult to meet if enrollments began to drop. They realize that if they add classrooms, they must make a number of other additions as well, including parking spaces, dormitory rooms, cafeteria space, and so on. Yet the present moment seems to be a golden opportunity to increase enrollment and income, and they are hesitant to keep enrollments capped at previous levels.

Into this situation comes a new factor. A company, which in the past only published books, has now decided to take the next step and sell courses as well. It has formed a for-profit online university, but it markets its products in a unique way. It approaches administrators in precisely this situation and offers to sell them, say, five sections of Intro to World Civilization. These courses could be taken online by the university's students, listed in the regular course schedule, and so on. Similarly with a range of other basic courses. The company offers to sell these courses to the university at, perhaps, $3,000 per section and a set cost per student—carefully calculated to be slightly less than the salary of a part-timer and slightly less than the tuition paid per student.[12]

To many administrators, this may seem to be the answer to their prayers. Suddenly they are able to offer a sufficient number of basic courses so that they can increase enrollment without adding classroom space. In fact, they can even make a bit of money in the process. This can be a very attractive proposition to those who are charged with guarding the financial well-being of the university.

This development has serious implications for academic integrity for several reasons. First, these are typically very standardized courses that in large measure "teach themselves," that is, there is a standard set of readings and assignments that students are taken through no matter who is the actual teacher of record. There is little room for individualized interaction or even personal contact between the student and the instructor.

Second, such courses typically will not be integrated into the life of the department. There is no discussion between the faculty who teach the online courses and the regular departmental faculty. The courses meet a requirement, but fail to be part of the undergraduate experience that universities hope to deliver.

Third, introductory courses are often quite important in terms of recruiting majors in a particular area. Often that process involves a student's identifying with a particular professor. It is not simply a matter of becoming interested in American history, but of wanting to be like a particular professor who is teaching that course. As we all know from our own experience in the classroom, students start coming to office hours, asking questions about the subject matter, and generally trying on the identity of a person who works in this particular area. Insofar as we have online courses for meeting general education requirements, we may well lose this valuable opportunity for helping students to gain a sense of what they want to pursue academically.

Finally, in most universities there is a well-defined process for approving both courses and teachers. This type of online course could still be approved for its content, but there would be little or no opportunity for departments to screen those who would be teaching the course, whereas departments would typically screen adjunct faculty who teach in their department. This undermines faculty autonomy in a very crucial area.

The Professorless Course. The next step is this process is easy to see. Once someone has developed a set of assignments and activities and tests and has also developed a way in which students' progress can be automatically assessed, it becomes possible to eliminate the instructor completely.[13] This seems to be a reasonable scenario in certain types of courses that aim at developing a proficiency or skill in a given area. (I sometimes think my students could take my introductory logic course without me: lectures are available on the Web, assignments and tests could be automatically scored, and I could spend my time doing something more interesting than teaching intro logic for the fiftieth time.)

The implications of this for academic integrity are quite significant. When we recall the five values of academic integrity, we see that most of them are relational—they define the optimal relationship between student and professor. What happens when the professor is removed from this equation? Consider, for example, the value of trust. Presumably students will still trust the accuracy of the material presented, but there will be no opportunity to develop a relationship of trust with a professor who might then guide one's academic progress. Trust in the *person* disappears. Similarly with respect. There is little room for respect to arise, simply because there may not be a professor to respect—or, for that matter, to manifest respect for the students.

THE END OF PRIVATE PROPERTY?

Let me conclude with a brief discussion of one of the additional way in which the Web has affected academic integrity issues, and this has to do with private property. There is something about the Web that breeds disrespect for private property, almost as though it were an irrelevant concept. Let me offer some examples.

File sharing has become popular on the Web. Napster certainly made the biggest splash in this area, but there were other, less well-known but more radical competitors. The best known of these is Gnutella.[14] In many cases, and this is clearly true concerning Gnutella, sharing is voluntary, although sometimes individuals may share material to which they have no rights.

On a number of occasions, I have found myself wanting to grab copies of photos off the Web without asking permission. (This is particularly true if I am doing a PowerPoint and need something visual for a particular slide.) If I were in a colleague's office and that colleague had a picture of Rawls on his desk, and I needed a picture of Rawls, I would never just take the picture without asking. I would ask and, if refused, would not pursue the matter. If, however, I found that same photo on my colleague's Web site, I might well grab the picture, even without asking.

What's the relevant difference here? In the case of a physical picture, my taking the picture diminishes the person to whom it belongs. On the other hand, with a virtual photo, the person who originally had the photo is not thereby deprived of his or her possession, although its value may be reduced by the production of copies. The math of copying and duplicating with virtual files is very different from what it has been in the past, for we can now make identical copies—indeed, it's unclear whether the concept of the "original" still has relevance here—instantaneously and without taking anything away from the original.

There is another relevant difference here as well. When colleagues put pictures on their desk, they are not thereby giving implicit permission to others to take the picture if they want it. However, when something is put on the Web, many people—perhaps incorrectly—believe that the act of placing it on the Web implies that it is available for everyone for free. Certainly much ambiguity could be eliminated if items on the Web had XML tags that indicated whether they were (a) available for free viewing but not download and reuse [say, a tag like this: PermissionFreeNoDownload-NoReuse and then EndPermission] or (b) available for download and reuse as well as viewing [with a tag like this: PermissionFreeDownload-OkReuseOK and then EndPermission]. Other tags could be added to indicate whether citation is necessary, if reuse is possible but requires either permission or notification, and so on. Furthermore, information about the permission holder [PermissionHolder and EndPermissionHolder] could be embedded on each page or through a server-side include file. All the tags, furthermore, could be made machine-readable for the new standards of the Semantic Web.[15] At that point, the intent of the author of the Web page would be unambiguous and that intent could be communicated in a highly efficient manner.

The XML/RDF solution is a reasonable way of responding to the kind of "policy vacuum," first described by Moor,[16] that is so common in computer ethics. It offers a clear and efficient way of demarcating the difference between what is merely publicly viewable and what is not only publicly viewable but also free for download and reuse.

The advantage of doing this in the realm of academic integrity is clear. It would clearly label authors' work as their own, provide an efficient mechanism for obtaining permission, and greatly reduce the size of the policy vacuum we are currently facing in regard to academic integrity and the World Wide Web.[17]

NOTES

1. Aristotle, *The Politics*, Book III, Jowett translation.

2. See, e.g., http://alexia.lis.uiuc.edu/~janicke/plagiary.htm.

3. See, e.g., http://www.plagiarism.com/, which sells plagiarism-detection software.

4. The site, http://www.plagiarism.org, still exists, but primarily points to the services offered at www.TurnItIn.com.

5. See http://rbsweb2.rutgers.edu/display.cfm?IDNumber=104; also see http://www.academicintegrity.org/cai_research.asp for a brief overview of McCabe's research.

6. See,e.g., McCabe's presentation at the 10th Annual Meeting of the Center for Academic Integrity: http://ethics.sandiego.edu/video/CAI/2000/Research/index.html.

7. See McCabe, Donald L., Linda Klebe Trevino, and Kenneth D. Butterfield, Academic Integrity in Honor Code and Non-honor Code Environments: A Qualitative Investigation, *Journal of Higher Education* (March 1, 1999) Vol. 70, No. 2: 211 ff.; also see McCabe, Donald L. and Linda Kiebe Trevino, Dishonesty in Academic Environments: The Influence of Peer Reporting Requirements, *Journal of Higher* Education (January 1, 2001) No. 1, Vol. 72: 29.

8. See http://ethics.sandiego.edu/video/CAI/2001/McCabe/index_files/slide0006.html.

9. The principal source of Aristotle's account of the virtues is to be found in Aristotle's *Nichomachean Ethics*, but important additional material is in the *Eudemian Ethics*, the *Politics*, and the *Rhetoric*. I have dealt in greater detail with Aristotle's ethics in chapter nine of my *Ethics: A Pluralistic Approach to Ethical Theory*, 3rd ed. (Belmont: Wadsworth, 2002). This chapter also includes an extensive bibliographical essay.

10. A PDF copy is available at http://www.academicintegrity.org/pdf/FVProject.pdf.

11. I am indebted to Michael Lissack for this suggestion at the Faculty Institute on Academic Integrity and the World Wide Web, sponsored by the Center for Academic Integrity, For information of the workshop, see http://ethics.sandiego.edu/Resources/cai/webworkshop/.

12. Lest this sound implausible, let me mention that I was actually present during precisely this kind of sales pitch. In that particular instance, it was unsuccessful.

13. I am particularly indebted to Jon Dorbolo for initially pointing this out during a presentation at CAP 2000.

14. See http://www.gnutella.com/.

15. On the Semantic Web, see http://www.w3.org/2001/sw/ and Tim Berners-Lee, James Hendler, and Ora Lassila, The Semantic Web, *Scientific American May 2001*: http://www.scientificamerican.com/article.cfm?articleID=00048144–10D2–1C70–84A9809EC588EF21&catID=2.

16. See James H. Moor, What Is Computer Ethics?, online at http://www.south-ernct.edu/organizations/rccs/resources/teaching/teaching_mono/moor/moor_defini-tion.html.

17. Some of these ideas were developed in a much shorter version and without the emphasis on virtues, Aristotle, and many of the policy recommendations in Academic Integrity and the World Wide Web, *Computers and Society* Vol. 31, No. 1 (March 2002): 33–42, and The Impact of the Internet on Our Moral Lives in Academia, *Ethics and Information Technology* Vol. 4 No. 1 (February 2002): 31–35.

FOUR

Enter Here—At Your Own Risk

The Moral Dangers of Cyberporn

SUSAN DWYER

"LUST MOTIVATES TECHNOLOGY."[1] Pornographers are always among the first to recognize and exploit the potential of each new wave of communication technology, from the printing press and early photography to film and video, and now the Internet.[2] So-called adult entertainment businesses led the way in the development of secure online credit-card transactions, and they have been at the forefront of database management. *Playboy* was one of the first companies to use digital watermarking; Virtual Dreams, a company that provides online striptease shows, pioneered the use of videoconferencing.[3]

Cyberpornography is one of the few reliably profitable online businesses. In 1997, there were 10,000 sex industry sites, the biggest of them generating about $1 million a month. By 1998, there were at least three sites returning more than $100 million a year. In 2000, one or more of 60,000 sex sites was visited by one in four Internet users at least once a month.[4]

None of this should come as a surprise: sex sells. However, we must not be misled into thinking that the Internet is awash with smut or saturated with pornography, as some panicky critics would have us believe. Cyberpornography accounts for only one-fifth of the total annual pornography business in the United States, variously put between $10 and $14 billion.[5] Hence, it might be doubted that there is anything to say about cyberpornography that has not already been said about more traditional types of pornography. What, if any, new moral questions does cyberpornography raise?

Bracketing off the fact that many children can access cyberpornography more easily than they can access video and print pornography, cyberporn presents us with fundamentally the same sorts of moral issues as its technologically less sophisticated cousins. Nevertheless, in a somewhat surprising twist, the experience of consuming pornography on the Internet helps to illuminate a moral critique of pornography that is yet to receive the attention it deserves. The twist is surprising because the moral critique I have in mind appears rather old-fashioned. Indeed, the critique has ancient precedent in Aristotle's account of the virtuous agent.

Put bluntly, the idea is that some pornography is morally problematic because it provides the raw material for and helps to nurture a class of morally bad actions—namely, sexual fantasizing about a variety of harms to oneself and/or to others. And, because of the unique phenomenology of consuming pornography online, certain kinds of cyberpornography are particularly effective in this regard. As I will argue, sexual fantasizing is something we deliberately and consciously *do*. We construct fantasies that please us and return to them over the course of our lives. Sexual fantasies are remarkably persistent; indeed, the empirical evidence suggests that they are among the most enduring elements of our respective psychologies. However, it is morally dangerous persistently and deliberately to engage in an activity that yokes sexual pleasure and satisfaction to conscious thoughts of degradation, humiliation, and violence.[6] To do so is to run a serious risk of compromising one's moral character. If I am right about the unique experience of consuming cyberpornography, then cyberpornography might be quite risky indeed.

This controversial thesis is apt to meet with significance resistance from a number of sources, most of which I will attempt to address later in this chapter. However, one such source can be dealt with quickly. My concern here is with the *moral evaluation* of pornography (more precisely, with the moral evaluation of consuming pornography). I make no claims about what, if anything, the state should do about pornography, its producers and distributors, or its consumers. Nor are any particular policy recommendations implied by the critique I offer.[7] Debates about the moral status of pornography need not and should not be construed exclusively as debates about free speech and censorship. Of course, moral analysis may play a legitimate role in the formulation of public policy, but there is a *point* to engaging in such analysis that is quite independent of that use. Morality concerns how we live our public *and* private lives; at the very least, it pertains to what kinds of people we aspire to be. To abjure moral analysis and evaluation that are not strictly in the service of making policy is, perversely, to divorce moral thinking from our everyday lives, where it has its natural home—another Aristotelian theme.

THE MORAL STATUS OF PORNOGRAPHY:
SOME EARLIER ACCOUNTS

Few of us are wholly indifferent to pornography, unless perhaps we have never seen any. Many people clearly like it a lot, while others hate it all. However, I suspect that any reasonably reflective and honest person will concede that there is *something* problematic about Web sites devoted to representations of sexual torture, or, to cite a more prosaic example, about the fact that a nontrivial number of our fellow citizens invest considerable resources to return over and over to images of women being ejaculated on. But what is the source of this unease, and is it justified?

Since pornography became an object of systematic study, three main lines of criticism have emerged. In historical order, theorists have argued for the moral problematicity of pornography on the grounds of (1) its sexual content, (2) its alleged harmful effects on women, and (3) its role in the social construction of sexuality and gender. Each new critique was prompted by the revealed inadequacies of the one(s) that preceded it. I think all three approaches are flawed. However, for current purposes I will discuss only the first two.

Employing the most value-neutral characterization of pornography— namely, explicit pictorial or verbal representations of human sexual activity designed to produce sexual arousal—some people have condemned pornography just on the basis of its sexual content. In particular, they believe that the sort of sexual behavior portrayed in pornography perverts some 'true' purpose of sex, claiming, for example, that sex ought always aim at procreation or that it should always involve a profound connection between two persons.

There is no denying that pornographic sex is, literally, sterile. While some women may have conceived as a result of intercourse had in front of the cameras, making babies is not what pornography is about. Moreover, a good deal of pornographic sex happens between persons of the same sex, penetrations are oral and anal as well as vaginal, and, more often than not, a typical heterosexual pornographic scene ends with the ejaculation of semen onto a woman's face or body. Neither can we deny that pornographic sex is largely impersonal. Some pornography has narrative structure, but for the most part it cuts straight to the sex, focusing intensively on genitalia. And while actors obviously interact in quite intimate ways, their pleasure (real or simulated) seems quite solipsistic: any penis, any vagina, any mouth, any anus will do.

Still, it is hard to see what is *morally* wrong about sex without procreative intent or with sex that is not at the same time an instance of profound interpersonal communication. Indeed, it was surely one result of the so-called sexual revolution of the 1960s that these sorts of worries about pornography began to seem quaint. Nevertheless, as feminists started to think about pornography, a new critique emerged. The focus of feminist concerns turned to the alleged connection between pornography, especially violent pornography, and violence against women. Robin Morgan's remark "Pornography is the theory, rape is the practice" captured a feminist perspective on pornography that was extremely influential for over a decade.[8] This perspective had a powerful strategic advantage. If pornography does cause demonstrable harm to women, then it is obviously morally bad. More important, the substantiated harms of pornography would justify its censorship. For the Supreme Court has long conceded that speech that constitutes a clear and present danger can be restricted consistent with the First Amendment.[9]

There are two main reasons why this approach fails. First, the empirical claim that pornography causes harm to women, say, by making men rape and commit sexual assault, has not been established. A vast amount of social science research has produced conflicting results, and the research itself is plagued by familiar problems of bias and selective interpretation.[10] The second reason we should abandon this particular critique of pornography is deeper. As Laura Kipnis puts it, "The argument that pornography causes violent behavior in male consumers relies on a theory of the pornography consumer as devoid of rationality, contemplation, or intelligence, prone instead to witless brainwashing, to monkey see/monkey do re-enactment of the pornographic scene."[11]

Since this idea will figure in what comes later, it is worth closer examination. The central point is this: humans are not simple stimulus-response machines. Merely seeing some representation cannot by itself cause action. Viewing or reading pornography usually does cause sexual arousal, even in people who find pornography morally troubling. But an erection is not an action.

ACTIONS

Actions are distinct from happenings. Contrast my shrugging to indicate that I don't know the answer to your question (an action) with the same movement, my shoulders going up and down, when I hiccup (a happening). Or, consider the comedian Chevy Chase and his hilarious pratfalls. His intentional and deliberate behavior is quite different from that of the person who is tripped up on the street or falls over during an epileptic fit. Chevy Chase's falling is funny precisely because he *means* to fall. A person's *actions* are explained in terms of that person's beliefs, desires, and intentions, whereas *happenings*—for example, the person's mere bodily motions—are fully explicable in terms of physiological goings-on. To complicate matters, we might also want to specify a middling range of movements that are neither quite actions nor merely happenings; for example, unthinkingly drumming one's fingers during a tedious meeting or bobbing one's foot while listening to music. Typically, we don't *decide* to move our bodies in these ways, but once we become aware that we are doing so, we can stop. Now, many of our physical responses to pornography are passive— they just happen to us—and perhaps some of our psychological ones are too. But *acting* on the basis of these responses is not something that just happens to a person; one has to choose or try to do certain things. Unless one is pathological, the consumer of pornography is not *compelled* to act in any particular way in light of what he sees.

Having said that, there are two types of action, which, while optional, are typically associated with the consumption of pornography: masturbation and sexual fantasizing. My main topic is the latter.

To reiterate: the proposition I want to consider is that some pornography is morally problematic insofar as it plays a role (perhaps a pivotal one) in morally dangerous sexual fantasizing. I suspect that the default position of many Americans is that a moral critique of sexual fantasizing is simply a non-starter. But precisely because this is the prevailing view, the assumptions on which it rests need to be scrutinized.

FANTASIZING AS INNER

A common view is that fantasizing is essentially 'inner.' Killing a rival is morally wrong; merely fantasizing about killing her is not. There is little rea-son to think that fantasizing about X-ing makes actual X-ing more likely. And, one might think that if fantasizing does 'spill over' into overt behavior, then the fantasizing can be criticized, but only derivatively, in terms of the badness of the behavior to which it led.

Fantasizing *is* inner, in some sense of that term that also describes think-ing in general. It is one among many ways in which we exercise our imagina-tions. And we engage in it in the privacy of our consciousness. Recalling the distinctions made earlier, fantasizing is not something that merely *happens* to us. It may be distinguished from having fleeting thoughts, daydreaming, or being subject to unbidden or intrusive images (the analogues in imagination of finger drumming). Rather, fantasizing is typically something we deliber-ately and consciously *do*. Undoubtedly, there are cases of compulsive fanta-sizing, just are there cases of compulsive hand washing. However, in the usual case, a person fantasizes for a reason: in order to distract, please, or motivate herself. Hence, despite its location inside our heads, fantasizing is properly described as a type of action and is therefore open to moral scrutiny. Of course, the grounds on which a person may be praised or blamed for fantasiz-ing remain to be articulated.

As I noted, it might be conceded that some fantasizing can be morally criticized, but only if that fantasizing leads to harmful overt behavior. About a man with sadistic sexual fantasies we might say "They're all in his head. He is not hurting anyone. And maybe his fantasizing in this way is what keeps him from actually doing such things." But this is just beside the point, once we recognize that fantasizing is a type of action. For the purpose of moral evaluation, it does not matter whether a particular instance of fantasizing is associated with *another* action. My stabbing you is morally wrong irrespective of whether, having enjoyed it so much, I go on to stab someone else, or whether, filled with new sense of your own mortality, you go on to be a great philanthropist. Similarly, we can make sense of the idea that you act wrongly when you break your promise to take me to a baseball game, even though our not going makes it possible for me to do more work on my book. Hence, an instance of fantasizing need not lead to some other bad action in order to be morally bad itself.

It will be clear at this point that I reject a thoroughgoing consequentialism that holds that the moral status of an action is determined exclusively and exhaustively by its actual consequences. Some actions, like those previously described, may be judged on the basis of their intrinsic features alone. The consequences of our actions are not morally irrelevant. However, they are not *all* that is morally relevant. If we focus exclusively on the consequences of our actions, we ignore a large part of what constitutes our moral lives. We respond not only to the results of one another's overt behavior but also to one another's beliefs, desires, intentions, and characters—in short, to each other's moral *agency*. If this is right, then it is at least arguable that a person's fantasizing can be morally bad whether or not the person acts out the fantasy.

SEXUAL FANTASIZING IS DIFFERENT

An objector might grant that, insofar as fantasizing is a type of action, it is open to moral evaluation, and yet balk at the idea that *sexual* fantasizing is ever morally wrong, or that a person can ever be blameworthy for engaging in sexual fantasizing. (Indeed, consider the apparent oddity of *praising* someone for sexual fantasizing.) I believe this reluctance stems from the understandable worry that the moral evaluation of sexual fantasizing puts us at the beginning of an unpleasant slippery slope. When it comes to making judgments about people's sexual lives, the track record is not good. For example, the erroneous judgment that homosexual sexual desire is morally perverse continues to play a significant role in the unjust treatment of homosexuals. Put this way, the objection is not that sexually fantasizing is always morally neutral or morally good, but rather that it would be better if we did not engage in the evaluation of sexual fantasies or desires, period.

I take this concern seriously.[12] However, it bears repeating that moral evaluation does not by itself warrant any particular state action. If we assume otherwise, if we forswear the moral evaluation of some human practices simply because we worry about what use might be made of those evaluations, then we effectively hold ourselves hostage to the irrationality and ill will of others. More important, as I will try to make clearer, when an agent engages in moral evaluation and moral judgment, he need not limit himself to evaluation of and judgment about the actions of *others*. Being a moral agent essentially involves turning those critical faculties on *oneself*, at least every now and then. This chapter, then, should not be read as invitation to point fingers at others whose sexual fantasizing one may find distasteful, but as an attempt to make space in the complex discussion of pornography for genuine first-personal—that is, self-assessment.

Nonetheless, there are deeper sources of resistance to the idea that sexual fantasizing can sometimes be morally bad, which are not always made explicit, in part, I think, because they are quite difficult to articulate. Since the thesis under consideration is so controversial, these assumptions are worth unpacking.

It will help to begin by considering some of the reasons a person might fantasize. First, fantasizing about an event can help us prepare for that event. Think of the teenager who fantasizes about losing both his parents, not because he wants them to die, but rather because doing so helps prepare him for loss. Second, fantasizing can motivate us. Think of the athlete who fantasizes about running in the Olympics. Third, we fantasize to entertain, please, or gratify ourselves. Quite often these reasons operate together; for example, the athlete might derive considerable pleasure by fantasizing about her Olympic performance. But, for present purposes, let us focus on the self-gratifying nature of fantasizing.

The gratification a person achieves by fantasizing may have several different explanations. First and most obviously, a person may simply have a desire to fantasize, which is then trivially satisfied when he does. Second, there are the familiar instances of fantasizing about something because one cannot, for practical reasons, bring it about; for example, I may fantasize about killing my noisy neighbor and derive a certain degree of satisfaction from doing so. And, within this class of cases we might draw a further distinction: I may actually have the full-blown desire that my neighbor die, such that I would kill her if I could dispense with the practical obstacles; or, I might have some merely prima facie desire that she die, such that even without any obstacles, I would never kill her. In the former, the satisfaction I achieve by fantasizing is the best I can get, given the circumstances. In the latter, the satisfaction I achieve by fantasizing is all the satisfaction I need. Lastly, there seem to be cases of fantasizing that are themselves about having certain desires that are satisfied in the fantasy. Examples here might involve desires that are radically at odds with desires the fantast has in either the full-blown or prima facie senses previously described, and which she positively doesn't want satisfied in any other way.[13] To be sure, even in these kinds of cases, the fantast derives some pleasure from her fantasizing, but it is a pleasure she can experience *only* in the realm of fantasy.

An objector might use these distinctions to argue that sexual fantasizing, while a type of action, can never be negatively morally evaluated, and indeed might sometimes be morally praiseworthy. Consider, for example, a man who has sadistic sexual fantasies. He may fantasize in this way because he has a full-blown desire to sexually torture women, where, recall, this means that he would sexually torture women in the absence of certain obstacles. In such a case, the man's fantasizing plays a role in his *refraining* from actually torturing women; for we imagine he can achieve some measure of satisfaction just through fantasizing. So, it seems this sort of fantasizing, which goes proxy or is a surrogate for harmful overt behavior, is praiseworthy since it has the positively good effect of making the actual commission of harm less likely.[14]

Alternatively, a man's desire to sexually torture women may only be prima facie; that is, even absent practical obstacles he would never actually harm anyone. Or, finally, his sexual fantasizing might be simultaneously the source and satisfaction of sexual desires that are odds with many of his full-blown desires: he doesn't want to have or satisfy these desires in any way other than by fantasizing. In each of the last two cases, the man's fantasizing and the gratification he achieves by it do not substitute for overt behavior. His fantasizing is idle and, it might be thought, for that reason morally neutral.

Of course, there is a difference between surrogate fantasizing and idle fantasizing.[15] However, this distinction does not support the claim that sexual fantasizing is always either morally good (because it goes proxy for overt harmful behavior) or else morally neutral (because it is idle). For this argument rests on an assumption that has already been rejected—namely, that the moral status of fantasizing is always a function of the connection between the fantasizing and overt behavior. But, as I have argued, fantasizing is a type of action, evaluable by itself and independently of any other actions to which it may be related.

Still, one might argue that sexual fantasizing must be distinguished from nonsexual fantasizing in the following way. We engage in sexual fantasizing as a way to satisfy our sexual desires, many of which are opaque to us. I am aware of my desire to kill my neighbor, and I know its origins—her having noisy parties three nights a week. This is a desire I can rid myself of. But many sexual desires don't seem to be so clear and they are not acquired in the same way; I just seem to *find* myself with them. Hence, it appears that I exercise far less control over my sexual desires than I do over my nonsexual desires. All this may be true. But it is irrelevant to the claim that sexual fantasizing may be morally evaluated. For even if we are not responsible for our sexual desires, which I doubt,[16] it is implausible to think of fantasizing as unavoidable. Fantasizing is a deliberate and intentional action. It is, therefore, generally an optional response to desire.[17]

This is borne out by the empirical evidence. Sexual fantasizing appears to be almost universal across the species. And psychologists suggest that it is the most common sort of fantasizing in which humans engage. Sexual fantasies are a type of a 'repeating' fantasy, meaning that individuals return to the same sexual fantasies over and over. Although there is considerable variation between people's sexual fantasies, all appear to be highly scripted and durable. Ethel Person likens a decision to fantasize to a decision to take down a favorite book from an inner and familiar library, and writes,

> Once a fantasy is invoked, the fantasizer savors, lingers on, or revises the most exciting, pleasing, or soothing part of his or her mental creation, whirling it around in the mind until arriving at the 'version' that is most gratifying, often slowing the fantasy down at the most stimulating point, and speeding it up at moments that have begun to seem boring, improving on the dialogue, adding new touches to glamorize the setting.[18]

We cannot assume that sexual fantasizing is inexorably driven by desires. We choose to fantasize: fantasizing is action. And when our fantasizing is in the service of desire satisfaction, we can be held responsible for it whether or not we are responsible for the relevant desires. It is crucial not to mistake the apparent helplessness of arousal and orgasm that accompanies sexual fantasizing for a lack of control over the fantasizing itself.

Whatever else it may be, fantasizing cannot be said to be off limits to moral evaluation just by dint of its being inner, private, or about sex.[19] Neither is it the case that the moral status of fantasizing (sexual and nonsexual) depends on the probability of its issuing in overt behavior. Still, to argue that sexual fantasizing is morally evaluable is not yet to give an account of what makes sexual fantasizing morally bad when it is. It is to that issue that I now turn.

MORALLY PROBLEMATIC
SEXUAL FANTASIZING: AN EXAMPLE

Dennis fantasizes about the following: he moves to a foreign city where he takes up residence in an abandoned building. He meets a young man in a club and brings him back to his place. For a sum of money, the young man agrees to allow Dennis to perform a sex act on him. After a while, Dennis kills him. This is just the first of several killings, some of which Dennis participates in with two other men. The killings all occur in a sexual context; Dennis and his collaborators either have sex with their victims or masturbate while one or the other of them beat or torture their victim.[20] Dennis becomes aroused when he engages in this fantasy and he deliberately calls it to mind when he masturbates. Sometimes he focuses on it when he has sex with a partner.

Now imagine two worlds, World A and World B, in all respects like the actual world, except that in World A, many people sexually fantasize about the sorts of things Dennis does, and in World B no one does. Take it as given

that the Dennis's of World A never act out what they fantasize about.[21]
Which is the morally preferable world?

Many people would *like* to be able to say "Neither." Given the option of
living in World A or World B, many would *like* to be able to say that it would-
n't matter. But if we are reflective and honest, I don't think we will find it is
a matter of indifference that people around us engage in such fantasizing.
Now, arguably, World A is the actual world, and so we do not have the option
of living apart from such fantasizers. If the fantasies and their authors bother
us, then the best we can do is not think about them. This is another piece of
the explanation for the reluctance to entertain the possibility that sexual fantasizing is open to moral evaluation: evaluation requires paying attention to
its objects—to fantasizers and the content of their fantasies.

The previous thought experiment does not establish very much. However, it helps brings to awareness an intuitive unease many people feel about
certain types of fantasizing.

Here is a different thought experiment. Art, Bob, and Chris each fantasizes about anal sex with young children and none of them acts out his fantasies. However, whereas Art is indifferent to his fantasizing, and Bob is distressed by his, Chris positively relishes his fantasizing. How do we judge these
men and their actions? Without more information it would be precipitous to
think they are all three reprehensible. But there is a sense in which we can
distinguish between them: being horrified or being delighted that one fantasizes in this way is arguably morally salient.

Taken together, the thought experiments suggest that two features of fantasizing are relevant to its moral evaluation. First, there is the content of the
fantasy, what it is about. Second, there is the attitude of the fantast toward
his fantasies. I will discuss each in turn.

Many people are skeptical about evaluating sexual fantasizing on the
basis of the content of the relevant fantasies because they doubt that the content of a fantasy, especially a sexual fantasy, is determinate.

In his paper, "A Child Is Being Beaten," Freud notes that the fantast herself can and does assume different roles in her fantasy. In the case he discusses,
sometimes she is a third-party spectator of a beating, sometimes she is the
child, and sometimes she is doing the beating.[22] From Freud we also inherit
the idea that our dreams are saturated with symbolism; they cannot be read
literally and are always open to interpretation. Many people are inclined to
believe that our sexual fantasies are like dreams in this respect.

It is telling, I think, that the (alleged) indeterminancy of fantasies is
invariably invoked when the fantasies in question concern events that are, in
some quite straightforward way, problematic. When someone fantasizes about
puppies and fresh apple pie, or about living a successful and happy life, the
urge to interpret diminishes to zero. This indicates that our first instinct is to
read fantasies literally. It is only when we don't like what we see that we wel-

come and come to find plausible our therapist's complicated story about 'narcissistic wounds' and the like.[23] When the content of our fantasizing disturbs us, it is natural to seek reassurances that neutralize the elements of those fantasies we do not like. However, there is little evidence to suggest that a cigar is not just a cigar most of the time.

We are unquestionably the authors of our fantasies: we consciously choose the scenario we imagine, we embellish it, edit it, and so on. It would be seriously disingenuous of me to say that I had no control over the elements of my fantasy, or that when I conjure up a particular scene its 'real' meaning is utterly opaque to me. After all, fantasizing is essentially self-gratifying: I fantasize about things that please me.

And Dennis fantasizes about what pleases him. He consciously and deliberately conjures up his favorite scenario of sexual debasement and torture, and he concentrates on it to have an orgasm. To say that the content of a fantasy pleases the fantast is to say that the fantast takes a pro-attitude toward that content. Sexual arousal on the basis of fantasizing would hardly be possible if we did not adopt such an attitude, if only for the duration of the fantasizing episode itself. The particular pro-attitude that a person takes to the content of his sexual fantasies can be usefully described by the term "eroticization," where, as John Corvino suggests, to eroticize an activity is to "actively regard . . . the activity with sexual desire."[24] Hence, whether the fantast delights in his fantasizing (as Chris does) or is horrified by it (like Bob), by eroticizing what he does, the fantast does adopt a pro-attitude toward the activity he fantasizes about.[25]

It is easy to be repelled by the content of Dennis's fantasy. But that repulsion by itself is not sufficient to warrant moral judgments about Dennis's fantasizing. Rather, it is the fact that Dennis's sexual fantasizing—an activity he deliberately engages in to experience intense pleasure—has that content that grounds the judgment that what Dennis does is morally problematic.

But why? This critique appears to be little more than a thinly veiled, nose-wrinkling disgust at the thought of what turns other people on—especially since the idea that fantasizing is morally bad (when it is) just in case either the fantasizing goes proxy for a harmful overt action or significantly raises the probability that the fantast will 'act out' his imaginings have been rejected. The view under consideration, recall, holds that some fantasizing is morally bad even if the fantast does not, in some sense of 'want,' want to do what he fantasizes doing, and even if his fantasizing does not make him more likely to carry out his fantasies. But how else can the moral badness of fantasizing be cashed out if not in terms of its causal or probabilistic consequences?

ACTIONS AND CHARACTER

As I mentioned earlier, at least on reflection, few of us believe that consequences are *all* that matter morally. We judge lying and the breaking of

promises morally wrong, whether or not those actions have bad consequences. But an appeal to the violation of moral principles or duties of the
sort that underpin our judgments about lying and promise-breaking will not
help here. For it is not really plausible to say that I transgress a specific moral
principle or that I violate a particular duty when I engage in certain kinds of
fantasizing. But, more to the point, it is hard to see how one could specify the
relevant principles or obligations in a nonquestion-begging way. We cannot
explain the moral badness of certain sorts of fantasizing by saying that those
activities violate the principle, "It is morally wrong to fantasize about harming others." For the truth of such a principle is precisely what is in question.

A more promising approach emerges if we think about the relations
between action, character, and moral agency. Moral agency refers to set of
abilities or capacities: the ability to deliberate between options for action,
taking into account not only one's own well-being, but the well-being of others; the capacity to recognize when a situation demands a moral response of
some kind, for example, rendering assistance to strangers, not serving prime
rib at a dinner for vegetarian friends; a sensitivity to the moods, emotions,
and commitments of others; the ability to persevere when the going gets
tough and resist distractions to important projects; the disposition to seek
coherence among one's commitments, expectations, and efforts (integrity).

Moral beings possess these abilities in varying degrees, and while some
seem naturally well endowed, others must labor to acquire and develop them.
Variability also exists in the ways in which the capacities and abilities that
constitute moral agency are exercised: there are moral virtuosi and moral
journeymen. Talk of a person's character is usefully construed as shorthand for
whatever grounds and enables these practical competencies, where we can
think of these grounds as the maxims—the regulative ideals—to which she
holds herself and to which she believes she ought to hold herself. It is crucial
to recognize that a person's character is not simply a laundry list of beliefs.
First, because it is not only the *content* of a person's moral beliefs that matter
but also her *attitudes* toward those beliefs. Central to the notion of character
is the idea that a person endorses—at the very least, accepts—certain principles of right action. Second, in order to ground moral competencies across a
life, the regulative ideals to which a person is committed (i.e., which she
endorses) must be ordered in some way; they might, for example, be hierar-
chically ordered from most general to most specific, or lexically ordered
according to some other principle. A mere concatenation of practical principles will not deliver the kind of stability over time that is a hallmark of character. Moreover, where there is no ordering of practical principles, inconsistencies are more likely; the kind of stability required for the exercise of moral
agency is absent.

But this does not mean that character is static. Indeed, precisely the
opposite is true. Although the experience of living a life as a reflective ratio-

nal being will have the effect of reinforcing some elements of our characters, each of us is always a work in progress. New challenges can reveal aspects of our character we had been unaware of; we might embrace these elements, or, finding them to be inconsistent with other more familiar and more important elements, we might seek to eliminate them. Even though human beings (as rational beings) are self-reflective, we are not utterly transparent to ourselves. In part, having a character involves the ongoing activity of self-scrutiny, self-discovery, and self-adjustment.

The dynamic nature of character indicates three ways in which actions and character are related. First and most obviously, a person's overt actions are evidence of the nature of his or her character. It is through observing the actions a person typically performs that we attribute to that individual a certain type of character. Less obviously, perhaps, a person's non-overt actions are evidence at least for *him* about the direction his character is taking. Second, some actions—actions for which the agent has a settled disposition, actions he reliably performs—are not merely evidence of his character; they express, in the sense of being constitutive elements of, that character. Finally, a person can attempt to perform a certain type of action because he wants eventually to acquire a settled disposition to perform that action. He wants, that is, for the maxim or practical principle determining that type of action to be an element of his character. We cannot construct a character out of nothing, and we are committed to some practical principles simply by virtue of being the kinds of creatures we are.[26] But, beyond the basics, we have considerable latitude in fine-tuning our characters, making certain traits part of who we are.

An example will help tie these claims about moral agency, character, and action together. Imagine that George, a man who has never paid much attention to the ways in which gender makes a difference in the world, develops a friendship with a feminist theorist whom he respects. She talks to him about the many subtle ways in which gender structures the social world, often to the advantage of men and the disadvantage of women. George believes that men and women are equal and that if women are badly treated just on account of being women, this is a very bad thing. George worries that he has been oblivious to the effects of gender hierarchy; he doesn't want to be a person who discriminates unfairly, offends, and so on. So George decides that he needs to pay to more attention to gender, and as a practical exercise to keep gender before his consciousness, he decides always to use the feminine pronoun in his writing, except for instances when to do so would be a blatant absurdity (e.g., he cannot refer to his brother as she.) Over time, the action of using the feminine pronoun makes George more sensitive to gender. He notices things he had not noticed before, and he formulates practical principles that constrain the way he acts in situations in which gender is relevant. Through habitually acting in a certain way, he improves his moral agency. He is now more sensitive to morally significant facts around him.[27]

George's story is, we might say, a success story. But the interplay between action, character, and moral agency that allows for human flourishing also allows for corruption. Habitually performing bad actions, or actions that desensitize one to morally salient facts, can seriously hinder the project of character development. Endorsing the wrong kinds of practical principles is corrosive of character. Consider again our sexual fantast Dennis. Here is a man who appears to endorse actions that might seriously undermine his character and thus his moral agency. He takes deep pleasure in fantasizing about harming others and he does so habitually. One ought not be the sort of person who takes sexual pleasure in the debasement of others. And one ought not act in ways that constitute being that sort of person.

These remarks hold outside the domain of sexual fantasizing. Consider other kinds of inner going-on, like emotions. Being overjoyed at and privately gloating about another's misfortune, irrespective of whether one actually laughs in the face of the other, are evil states of mind. Voluntary gloating is morally bad action. One ought not be the kind the kind of person who performs such actions.[28]

The last sentence bears emphasis, if only to forestall the misunderstanding that, after explicitly rejecting consequentialism, I am now relying on precisely such a moral approach in speaking of the ways in which a person's actions affect his or her character. Of course our actions affect our characters. But to stress the moral significance of this truism is not to commit oneself to consequentialism. For the relation between a person's actions and that person's character is a constitutive relation. In this sense, it might be better to say that a person's actions *effect* part of that person's character.

So far I have been considering the proposal that certain types of sexual fantasizing are morally risky on account of the ways in which they constitute the undermining of moral agency and the corruption of character. But precisely how does this bear on pornography?

PORNOGRAPHY AND SEXUAL FANTASIZING

As enjoyable as sexual excitement is, pornography's popularity would be surprising if all it did was provide the color and sound for our inner black-and-white silent movies. Undoubtedly, pornography supplies its consumers with novel elements for their sexual fantasies as well as new ideas for their flesh-and-blood sexual encounters. More significantly, pornography concretizes existing sexual fantasies, providing enduring and substantive representations of what might otherwise exist 'just' in people's heads.

The implications of the publication and distribution of representations of sexual fantasies must not be underestimated. Like many other cultural discourses, pornography provides us with language and concepts, a framework within which to ground and organize our sexual experience. In this way, pornography and sexual fantasizing are mutually legitimating. The very existence of an industry devoted to producing sexual arousal—even though some people persist in thinking that pornography is marginal—tells us that it is okay to derive sexual pleasure from fantasizing in certain ways. Moreover, when a person sees the major elements of their favorite sexual fantasy acted out with real people, he can rest assured that he is not deviant; he can infer that others are turned on in similar ways. (Hence the widely used therapeutic strategy of normalization, which involves dealing with a client's distress about her sexual desires and fantasies by suggesting that she is not alone in having them.) Ethel Person sums up the relation between pornography and sexual fantasizing in the following way:

> . . . works like the Story of O and the writings of the Marquis de Sade have become part of a cultural debate on the prevalence, meaning, and legitimacy of sadomasochistic fantasies and practices. But these works could never have achieved their popularity if they did not speak to deep-seated fantasies shared by large numbers of people. Probably their popularity helped legitimize such fantasies, which in turn helped to make them even more available to consciousness and therefore more widespread.[29]

By supplying us with a constant supply of new and old sexual ideas, pornography permits and encourages us to engage in unbounded sexual fantasizing. This is precisely why some theorists defend pornography, seeing it as a tool of liberation. No doubt that it can be. But some pornography—like Dennis Cooper's described earlier—facilitates and helps to legitimize sexual fantasizing that is morally risky.

An objection might be made at this point based on the fact that a good deal of bondage and discipline and sadomasochistic pornography is produced by and for members of the BDSM community—adults who consensually engage in sexual practices like various kinds of sexual torture. Visit a Web site or discussion group for this community and one will typically find—alongside pictures of "slaves"—some statement about "play" etiquette; that is, a list of do's and don't's for sexual scenes that emphasize the importance of mutual consent. The objection would be that since such pornography is about *pretend* or *simulated* degradation, humiliation, and abuse, it is not to be associated with the material that I have claimed is morally risky. For the fantasies that this material stimulates and reinforces are not fantasies about doing real harm to anyone.[30]

All this might be so, but it is beside the point. No one can say with certainty that *all* members of the BDSM community are "only playing." However, even if this is true, there is still room for concern. For what is it to be sexually aroused by fantasies of simulated degradation and abuse (or, by extension, by the 'actual simulation' of sexual torture)? Responding to Patrick Hopkins's defense of sadomasochism,[31] Corvino insightfully undermines any confidence we might have that sadomasochists are turned on only by the simulation of certain practices. He questions the psychological possibility of eroticizing a "simulation qua simulation." He writes,

> True, SM participants frequently attend to the pleasure of their partners, and to that extent, they are mindful of features that distinguish their activities from actual violence. But they are also mindful of features that occur in the "real" case: the spanking, the quickened heartbeat, the gasps and groans. When they eroticize these features, SM participants . . . seem to be eroticizing not simulations qua simulations, but domination and its manifestations. The simulation is not the object of arousal; rather, it is the vehicle for the object of arousal.[32]

I have suggested that the moral evaluation of sexual fantasizing depends on two things: the content of the fantasies in question and the attitude that the fantast takes toward that content. I argued earlier that, regardless of whether a person delights in or is horrified by his fantasizing, if he does indeed fantasize about an activity to achieve sexual arousal, then he ipso facto takes a pro-attitude toward that activity—at least for the duration of the fantasizing episode. If Corvino is right, then, to some extent, even members of consensual BDSM practices take pro-attitudes toward (variously) sexual torture, bondage, submission, and domination. Adopting such attitudes, and, more to the point, actively encouraging them in oneself are not obviously consistent with the maintenance of a sound character.

There is certainly much more to say about sadomasochistic and other fetishistic sexual practices. The moral status of these practices and the pornography that depicts them have been a hotly debated topic for decades. I do not pretend to have settled any of the central questions here. My contingent conclusion, however, in answer to the question I tabled in note 6, is that the moral critique I have offered here probably does extend to the sexual fantasizing associated with consensual BDSM practices.

CYBERPORNOGRAPHY

Cyberpornography may be more effective in facilitating and legitimizing sexual fantasizing than traditional forms of print and video pornography. This is not just because cyberporn is more accessible than other forms of pornography, though that is a factor. Rather, the very form of cyberporn determines a unique experience of consumption. Accessing and enjoying cyberporn implicates the consumer's agency in interesting ways.

Cyberporn *is* far more accessible than other types of pornography in at least two senses. First, it is easier to get at the material; opening Netscape Navigator takes less time than driving to the local video store or sex shop. Second, cyberporn can be delivered directly and privately to one's home.

Hence, one traditional barrier to getting hold of pornography—embarrass-ment—is removed. But while these facts might prompt more people to try pornography and others to try more pornography, they do not yet suggest that cyberporn is morally more risky than print and video pornography.

Some critics have argued otherwise, claiming that the ready availability of porn online gives rise to addiction. The research and literature on Internet addiction—of a sexual and nonsexual kind—are highly controversial. But, in any case, it is beside the point for the argument under consideration here. If cyberporn is addictive, that would be unfortunate; but only in the sense that *any* addiction is a bad thing. Addiction compromises a person's agency, and distracts or prevents the person from engaging in a full range of valuable life projects. The present thesis is narrower, having to do with morally risky sex-ual fantasizing. Moreover, as I have been at pains to point out, the sexual fan-tast is *responsible* for his fantasizing and for the actions that support that fan-tasizing. He is not helpless in the face of an addiction that his 'agential self' cannot penetrate. (I will return to this point briefly.)

It is trivial to note that the Internet has changed and continues to alter the ways in which many people obtain information and communicate with one another. However, what has gone relatively unexplored are the ways in which individual use of the technology changes the *user*.[34] It is, therefore, worth thinking about the phenomenology of computer-mediated communi-cations and other human–Internet interactions. In what remains, I will offer some speculative remarks about two features of consuming cyberporn that, I believe, serve to buttress the claim that cyberporn is more morally dangerous than traditional print and video pornography.

First, consider the experience of browsing the World Wide Web. The ease of browsing (for *anything*) online, the speed at which vast quantities of information can be procured, might lead us to think that the Web is the ulti-mate desire-satisfaction machine. Want something? Open your favorite search engine or database, and what you desire is only a click or two away. This is certainly true when the desire in question is quite specific, for exam-ple, when I want to know the business hours of my local IKEA store or the directions to a restaurant. Such a desire is easily satisfied and, once it is, I have little motivation to continue browsing.

However, typically, we browse the Web precisely because we do not quite know what we want. Either we have no specific question for which we seek an answer, or we do not know what is 'out there' about particular topic. Con-sider finding out about alternative treatments for some recently diagnosed medical condition. The experience of this type of browsing is quite different. When I don't have a particular question in mind, I have to work harder to get useful information. And, in some cases, what counts as useful information is constructed as I browse, somewhat after the fashion of the game Twenty Questions. When I browse, I am continually offered new links to different sites. My desire, inchoate to begin with, is tweaked, refined, heightened; each link promises that the next site will be what I am looking for. In this way, my motivation for staying online is continuously energized.

The genius of Web browsing is that it feeds off desires, many of which the activity of browsing itself helps to create and to amplify, and some of which, by design, will never be satisfied. Purveyors of cyberporn exploit this aspect of the technology quite effectively. Go to the Web with a general curiosity about sexually explicit material (search engine keyword: "XXX") or with a specific sexual interest (search engine keyword: "BBW" or "BCT")[35] and you will be provided with more sites than you know what to do with. More important, cyberpornographers have deliberately built their sites in ways that make it very difficult for a consumer to leave them. Open a pornography site and try to close the browser window. The chances are that you will be bumped to another (pornography) site. Soon you will have dozens of browser windows open on your desktop. And the escalation of unsatiated desire continues.[36]

Browsing cyberporn is rarely just like browsing racks of print pornography or watching a lot of videos. To be sure, it has two similar effects—namely, it provides content for many new and different fantasies and, by its very existence, serves to legitimize the fantasies of its consumers. However, cyberporn also has the effect of keeping consumers engaged in the business of sexual fantasizing longer. First, the ways in which cyberporn is delivered to consumers helps to construct desires that are in turn prevented from being satisfied; one is always encouraged to go to another and then another site. Such 'movement' is relatively effortless, and the chain of new sites to which consumers are bumped is often characterized by increasingly 'extreme' content. (The term is the industry's own.) Furthermore, this rapid delivery of images keeps alive fantasies that the consumer might otherwise have ceased having for want of imagination or because they strike him as 'too bizarre.' Because of the unique nature of consuming pornography online, consumers' sexual fantasizing is facilitated in previously unimaginable ways.

A potential objection at this point helps to highlight a second relevant aspect of the experience of consuming cyberporn. Someone might say that consumers of cyberporn can hardly be held responsible for the sexual fantasizing in which they engage while online or as a result of viewing cyberporn. For haven't I just suggested that the medium itself compromises agency? Cyberporn consumers are deliberately manipulated. As a result of being 'trapped' in Web sites, certain fantasies are forced on them. In other words, precisely how is the account I offer here different from an addiction account?

It must be conceded that users of technology are changed in more or less significant ways by their experience. But even cyborgs—those who see their machines as literal sexual prostheses—do not for that reason cease to be responsible agents. Nonetheless, I think that the cyberporn consumer's *sense* of his own agency is compromised. The genuine and deliberate activities of opening the first site, consciously following links, downloading images, and repeating the exercise can feel quite passive. The material is delivered to one's desktop. Most of the time, one doesn't have to do anything (except stay online) to find out about new sites. And opening a site requires just a click of the mouse. Moreover, the intense privacy of consuming porn online can make it seem as if one is not actively engaged in any way. Rather it appears that one's fantasizing and online pornography have serendipitously converged. In this way, the consumer is positively discouraged by the medium itself from keeping his own agency and responsibility for fantasizing in focus. It is not as if a consumer of online pornography is rendered helpless with respect to his actions. It is just that the experience itself serves to create the *illusion* that his agency is not engaged. In this way, we can say that the character of the consumer of cyberpornography-with-morally-problematic-content is *doubly* compromised. First, his actions threaten to make him a person of less desirable sort; second, the experience of consuming cyberpornography tends to render the very question of his own complicity otiose to *him*.

To summarize these speculations: consuming cyberporn, by its very nature, facilitates sexual fantasizing, often, of a morally problematic sort (when consumers are bumped to more extreme sites) and it simultaneously masks from the consumer his own agency in the act of consumption. The consumer's character is thus doubly threatened: morally risky sexually fantasizing is facilitated in quite aggressive ways, and the fantast's agency, his own complicity in such actions, is rendered obscure.

CONCLUSION

The overall agenda of this chapter has been to make room for a particular kind of moral critique of pornography, one that pays close attention to the moral effects pornography can have on its consumers. At the heart of that critique is the idea that it is morally risky to engage in certain kinds of sexual fantasizing on the grounds that to habitually link sexual pleasure and satisfaction with thoughts of degradation, abuse, and humiliation can undermine the development and maintenance of a sound moral character. Any pornography that encourages and facilitates such fantasizing—and it is plausible that cyberpornography is particularly efficacious in this regard—can thus be morally criticized. It bears emphasis yet again that this line of argument does not by itself imply restrictive public policies concerning pornography either on or offline. If anything, this particular moral critique of pornography would seem to make the prospects of state intervention quite poor. For we are and should be skeptical of *state*-imposed limitations on our freedom directed at the goal of making us better moral agents. That said, the present discussion is not without practical relevance. Each of us has a responsibility to make judgments about *our own* actions and attitudes. This is the sense in which morality is as much self-regarding as it is other-regarding. For the moral status of any social activity, like the consumption of pornography, may be analyzed in terms of its effects on its practitioners as well as on others.[37]

NOTES

1. Michael Saenz, "The Carpal Tunnel of Love: Virtual Sex with Mike Saenz" (interview with Jeff Milstead and Jude Milhon), *Mondo 2000* 4 (n.d.), cited in Claudia Springer, *Electronic Eros: Bodies and Desire in the Postindustrial Age* (Austin: University of Texas Press, 1996), p. 80.

2. For a survey of the entangled history of pornography and technology see Peter Johnson, "Pornography Drives Technology: Why *Not* to Censor the Internet," *Federal Communications Law Journal* 49 (1996): 217–226.

3. See Frederick S. Lane III, *Obscene Profits: The Entrepreneurs of Pornography in the Cyber Age* (New York and London: Routledge, 2000).

4. Timothy Egan, "Technology Sent Wall Street into Market for Pornography," *The New York Times*, Monday, October 2000, A1, A20.

5. Frank Rich, "Naked Capitalists," *The New York Times Magazine*, Sunday, May 20, 2001, pp. 51–54.

6. Does the risk I allude to track only sexual fantasizing about *actual* degradation, humiliation, or violence, or does it attend sexual fantasizing about *simulated* degradation, humiliation, or violence? That is, does the critique I offer here extend to the sexual fantasizing of practitioners of *consensual* bondage/discipline/sadomasochistic practices, say? This is a very difficult question. I suspect that the answer is "Yes"; see the end of the section titled "Pornography and Sexual Fantasizing."

7. For the record, I am somewhat of a free speech absolutist. See my "Free Speech: A Plea to Ignore the Consequences," *Computer-Mediated Communication*, vol. 3, no. 1 (www.december.com/CMC/mag/1996/jan/toc.html), and my "Free Speech" *Sats: The Nordic Journal of Philosophy* 2 (2001): 80–97.

8. Robin Morgan, *Going Too Far: The Personal Chronicle of a Feminist* (New York: Random House, 1977), p. 169.

9. The so-called clear and present danger test as a tool in evaluating First Amendment challenges has its roots in *Schenck v. United States*, 249 U.S. 47 (1919), in which Justice Holmes wrote: "The question in every case is whether the words used are used in such circumstances and are of such a nature that they will bring about the substantive evils that Congress has a right to prevent" (p. 52).

10. See, e.g., Ferrell M. Christensen, "Cultural and Ideological Bias in Pornography Research," *Philosophy of the Social Sciences* 20 (1990): 351–375; Alison King, "Mystery and Imagination: The Case of Pornography Effect Studies," in *Bad Girls and Dirty Pictures*, eds. Alison Assister and Avedon Carol (London: Pluto Press, 1993), pp. 57–87; and Daniel G. Linz, Edward Donnerstein, and Steven Penrod, "The Findings and Recommendations of the Attorney General's Commission on Pornography: Do

the Psychological 'Facts' Fit the Political Fury?" *American Psychologist* 42 (1987): 946–953.

11. Laura Kipnis, *Bound and Gagged: Pornography and the Politics of Fantasy in America* (New York: Grove Press, 1996), p. 175. For a more detailed treatment of the objection see Deborah Cameron and Elizabeth Frazier, "On the Question of Pornography and Sexual Violence: Moving Beyond Cause and Effect," *Pornography: Women, Violence, and Civil Liberties*. Ed. Catherine Itzin (Oxford: Oxford University Press, 1992), pp. 359–383.

12. Consider the case of twenty-two-year-old Ohio resident Brian Dalton. Having served a few months for a child pornography conviction in 1998, Dalton was on parole in July 2001 when his parole officer discovered Dalton's journal during a routine search. The journal contained descriptions of Dalton's violent sexual fantasies involving fictional children said to be ten or eleven years of age. A grand jury indicted Dalton of two felony counts under an Ohio law that prohibits the creation of obscene material involving minors. He was sentenced to seven years in prison. See Bob Herbert, "The Thought Police," *The New York Times*, Thursday, July 19, 2001, A25.

13. Arguably, certain masochistic sexual fantasies are like this. See, e.g., Lynne Segal's illuminating discussion, "Sensual Uncertainty," in *Sex and Love: New Thoughts on Old Contradictions*. Eds. Sue Cartledge and Joanna Ryan (London: The Women's Press, 1983), pp. 30–47.

14. This is part of what underlies the so-called catharsis defense of violent pornography: the availability of sadistic pornography permits those men who have violent sexual desires to deal with them safely. See, e.g., G. L. Simons, *Pornography Without Prejudice* (London: Abelard-Schuman, 1973), pp. 85–103.

15. The terminology is Christopher Cherry's. For a thorough discussion see his "The Inward and the Outward: Fantasy, Reality and Satisfaction," *New Essays in the Philosophy of Mind*. Eds. D. Copp and J. J. MacIntosh (Calgary, Alberta: University of Calgary Press, 1985), pp. 175–193, and "When Is Fantasizing Morally Bad?" *Philosophical Investigations* 11 (1988):112–132.

16. It is not at all clear that we have *no* control over our sexual desires. Given the kinds of creatures we are, our sexuality, like other aspects of our being, is mediated by both biological and cultural factors. There is little reason to think that our sexual desires are any 'purer' than our nonsexual desires, in the sense that they are wholly biologically determined. See, e.g., Martha C. Nussbaum, "Constructing Love, Desire, and Care," in *Sex, Preference, and Family*. Eds. David M. Estlund and Martha C. Nussbaum (New York: Oxford University Press, 1997), pp. 17–43.

17. Leitenberg and Henning write: "In general . . . most sexual fantasies appear to be *deliberate* patterns of thought designed to stimulate or enhance pleasurable sexual feelings regardless of whether the fantasies involve reminiscing about past sexual experiences, imagining anticipated future sexual activity, engaging in wishful thinking, or having daydreams that are exciting to imagine without any desire to put them into practice" (p. 470, emphasis added).

18. Ethel Person, *By Force of Fantasy: How We Make Our Lives* (New York: Basic Books, 1995), p. 35.

19. For more on the idea that we can be blameworthy for some of our thoughts and fantasies see Ishtiyaque Haji, *Moral Appraisability: Puzzles, Proposals, and Perplexities* (New York: Oxford University Press, 1998), esp. chapter 14.

20. The content of this fantasy is drawn from an excerpt of Dennis Cooper's story "Numb," originally published in his *Frisk* (New York: Grove/Atlantic, 1991) and reprinted in *Forbidden Passages: Writings Banned in Canada*, introductions by Pat Califia and Janine Fuller (Pittsburgh: Cleis Press, 1995), pp. 151–160. I do not know whether this story describes the content of a sexual fantasy Mr. Cooper himself has. However, the story is intended as a piece of gay erotica, and it might be someone's fantasy.

21. Some readers might find what the narrator of Cooper's story says interesting: "Then I crawled across the room and sat cross-legged, watching him bleed to death. I stayed there all night, worn out, and vaguely wondering why I didn't go phone the police, or feel guilt or sympathy for his friends. I guess I'd fantasized killing a boy for so long that all the truth did was fill in details" (ibid., p. 153). Perhaps this is a just flash of irony.

22. Sigmund Freud, "A Child Is Being Beaten," *Selected Writings*, vol. 10 (Harmondsworth: Penguin, 1979). See also the discussion in Jean Grimshaw, "Ethics, Fantasy, and the Self-Transformation," *Ethics* (Royal Institute of Philosophy Supplement, 35). Ed. A. Phillips Griffiths (Cambridge: Cambridge University Press, 1993), pp. 145–158.

23. For a summary of what she aptly describes as the "chaos of theories," each purporting to explain women's masochistic sexual fantasies, see Sandra Bartky, *Femininity and Domination: Studies in the Phenomenology of Oppression* (New York: Routledge, 1990), pp. 52–54.

24. John Corvino, "Naughty Fantasies," *Southwest Philosophy Review* 18 (2002): 213–220, p. 214. Corvino also advances a nonconsequentialist moral critique of some kinds of sexual fantasies. His central intuition is that "any seriously wrongful activity merits an attitude of disapproval, and eroticization of such an activity is inconsistent with this attitude" (216–217).

25. Notice that this point about the sexual fantast's necessary pro-attitude toward the content of his fantasy serves to reinforce my earlier claim that, for the purposes of moral evaluation, it matters not whether the fantast seeks to satisfy a full blown or 'only' prima facie desire.

26. The idea that humans have some native moral endowment is an ancient though controversial one. For a defense see my "Moral Selves and Moral Parameters," *Becoming Persons*. Ed. Robert N. Fisher (Oxford: Applied Theology Press, 1995), pp. 471–500, and "Moral Competence," *Philosophy and Linguistics*. Eds. Kumiko Murasugi and Robert Stainton (Boulder: Westview Press, 1999), pp. 169–190. And see Sissela Bok, "What Basis for Morality? A Minimalist Approach," *The Monist* 76 (1993): 348–359 for a nonnativist account of a universal morality.

27. For a more detailed account of what we can imagine to be George's developmental trajectory and of the relation between character and practical rationality see Martha C. Nussbaum, "The Discernment of Perception: An Aristotelian Conception

of Private and Public Rationality." *Love's Knowledge: Essays on Philosophy and Literature* (New York and Oxford: Oxford University Press, 1990), pp. 54–105.

28. See, e.g., A. C. Ewing, "The Justification of Emotions," *Proceedings of the Aristotelian Society,* supp. Vol. 31 (1957): 59–74; S. I. Benn, "Wickedness," *Ethics* 96 (1985): 795–810; and Robert Merihew Adams, "Involuntary Sins," *The Philosophical Review* 94 (1985): 3–31.

29. Ethel Person, *By Force of Fantasy,* p. 94.

30. Members of the BDSM community are quick to condemn those who seek sexual satisfaction from the actual debasement and abuse of others.

31. Patrick Hopkins, "Rethinking Sadomasochism: Feminism, Interpretation, and Simulation," *Hypatia* 9 (1994): 116–141.

32. Corvino, ibid.

33. See Alvin Cooper, Coralie R. Scherer, Sylvain C. Boies, and Bary L. Gordon, "Sexuality on the Internet: From Sexual Exploration to Pathological Expression," *Professional Psychology: Research and Practice* 30 (1999): 154–156; Stephen F. Davis, Brandy G. Smith, Karen Rodrigue, and Kim Pulvers, "An Examination of Internet Usage on Two College Campuses," *College Student Journal* 33 (1999): 257–261; and Jennifer P. Schneider, "Effects of Cybersex Addiction on the Family: Results of a Survey," *Sexual Addiction and Compulsivity* 7 (2000): 31–58.

34. Some preliminary research indicates that we are likely to say things online that we would never dare say in face-to-face situations. For example, conversations in company chat rooms, where users are anonymous, have come close to being libelous. See Reed Abelson, "By the Water Cooler in Cyberspace, the Talk Turns Ugly," *The New York Times,* Sunday, April 29, 2001, A1. See also Sherry Turkle, *Life on the Screen: Identity in the Age of the Internet* (New York: Simon and Schuster, 1995).

35. For cyberporn neophytes, these are the standard acronyms for Big Beautiful Women and Ball and Cock Torture.

36. "Porn sites now, some 30% of which are estimated to be content-free are little more than ads for other sites, electronically 'booby-trapped' with blind links and pop-up consoles and windows designed to gain hits and to send the surfer to other sites. This practice, known as 'click-through farming,' marks a relatively new development in advertising strategy, supplanting the old banner system, where one 'click-through,' that is, the act of mouse-clicking on an ad banner, might pay as much as 15 cents for sending a potential customer to a specific site. Now, if you hit a so-called free site, full page ads that look like tables of contents pop up, or new browser windows open spontaneously in dizzying layers, sending you to several other sites. . . . Attempts to close the windows only generates more of them, including JavaScript-launched 'consoles' that linger long after the original site has been left. The race to close windows faster than they pop-up is on. Clicking on thumbnail images or buttons on a slick console page that might offer 'amateur orgy' or 'naughty schoolgirl' images, instead of linking you to any images, will send you to another site, whose URL, normally appearing in the browser's status bar, has been obscured by a JavaScript program. And should you decide that you have had enough, and exit the original page, an exit

console will pop up which usually points surfers back to the first site. Trapped in a loop, surfers return to the original site again and again without realizing it" (Michael Uebel, "Toward a Symptomatology of Cyberporn," *Theory and Event* 3 (2000) at http://muse.jhu.edu/journals/theory_and_event/v003/3.4uebel.html, para.55).

37. Many thanks to the following for useful discussion and provocative questions: Robert Cavalier, Felmon Davis, Christine Koggel and her students at Bryn Mawr College, Alex London, Patrick McCroskery, Eduardo Mendieta, Paul Pietroski, Mandy Simons, Sarah Stroud, and Carol Voeller.

REFERENCES

Abelson, Reed. 2001. By the Water Cooler in Cyberspace, the Talk Turns Ugly, *The New York Times*, April 29, A1.

Adams, Robert Merihew. 1985. Involuntary Sins, *The Philosophical Review* 94: 3–31.

Bartky, Sandra. 1990. *Femininity and Domination: Studies in the Phenomenology of Oppression*. New York: Routledge, p. 54.

Benn, S. I. 1985. Wickedness, *Ethics* 96: 795–810.

Bok, Sissela. 1993. What Basis for Morality? A Minimalist Approach, *The Monist* 76: 348–359.

Cameron, Deborah, and Elizabeth Frazier. 1992. "On the Question of Pornography and Sexual Violence: Moving Beyond Cause and Effect," in *Pornography: Women, Violence, and Civil Liberties*, edited by Catherine Itzin. Oxford: Oxford University Press, pp. 359–383.

Cherry, Christopher. 1985. "The Inward and the Outward: Fantasy, Reality and Satisfaction," in *New Essays in the Philosophy of Mind*, edited by D. Copp and J. J. MacIntosh. Calgary, Alberta: University of Calgary Press, pp. 175–193.

———. 1988. When is Fantasizing Morally Bad? *Philosophical Investigations* 11: 112–132.

Christensen, Ferrell M. 1990. Cultural and Ideological Bias in Pornography Research, *Philosophy of the Social Sciences* 20: 351–375.

Cooper, Alvin, Coralie R. Scherer, Sylvain C. Boies, and Barry L. Gordon. 1999. Sexuality on the Internet: From Sexual Exploration to Pathological Expression, *Professional Psychology: Research and Practice* 30: 154–156.

Cooper, Dennis. 1995. "Numb." Reprinted in *Forbidden Passages: Writings Banned in Canada*, introductions by Pat Califia and Janine Fuller. Pittsburgh: Cleis Press, pp.151–160.

Corvino, John. 2002. Naughty Fantasies, *Southwest Philosophy Review* 18: 213–220.

Davis, Stephen F., Brandy G. Smith, Karen Rodrigue, and Kim Pulvers. 1999. An Examination of Internet Usage on Two College Campuses, *College Student Journal* 33: 257–261.

Dwyer, Susan. 1995. "Moral Selves and Moral Parameters," in *Becoming Persons*, edited by Robert N. Fisher. Oxford: Applied Theology Press, pp. 471–500.

———. 1996. Free Speech: A Plea to Ignore the Consequences, *Computer-Mediated Communication* vol. 3, no. 1 (www.december.com/CMC/mag/1996/jan/toc.html).

———. 1999. "Moral Competence," in *Philosophy and Linguistics*, edited by Kumiko Murasugi and Robert Stainton. Boulder: Westview Press, pp. 169–190.

———. 2001. Free Speech, *Sats: The Nordic Journal of Philosophy* 2: 80–97.

Egan, Timothy. 2000. Technology Sent Wall Street into Market for Pornography, *The New York Times*, October 23, A1, A20.

Ewing, A. C. 1957. The Justification of Emotions, *Proceedings of the Aristotelian Society*, supp. Vol. 31: 59–74.

Freud, Sigmund. 1979. "A Child Is Being Beaten," in *Selected Writings*, vol. 10. Harmondsworth: Penguin.

Grimshaw, Jean. 1993. "Ethics, Fantasy, and the Self-Transformation," in *Ethics* (Royal Institute of Philosophy Supplement, 35) edited by A. Phillips Griffiths. Cambridge: Cambridge University Press, pp. 145–158.

Haji, Ishtiyaque. 1998. *Moral Appraisability: Puzzles, Proposals, and Perplexities.* New York: Oxford University Press.

Herbert, Bob. 2001. The Thought Police, *The New York Times*, July 19, A25.

Hopkins, Patrick. 1994. Rethinking Sadomasochism: Feminism, Interpretation, and Simulation, *Hypatia* 9: 116–141.

Johnson, Peter. 1996. Pornography Drives Technology: Why *Not* to Censor the Internet, *Federal Communications Law Journal* 49: 217–226.

King, Alison. 1993. "Mystery and Imagination: The Case of Pornography Effect Studies," in *Bad Girls and Dirty Pictures*, edited by Alison Assister and Avedon Carol. London: Pluto Press, pp. 57–87.

Kipnis, Laura. 1996. *Bound and Gagged: Pornography and the Politics of Fantasy in America.* New York: Grove Press.

Lane, Frederick S. III. 2000. *Obscene Profits: The Entrepreneurs of Pornography in the Cyber Age.* New York and London: Routledge.

Leitenberg, Harold, and Kris Henning. 1995. Sexual Fantasy, *Psychological Bulletin* 117: 469–496.

Linz, Daniel G., Edward Donnerstein, and Steven Penrod. 1987. The Findings and Recommendations of the Attorney General's Commission on Pornography: Do the Psychological "Facts" Fit the Political Fury? *American Psychologist* 42: 946–953.

Morgan, Robin. 1977. *Going Too Far: The Personal Chronicle of a Feminist.* New York: Random House.

Nussbaum, Martha C. 1997. "Constructing Love, Desire, and Care," in *Sex, Preference, and Family*, edited by David M. Estlund and Martha C. Nussbaum. New York: Oxford University Press, pp.17–43.

———. 1990. "The Discernment of Perception: An Aristotelian Conception of Private and Public Morality," in *Love's Knowledge: Essays on Philosophy and Literature*. New York and Oxford: Oxford University Press, pp. 54–105.

Person, Ethel. 1995. *By Force of Fantasy: How We Make Our Lives*. New York: Basic Books.

Rich, Frank. 2001. Naked Capitalists, *The New York Times Magazine*, May 20, pp. 51–54.

Schneider, Jennifer P. 2000. Effects of Cybersex Addiction on the Family: Results of a Survey, *Sexual Addiction and Compulsivity* 7: 31–58.

Segal, Lynne. 1983. "Sensual Uncertainty," in *Sex and Love: New Thoughts on Old Contradictions*, edited by Sue Cartledge and Joanna Ryan. London: The Women's Press, pp. 30–47.

Simons, G. L. 1973. *Pornography Without Prejudice*. London: Abelard-Schuman.

Springer, Claudia. 1996. *Electronic Eros: Bodies and Desire in the Postindustrial Age*. Austin: University of Texas Press.

Turkle, Sherry. 1995. *Life on the Screen: Identity in the Age of the Internet*. New York: Simon and Schuster.

Uebel, Michael. 2000. Toward a Symptomatology of Cyberporn, *Theory and Event* 3, http://muse.jhu.edu/journals/theory_and_event/v003/3.4uebel.html.

FIVE

Trust in Cyberspace

JOHN WECKERT

FROM AN ARISTOTELIAN point of view, an important component of leading a good life, or of human flourishing, is friendship. And trust plays a central role in friendship, although Aristotle himself does not explicitly say much about it. Trust, then, is central in human flourishing, and given that an increasing proportion of our lives is being spent online, trust in that environment is also becoming of more concern. However, online trust presents a somewhat confusing picture. Often there is thought to be too little trust in this environment, and this has produced a variety of methods and suggestions aimed at creating trust, particularly in and for e-commerce. Sometimes, however, there seems to be too much trust, and many people are deceived, hurt, and even harmed. For example, the well-known Kaycee Nicole hoax deceived many (Dunne, 2001), as did that of Joan, the supposed disabled female neuropsychologist (van Gelder, 1991), and too many e-mail users willingly open possibly virus-infected attachments from unknown senders. It is also not clear what the object of online trust is—that is, *what* is trusted. Commonly it is trust of people or companies, but it might be trust of Web sites, systems, terminals, and so on, and perhaps even trust of people by systems and routers by other routers (Camp, 2000). Sometimes, too, trust is seen as just an issue of security (Schneiderman, 1999), but at other times it is rather something that concerns human behavior. In addition, it has been argued that no real online trust is possible because the conditions necessary for trust cannot be found in that environment.

A few of these points can be clarified immediately. First, in this discussion the main concern is with trust between individuals, and not trust of Web sites, and so on, although trust of organizations, both by individuals and by other organizations, is also relevant. Second, trust is not, or is not merely, security. Although a secure network and system might be necessary for trust, such security is not the same as trust. This will be elaborated later. Third, it is true that not all online contexts are exactly the same with respect to trust, for example, distinctions can be drawn between e-commerce, chat groups, and cooperative research groups, at least. Some of these distinctions will arise again, but for the purposes of the argument of this chapter, they do not matter too much. Our concern is with online trust in general. Trust is important perhaps for different *reasons* in different contexts—for example, for commerce in one and for the development of personal relationships in another, but it is nevertheless *trust* that is important, and the contention here is that that is essentially the same across contexts. Finally, the question of whether online trust is possible will be examined in some detail.

THE IMPORTANCE OF TRUST, ONLINE AND OFF

The most common reason given for the importance of online trust is that "without trust, development of e-commerce cannot reach its potential" (Cheskin, 1999, p. 2). And again "Trust encourages organisations to make investments necessary for electronic information exchange. . . . It discourages opportunistic bahaviour which clearly reduces the opportunity for greater information sharing over time" (Ratnasingam, 2000, p. 61). This is really just one aspect of the larger picture. Trust is necessary for the successful functioning of any community. But trust is also important for personal relationships, and for the individual's good, particularly with respect to self-esteem. Personal relationships and the individual's good will be considered following a discussion of the pragmatic reasons why trust is important for communities.

COMMUNITIES

Successful living within groups requires some trust. I must trust that others will act in ways that are conducive to harmonious living, and they must trust that I will do the same. Societies function better the more trust that there is, and without any trust could not function at all (Putnam, 1994). This need for a moderately high level of trust for the smooth and efficient functioning of a society includes the functioning of its economy, whether on or offline. The reason for this is that things are more efficient when there is a high level of trust. When there is lack of trust, there must be monitoring and surveillance, filling out of documents and keeping of records, and somebody must read at least some of these, which is all largely unproductive work. Putnam, Coleman, and others talk of trust as social capital, the ability of people to work together for common purposes:

Like other forms of capital, social capital is productive, making possible the achievement of certain ends that would not be attainable in its absence. . . . For example, a group whose members manifest trustworthiness and place extensive trust in one another will be able to accomplish much more than a comparable group lacking that trustworthiness and trust. (Coleman, 1990, pp. 302, 304)

Without trust people cooperate only under a system of formal rules or con-tracts and these are often called "transactions costs." These costs are in effect a tax on lack of trust. Fukuyama, talking about trust in society in general, says that costs incurred by police, lawyers, prisons, and so on are "a direct tax imposed by the breakdown of trust in society." He continues:

People who do not trust one another will end up cooperating only under a system of formal rules and regulations. . . . This legal apparatus, serving as a substitute for trust, entails what economists call "transaction costs." Wide-spread distrust in a society, in other words, imposes a kind of tax on all forms of economic activity, a tax that high-trust societies do not have to pay. (Fukuyama, 1995, pp. 11, 27–28)

This is not a totally new idea of course, and there is a hint of it in Aristotle, as we will see when the role of goodwill is discussed.

Presumably this is all just as true online as offline. As already seen, there is plenty of discussion regarding e-commerce and trust, and some degree of trust is necessary in so-called virtual communities as well—that is, online chat groups and the like—if they are to be successful. However, the online situation is more tenuous than the offline, and requires further examination.

PERSONAL RELATIONSHIPS

Trust is not only important for a community to function smoothly, it is also necessary in personal relationships. It is difficult to see how the important relationships of love and friendship can even get started without trust. Love, even deep love, is of course possible where trust is lacking. A prodigal child can be loved unreservedly, even if there is little trust given or deserved, and there can be strong love for a partner, or desired partner, without trust (after Iago's success, Othello loved, but did not trust, Desdemona). But this trust-lacking love is hardly conducive to a loving *relationship*. Trust is also impor-tant in friendship. I trust that my friend will have, at least to some significant degree, my interests at heart. Without that, it is difficult to know what to make of friendship, a sentiment it seems, that would be endorsed by Aristo-tle, as we will see shortly.

Individuals

There seems also to be a connection between trust and self-esteem, and even perhaps self-respect. We feel better about ourselves when we believe that we are trusted. If I know that someone, an acquaintance, does not trust me, I know, or have good reason to believe, that that person considers me to have some serious character deficiencies. I am seen as being deficient in one or more characteristics such as reliability, caring, loyalty, honesty, selflessness, and the like. While it seems not to bother some people too much what others think about them, most of us do want to be seen favorably. I feel better about myself if others have a good opinion of me. I do like to be trusted, and I do not like to be distrusted. Being trusted is, of course, not merely being liked, and in some cases the two do not go together. I can trust someone without liking her (she may be trustworthy but boring and arrogant). Similarly, I may like someone whom I do not trust (she may be intelligent and witty but not at all trustworthy). This link between being trusted and self-esteem is not a tight one. It is certain possible to have high self-esteem regardless of what others think about us and how they behave toward us. We might just not care. Nevertheless, a strong case can be made that there is some link.

Being trusted also contributes to our autonomy. If I am trusted, I can make decisions to act in certain ways with respect to others that I cannot if I am not trusted. I cannot *choose*, in any real sense, to do the right thing by my employer if I am regularly monitored rather than trusted. If I am trusted, I am not monitored to ensure that I do what I am told. (See Weckert, 2002, for more on workplace monitoring.) This increased autonomy and concomitant responsibility in turn can contribute to self-esteem and a general feeling of well-being, and Fukuyama reports that this has been found to be the case in workplaces: "Workers usually find their workplace more satisfying if they are treated like adults who can be trusted to contribute to their community rather than like small cogs in a large industrial machine designed by someone else" (Fukuyama, 1995, p. 31).

WHAT IS TRUST? WHY IT MATTERS

Concerns about trust arise in various contexts on the Internet, for example, in e-commerce and in so-called virtual communities such as chat groups. How we cope with these concerns depends partly on what we take trust to be. Our account of trust matters because different types of account have different consequences. If, for example, we believe that trust is to be explained in terms of rational expectations, then we might be tempted to design networks with a large amount of monitoring capability, so that wrongdoing is easy to detect and deception difficult. The same could be true if we consider trust as fragile. On the other hand, if trust is taken as quite robust, fewer safeguards for maximizing correct behavior would be necessary. Before looking explicitly at trust on the Internet, therefore, we will consider more generally what trust is. Once we have an account, we will be in a better position to proceed.

TRUST, RELIANCE, AND GOODWILL

First, trust must be distinguished from mere reliance, although the latter is part of trust. I rely on my glasses to see, but in no interesting sense do I trust them. A beggar may rely on passersby for sustenance, but have no trust that his needs will be met—he simply has no choice. Annette Baier argues that trust is a special sort of reliance—reliance on a person's goodwill toward one. If A trusts B, then A relies on B's goodwill toward A. As it stands, this cannot be quite right, as Holton (Holton, 1994) has shown. First, a confidence trickster might rely on one's goodwill without trusting one, therefore reliance on goodwill cannot be a sufficient condition for trust (although perhaps this could be what a case of what Baier calls "bad trust" [Baier, 1986, pp. 255–256]).

Holton next points out that if I trust someone, I do not necessarily rely on that person's goodwill toward *me* (Holton, 1994, p. 65). I could trust someone to care for my children, relying on his goodwill toward *them*, but not necessarily toward me. He might consider me a very poor parent and have no goodwill toward me at all. Therefore, it might be the case that there is always goodwill toward the trustor *or* toward the object of the trust (i.e., toward me or toward my children). Holton considers this disjunction but dismisses the view that any goodwill at all is necessary, using one of Baier's own examples. This example is that "we trust our enemies not to fire at us when we lay down our arms and put up a white flag" (Baier, 1986, p. 234). His comment on this is that while we rely on our enemy not to fire, talk of goodwill is out of place, but talk of trust is not. We might trust our enemy here, but we certainly cannot assume any goodwill toward us, he thinks.

This seems rather too quick, and there are two possible responses. Some goodwill would seem to be possible. The enemy feels good about defeating us, and perhaps some gratitude that we surrendered and did not fight to the death, thus reducing their casualties too. Talk about some degree of goodwill does not seem out of place. On the other hand, it may not always make sense to talk of trust in this situation. Perhaps I do not trust them not to shoot, but I do rely on them not shooting because of international agreements and the threat of punishment if they do. So Holton has not demonstrated that goodwill is not a component of trust. Even in these difficult cases, a plausible story can be told that trust involves reliance on goodwill.

GOODWILL, ARISTOTLE, AND FRIENDSHIP

A moment ago Aristotle was mentioned in relation to friendship. Although he says little about trust explicitly, his account of friendship, which has the goodwill of someone as a central component, would seem to implicitly involve trust between friends, as trust is described here. He says, in *Nicomachean Ethics (NE)*: "To be friends, then, they must be mutually recognized as bearing goodwill and wishing well to each other" (*NE*, 1156a 5). Whether this is a component in all friendship, or only in the highest sort, is debatable, although Cooper argues that it is (Cooper, 1980), a view that will be accepted here. (It must be noted that Alpern is not in complete agreement with Cooper's interpretation, but still believes that "dependence, cooperation, trust, and some degree of communion and sharing" can be found in Aristotle's inferior friendships [Alpern, 1983, p. 315].) Trust, then, is a component of all friendships to the extent that friends rely on the goodwill of each other. Aristotle himself does in fact say, talking of the friendship of the good, that " it is among good men that trust and the feeling that 'he would never wrong me' and all the other things that are demanded by true friendship are found" (*NE*, 1157a 20), without saying anything further about trust. This is not to imply that trust only occurs in friendships. We can have goodwill toward those who are not, in any recognizable sense, our friends. However, trust within relationships of close friendship and love (including couples, and parents and children), could perhaps be seen as the paradigm cases of trust.

We saw earlier Fukuyama's claim that more legal apparatus and law enforcement are necessary when there is less trust. Although Aristotle does not talk in these terms, there seems to be a similar idea underlying some of his comments on friendship and justice. Just as a high level of trust in a community is a force for coherence, and reduces the need for various sorts of laws and law enforcement, so friendship reduces the need for justice, at least in the sense that justice needs to be enforced. "Friendship seems too to hold states together . . . and when men are friends they have no need of justice" (*NE*, 1155a 25). Cooper describes Aristotle's *civic* friendship in a manner that makes it look very similar to what Fukuyama and others say about trust in a community:

> . . . civic friendship exists where the fellow-citizens, to one another's mutual knowledge, like . . . one another, that is, where each citizen wishes well . . . to the others, and is willing to undertake to confer benefits on them, for their own sake, in consequence of recognizing that he himself is regularly benefited by the actions of the others. In a community animated by civic friendship, each citizen assumes that all the others . . . are willing supporters of their common institutions and willing contributors to the common social product. . . . So they will approach one another for business and other purposes in a spirit of mutual good-will. . . . They will be accommodating rather than suspicious, anxious to yield a point rather than insisting on the full letter of their rights. (Cooper, 1977, p. 646)

Although the relationship between friendship and justice in Aristotle is, of course, complex (see Sokolowski, 2001), and justice cannot be related to friendship in the way that it has been suggested that "transaction costs" are related to trust, if Cooper is right about civic friendship, there does seem to be some resemblance. A society with a high level of civic friendship, and therefore trust, is more successful and happier than one with a low level.

COGNITIVE AND NONCOGNITIVE ACCOUNTS

It has been argued that trust involves reliance on the goodwill of the trustee—that is, if A trusts B, then A relies on B's goodwill toward A or toward the object of the trust. It now remains to be seen if A's reliance on B is a matter of A's beliefs about B, or more about A's attitudes (or something like them) toward B. This distinction between cognitive and noncognitive types of accounts has been explained by Becker thus: "let us call trust 'cognitive' if it is fundamentally a matter of our beliefs or expectations about others' trustworthiness; it is noncognitive if it is fundamentally a matter of our having trustful attitudes, affects, emotions, or motivational structures that are not focused on specific people, institutions, or groups" (Becker, 1996, p. 45). On a cognitive account "A trusts B" amounts to something like "A believes (expects) that B will do X in situation S." If A trusts B to take care of his cat while A is on vacation, A believes or expects that B will look after the cat during that time. On a noncognitive account, "A trusts B" is something like "A's attitude toward B is Y," or "A takes a certain stance, Y, toward B" (see, e.g., Govier, 1997, Holton, 1994, and Jones, 1996, although Becker might not call all these noncognitive).

Coleman emphasizes the cognitive:

> . . . the elements confronting the potential trustor are nothing more or less than the considerations a rational actor applies in deciding whether to place a bet. . . . The potential trustor must decide between not placing trust, in which case there is no change in his utility, and placing trust, in which case the expected utility relative to his current status is the potential gain times the chance of gain minus the potential loss times the chance of loss. A rational actor will place trust if the first product is greater than the second. (Coleman, 1990, p. 99)

There are, however, problems with cognitive accounts. Accounts of trust that depend heavily on knowledge and expectation seem inadequate. Although trust has a cognitive element, it is more than that. A child's trust in its parents cannot be explained in terms of belief alone, nor can that between friends. Young children are not capable of the right sorts of beliefs. And trust between friends is also not based on a careful weighing of risks and benefits, particularly if we accept an interpretation of Aristotle's friendship in which goodwill is always a component. There is also a paradox inherent in cognitive accounts of trust of the Coleman type. This will be discussed in more detail later, but essentially the issue is that particular conditions that increase certainty regarding our beliefs and expectations about someone's actions also reduce the space for trust. It is commonly claimed, too, that trust is fragile—for example, by Dasgupta (Dasgupta, 1988, p. 50)—but that is far from obvious. Trust, it will be argued, is actually rather robust, but this is not easy to explain on a cognitive account. The account to be developed here has more in common with those based on attitudes or stances, and has both cognitive and noncognitive aspects, something that seems necessary, as Baier agrees: "trust is one of those mental phenomena attention to which shows us the inadequacy of attempting to classify mental phenomena into the 'cognitive,' the 'affective,' and the 'conative.' Trust, if it is any of these, is all three" (Baier, 1994, p. 132). This sort of account also seems to fit much better the facts that we know about trust, and it does have implications for trust on the Internet.

TRUST AS SEEING AS

For our purposes, if A trusts B, then A *sees* B's behavior *as* being trustworthy, or A *sees* B *as* trustworthy, or A *sees* B *as* a person to trust. In order not to beg any questions, it can be said that A sees B as someone who will, typically, do as he or she says, who is reliable, who will act with the interests of A in mind, has some goodwill toward A or A's dependents, and so on. For the sake of brevity, however, we will talk of A's seeing B as someone trustworthy. Looking at trust in this way makes it resemble a Kuhnian paradigm (Kuhn, 1970). While not wanting to push this analogy too far, this approach does highlight some of the important features of trust, in particular the intertwining of the attitudinal and the cognitive, and the robustness of trust. Trust also contains an element of commitment that is often overlooked, although many writers talk about the risk and uncertainty aspects. If I trust someone, then I am willing to "put myself in his hands," to make myself vulnerable to him in some way. If I am not willing to do this, it is not clear that there is any force in my supposed trust. Although these and other features are not incompatible with accounts couched in terms of attitude or stance, the seeing as approach does make them more obvious.

If A sees B as trustworthy, then there is more involved than merely believing or expecting him to be trustworthy. There could even be cases in which A sees B as trustworthy but does not believe that he is, in a way similar to the manner in which we see the moon larger near the horizon than at its zenith, even though we do not believe that it varies in size. I do not want to suggest that this is the normal state of affairs. Normally we believe that things are, more or less, the way that we see them. But on occasion this is not so. While it might be difficult to imagine a case in which I could see someone as trustworthy *and* believe that he or she was not, there is little doubt that

I can see someone in that way without having any specific beliefs, certainly not *explicit* ones, about the matter. In fact, we do not normally think about trust too much, or someone's trustworthiness, except when we are disappointed. It is similar to normal science being conducted within an unquestioned paradigm (Kuhn, 1970). These ideas also have something in common with Lagerspertz, who says that to trust "is to present behaviour in a certain light" (Lagerspertz, 1998, p. 5). Another way of looking at trust as seeing as, is this: if A sees B as trustworthy (with respect to A), he interprets B's behavior as showing goodwill, or at least not ill will, toward A. If A see B as untrustworthy, that is, he *distrusts* him as opposed to having no views on the matter, he interprets B's behavior as showing ill will toward him (a typical characteristic of the paranoid).

One commonly supposed but rarely supported feature of trust, mentioned already, which this model does challenge, is that while trust is difficult to build, it is rather fragile and easy to demolish. (Govier does raise this issue in the first sentence of her book, when she writes, "The human capacity for trust is amazing" [Govier, 1997, p. 3].) That trust is difficult to build is not in question, that it is fragile is. This view of the fragility of trust seems to be based on something like a Popperian falsificationist view of science. While a theory cannot be verified, an incompatible observation falsifies it. We know that in science the situation is more complicated than that, and so it is with respect to trust. It is probably true that if I know that A has *deceived* me in a situation in which I trusted him, my trust will be weakened or, perhaps, extinguished. But most cases are not like this. When expectations are not met, deceit is not always, and probably not usually, involved. Suppose that I trust A to do X, but he does not do X. It is unlikely that I will stop trusting him on the basis of one, or even a few, lapses of this kind, unless, of course, I do suspect deceit. There could be many reasons why A did not do X. There may have been some misunderstanding between us and he did not realize that I expected him to do it. He might have had good reasons for not doing it that are unknown to me, but such that if I did know of them I would approve of his not doing it. I do *not* immediately see A's behavior as being untrustworthy. This is similar to science where, if there is incompatibility between an observation and a theory, there is more than one way to explain the incoherence. One need not reject the theory, or the trust, outright. Quine's *maxim of minimum mutilation* is relevant here (Quine, 1970, p. 7). My most cherished beliefs and attitudes are affected least, or mutilated least, and trust in someone is frequently cherished. I will, if I can, find some explanation that does not involve rejecting my trust. John Updike illustrates this robustness of trust in his short story "Trust Me" as he writes of a small boy, Harold, who jumps from the side of a pool into the supposedly waiting arms of his father. Unfortunately the father did not catch him, with unpleasant, though not fatal, consequences for the boy. But "Unaccountably, all through his growing up he continued to trust his father." He continued to trust him because he had plausible explanations at hand: "perhaps [he] had leaped a moment before it was expected, or had proved unexpectedly heavy, and had thus slipped through his father's grasp" (Updike, 1987, p. 4). This view of trust is supported by some empirical research as well. According to Rempel, Ross, and Holmes, talking of trust in close relationships, "trust can act as a filter through which people interpret their partner's motives" (Rempel et al., 2001, p. 58). People in high trust relationships interpret their partner's actions "in ways that are consistent with their positive expectations," while those in low trust relationships "are less likely to attribute their partner's behavior to benevolent motives."

There will always be some risk and uncertainty associated with trust. If A trusts B, then A takes some risk with respect to B, and, in a sense, the greater the trust, the greater the risk. I risk a lot more in a loving relationship than I do in a casual friendship. The commitment is greater so there is much more at stake. The *seeing as* account of trust accommodates this, as can be noted in the following discussion of reasonable trust.

When is it reasonable to trust? On a purely cognitive account of trust, it might be argued that trust is reasonable if A has a contract with B to do X and there is some authority that can ensure adherence to the contract. Another situation is that in which A has the power to ensure that B does X, B knows that A has the power, and A knows that B knows that he has that power. In these cases, however, there is not really trust. Trust is not necessary when an action is inevitable. A better way to approach the question is to say that A's trust in B is reasonable if A knows or justifiably believes that B is trustworthy, or if A justifiably believes that most people are trustworthy most of the time and justifiably believes that he has no reason to distrust B on this occasion. The next step is to spell out the conditions under which it is justifiable to believe in B's trustworthiness.

An even better approach, if "A trusts B" is couched in terms of "A sees B as Y," is that the reasonableness is in terms of the reasonableness of the *seeing as*. A's seeing B as trustworthy is reasonable to the extent that A's seeing B in this way gives a coherent account of B's behavior. If A sees B's behavior as trustworthy, there is little that requires explanation. On the other hand, if A interprets B's behavior as untrustworthy, he must attribute to him many devious motives and intentions for which there is no evidence. With this view, a few cases of possibly untrustworthy behavior will not count against the reasonableness of the overall trust. They can be counted as just anomalies to be explained away. A will try to 'minimally mutilate' his view of B. If there are too many anomalies, of course, such a stance becomes no longer viable. This is similar to Kuhn's view of paradigm change in science. Where the threshold is will vary, depending on the strength of the trust. When the trust is very strong—say, the trust in a parent or a close friend—the trust "paradigm" will be very resistant to challenge. Too much is at stake. Where the trust is less, there will be a correspondingly weaker resistance to change.

On this account, when trust is lost, there will be something like a "gestalt switch." After the switch, A will see B as untrustworthy, and possibly trustworthy actions will be interpreted as anomalies and explained away, something that a paranoid person will typically do.

Finally, let us comment on the application of this model. So far it has been applied to trust relationships between individuals only, but this requires qualification. Often we trust a person in some respect rather than in all. A might trust B to care for his children, but not to stay sober at a party. Trust is frequently relative to contexts, but that is compatible with the seeing as model. A sees B as trustworthy in context C, but not necessarily in context D. This model of trust can also accommodate trust of institutions. For example, A sees the government as trustworthy, or A sees business X as trustworthy. Again, these could be relativized to particular contexts.

IS TRUST ONLINE POSSIBLE?

Armed with this account of trust, we are now in a position to examine online trust. It should first be noted that it could be argued that computer systems and networks are hardly neutral with respect to trust. They might not cause lack of trust, but when people are inclined not to trust, these systems facilitate its reduction or even elimination. It is very easy to check on what someone is doing if they use a computer system in the workplace. For example, e-mail sent and received, Web sites visited, and listserver activity can be examined with ease. On the other hand, deceit is easy, at least with respect to the "average" user, and a large degree of anonymity is possible in some contexts. Someone with a good knowledge of the way in which computer networks are constructed and operate can fairly easily remain anonymous, for most practical purposes. Does, or can, trust play a role here? To answer this it is necessary to consider more carefully what problems the online world does pose for trust.

OBSTACLES TO TRUST ONLINE

It has been argued that trust is important, both on and offline, and there are many discussions suggesting that if e-commerce is to be successful online, trust is essential. But is trust possible online? A number of arguments suggest that there are problems. Four types of supposed obstacles can be identified: community values, Internet context and roles, disembodiment, and security.

COMMUNITY VALUES

According to Fukuyama, who does not talk about online trust explicitly, trust arises in a community with a set of shared moral values: "Trust is the expectation that arises within a community of regular, honest, and cooperative behavior, based on commonly shared norms, on the part of other members of that community" (Fukuyama, 1995, p. 26). The difficulty posed here is that the Internet is not a localized community with commonly shared norms. Rather, it encompasses many communities with many different values. The online "community" crosses cultures, so can there be a shared set of moral values? Given this, it seems that the right conditions for the development of trust do not exist online. Perhaps this is not an important obstacle. There can certainly be localized, or special interest, online "communities" that seem to share enough values in order to be successful, and in those there often appears to be plenty of trust. That, of course, does not help the situation much with respect to e-commerce, in which the "community" is global, and fewer values are shared. It is possible, however, that this is a relatively short-term situation. It is plausible to think that if people see the value in doing business online, they will accept the values necessary for that business to proceed, at least while they are online. They may or may not accept those values in other aspects of their lives, but that is irrelevant. That there are shared values online is enough.

INTERNET CONTEXT AND ROLES

Nissenbaum raises the problem of "inscrutable contexts" (Nissenbaum, 2001, p. 114). The online context is different from the offline, and in particular the normal role definitions do not apply. The contexts within which we interact are largely unfamiliar and unformulated, and so do not generate the same assurance in the trustworthiness of others that more familiar contexts do.

Although this may be a problem now, it is not clear that it is a very long-term one. As more people use the Internet, and as their experience with it grows, the various online contexts will become commonplace and familiar, and probably more structured, even if informally. New roles will emerge, and these will become as familiar as those that we are comfortable with now.

DISEMBODIMENT

Disembodiment would seem to be the most serious obstacle, so it will receive a little more attention. Our bodies are important for a variety of reasons, and in the context of online trust three stand out. First, they, to a significant extent, anchor identity; second, they convey and receive much information—that is, they play an important role in communication; and, third, they are vulnerable. The first two reasons are discussed by Nissenbaum as problems for online trust. She argues that the conditions necessary for the creation and maintenance of trust offline are not present online (Nissenbaum, 2001, pp.

113–114). The first of these is missing identity. Online it is not clear whom we are communicating with, so it is difficult to know whether it is someone trustworthy. And because they are anonymous, more or less, for practical purposes, there is less reason to believe that they will act responsibly. In addition, it is often difficult to know whether we are communicating with the same person over time. All that there is to go on is what is on the screen. The second problem is missing personal characteristics. Not only can we not be sure of the identity of the person whom we communicate with, but we also know few of their personal characteristics. Hence, many of the cues that we use to assess trustworthiness are missing. Indeed, the communication channels are very narrow. No body language is conveyed, so reliance is purely on the verbal, and that itself is limited to the written word.

A similar argument is presented by Cocking and Matthews in their discussion of online friendship. They argue that

> what is lacking here is not merely a partial, or marginal set of factors, but a significant global loss and distortion of the real case. What is distorted and lost, in particular, are important aspects of a person's character and of the relational self ordinarily developed through those interactions in friendship which . . . are precisely the kinds of interactions largely weakened or eliminated by the dominance of voluntary self-disclosure found in the virtual world. (Cocking and Matthews, 2000, p.231)

Their core point is that online we have an amount of control over how we present ourselves to others that is not possible in the offline world. Therefore, nobody can get to know our characters in the way that is common in friendship. I know my friends' strengths and weaknesses, and they know mine, but we are friends nonetheless. Although this is an argument about friendship, it is relevant also to trust. If we have a high level of control over how we present ourselves to others, it is highly likely that the presentation will contain more of our favorable attributes than the less favorable ones. The possibility of deception is also increased. So not only is the possibility of true friendship lessened, but so is the possibility of trust.

Dreyfus's problems with online trust are related to both communication and vulnerability (Dreyfus, 2001, pp. 70–71). His main concern with communication, however, seem to be with gaining information through the body. From childhood experience we acquire a disposition to trust those who touch us tenderly. Trust is based on feelings of security that babies get in their caretakers' arms. But this experience is missing in the online world. His second point is based on the fact that trust involves vulnerability. If I trust someone, I am to some extent vulnerable. However, I must be in the same room as someone to be really vulnerable with respect to that individual, and to know that he or she will not take advantage of me. If our only contact is online, the potential for harm, and hence my vulnerability, is not great.

SECURITY

The fourth kind of obstacle to online trust, again raised by Nissenbaum (2001), is that the security measures necessary to make the online environment safe leave little space for trust. This will be discussed further shortly, under Solution 1.

SUMMARY OF OBSTACLES

Of the four types of obstacle raised, it has been suggested that the first two are not much cause for concern, but no answers have yet be given for the last two. Two proposed solutions will be examined. The first follows from the final obstacle, security. It will be argued that while security is not a solution, neither is it necessarily an obstacle. The second proposed solution suggests ways of engendering online trust, but, given the disembodiment problems, this seems to lead to a conflict. On the one hand, there are arguments suggesting that online trust is not possible, and, on the other, people are proposing ways of creating it. To resolve this conflict it will be argued that the problems raised with respect to disembodiment are not as destructive to trust as claimed.

PROPOSED SOLUTIONS

SOLUTION 1

One solution is to treat online trust purely as a technical security issue. What matters is to make the network secure. This, however, is unsatisfactory on its own. First, in practice, human behavior, and not only network security, is important (ICAC, 2001); second, overemphasis on security reduces space for trust (but perhaps this does not matter); and third, security is costly in both money and individual freedom. To highlight these problems, consider a fairly restricted network rather than the whole Internet, just a network in a workplace, and the monitoring of employees on this network. Suppose that an employer, A, does not monitor B, her employee, on the assumption that if B is not doing her job properly, she will learn about it soon enough. This requires a reasonable level of trust on A's part. Suppose now that she does acquire monitoring equipment that gives her the capability to keep track of B's activities. Obviously, the more that this equipment is used, the greater will be her certainty that B is carrying out her work properly. On this security model of trust, her trust in B should be stronger the more that she monitors B's activities. But this is not so. The more that B is monitored, the less space there is for trusting her. The paradox inherent in this type of account of trust is that the conditions that should make trust stronger—the monitoring—diminish it and make it redundant. The more monitoring there is, the less need there is for trust. In a situation of total monitoring—say, a maximum security prison—trust disappears, or almost. This is the thrust of Nissenbaum's second type of worry about online trust (Nissenbaum, 2001, pp. 114 ff.). The problem can be highlighted, too, by considering the situation from a slightly different angle. Suppose that the workplace had a completely secure computer network. What would such a network be like? It would be completely reliable—that is, there would be no breakdowns. All firewalls would be completely safe, so no intruders could ever get through. Encryption would be undecipherable without the appropriate keys, those keys would be safe, and authentication techniques would be foolproof. Would trust matter? It would, because while intruders would be kept out, there would be no guarantee that legitimate users were behaving properly. They could be practicing deceit, stealing information, and so on. Suppose that there was a perfect system of monitoring. All activity is logged and all inappropriate behavior punished. Everything that all insiders do is monitored, so there is no chance that they can do anything undetected. Is trust required now? Some is. Although it may not be necessary to trust the general users, the employees, simply because they are not in a position to misbehave, those undertaking the monitoring and surveillance must still be trusted to do the right thing. Perhaps they are monitored too, but that just moves the trust to another level, and so on ad infinitum. This regress can perhaps be avoided by automating the monitoring. When anything untoward is noticed, the perpetrator will automatically be punished in some way, and their deeds made public. In such a system perhaps trust would not be necessary within the system, but it would still be necessary to trust the developers and maintainers of the monitoring system. Is it implemented in a manner that is fair, or does it favor certain people? But even if such a system were fair, would anyone really want to work in a workplace with this kind of environment? Probably not. It seems to be a very high price to pay to avoid the need to trust other human beings. The system would have modeled a very efficient police state. Trust, consequently, cannot be engendered by security alone; in fact, too much security stifles trust.

SOLUTION 2

A second type of solution attempts to create an online environment that, at least for electronic commerce, instills confidence in people. A variety of methods have been devised to achieve this. Wallace describes one attempt:

> To help build trust [eBay, an online auction house] developed an electronic feedback database to help buyers and sellers evaluate a potential partner's integrity and reputation. Any registered user can post a positive, neutral, or negative comment about any other user and a person who is contemplating a transaction can check the files to see if other eBay users thought highly of that individual. (Wallace, 1999, pp. 244–245)

Another common strategy is the use of Internet seals issued by trusted third parties. An example is WebTrust, a seal issued by various institutes of chartered accountants, including those in the United States, Canada, and Australia (WebTrust, 2002). If a business satisfies certain requirements, it can display the WebTrust seal on its Web sites. The requirements that need to be met for the right to display such seals usually relate to privacy and security issues. Yet another device is the use of so-called embodied conversational agents. These agents, usually cartoon-like characters, give advice and information, and can interact with users in a manner similar to human interaction (Cassell and Bickmore, 2000).

These and other methods and guidelines have been developed and implemented to encourage trusting behavior in electronic commerce. Obviously there still needs to be good network security, but of the blocking kind (e.g., firewalls and encryption) rather than the monitoring kind (although these are not completely mutually exclusive).

The discussion in this section has been purely related to electronic commerce because this is the area in which there has been the most concern about the lack of trust, and in which efforts have been made to develop strategies and methods for strengthening trust. In some other online contexts—for example, chat groups—the development of trust does not seem to be such a problem, possibly because there is not so much at stake, at least financially.

POSSIBLE CONFLICT?

Earlier several arguments were considered that suggested that conditions for trust do not exist online. However, as we saw in the previous section, many people offer suggestions regarding how online trust can be generated, and this seems to create a problem. In summary, the problem is that for e-commerce and other online activities to be successful, a moderately high level of trust is necessary, but, for the reasons given earlier, it seems difficult, if not impossible, for such trust to develop. So those offering suggestions regarding how to create trust are embarking on an impossible task. This question of possible conflict must now be explored further.

DISEMBODIMENT REVISITED

From a theoretical point of view, disembodiment appears to be a considerable obstacle to trust, yet the empirical evidence presents a more ambiguous picture. There is certainly evidence for lack of trust online. Reid, for example, in discussing betrayal in online communities, writes that "participants feel that they cannot trust anyone, that everything can be a lie, and that no one tells anyone who they really are" (Reid, 1998, p.36). Wallace notes that "we are a little cooler online" (Wallace, 1999, p. 17), and Kiesler and Kraut say that "people generally feel less close to online communication partners than to those with whom they have formed real-world relationships" (Kiesler and Kraut, 1999, p. 783).

On the other hand, there is also evidence, admittedly anecdotal, that trust and genuine relationships can and do develop. Parks and Floyd note that "online relationships are genuine personal relationships in the eyes of the participants" (Parks and Floyd, 1996, p. 82). And Wallace writes that

> you sometimes feel closer to people on other side of your screen whom you have never seen than to the people in the next room. You may reveal more about yourself to them, feel more attraction to them and express more emotions. . . . At the keyboard you can concentrate only on yourself, your words, and the feelings that you want to convey. You don't have to worry about how you look, what you're wearing, or those extra pounds you meant to shed. (Wallace, 1999, p. 151)

It is worth noting that disembodiment is here considered a virtue and not a problem for meaningful communication. Again, from Deuel we hear:

> For participants who are emotionally invested in such activities, a number of additional factors come into play to enhance the experience: the slow development of real-time interaction and mutual stimulation between the two participants. . . . Most experienced participants describe a point at which the screen disappears, when one is no longer sitting at a terminal but is perceptually in another space and the imagination has taken over entirely. (Deuel, 1996, p. 138)

While Deuel is here talking of virtual sex and not necessarily any genuine friendship, her research does indicate that meaningful relationships that involve some level of trust are not uncommon online. There is also evidence that project or research teams working purely online can and do develop trust between their members (Wallace, 1999, pp. 85–86). Although this evidence of the formation of close relationships online that involve some trust is important, perhaps more important are the *explanations* of how this is possible in the light of disembodiment. Parks and Floyd claim that time is an important factor: "The important point . . . is not that CMC [computer mediated communication] is unable to convey relational and personal information, but rather that it may take longer to do so" (Parks and Floyd, 1996, p. 82). They continue: "the emphasis placed on factors like physical appearance or proximity may reflect less of a theoretical necessity than a consequence of the fact that most theories of relational development predate the current explosion in computer-mediated communication technology" (Parks and Floyd, 1996, p. 84).

There is also some evidence that text itself can provide some cues for truthfulness: "There was a tendency for truthful subjects to use words in a slightly different way compared to nontruthful ones. Their words were somewhat more likely to be complete, direct, relevant, clear, and personalized" (Wallace, 1999, pp. 52–53).

What can be concluded from the studies just mentioned? The evidence suggests that close and meaningful relationships do form online, and many of these relationships involve at least some degree of trust. Although disembodiment can be a deterrent to the development of online trust, it is not an overwhelming one. It can be, and is, overcome. Even though there is deception—for example, in the Kaycee Nicole hoax—these cases seem to be the exception. This case illustrates, too, that, despite disembodiment, there can still be a high degree of vulnerability online (van der Woning, 2001). Where there is emotional commitment, there is the chance of emotional hurt, online or off.

This section has concentrated on online contexts other than e-commerce, but if the problem here is not as great it is sometimes thought, there seems no reason why it should be in the e-commerce context either.

THE CREATION OF ONLINE TRUST

An earlier section discussed some suggested ways of generating online trust. In general, these involve making more information available to people so that they are better informed about those whom they communicate with online, and, where possible, emulating a situation that is not too different from their experience in the offline world. This extra knowledge, together with confidence in the security of the system, will, it is hoped, encourage people to take risks online, in the expectation that these risks are not too great. I will interact with other people and with businesses online in those cases in which I believe that the benefits outweigh the risks. I calculate the risks and benefits in a Coleman-like way (see the earlier Coleman quotation), and make my decision on that.

While this might be a reasonable way to proceed in some instances, it is not obvious that it is in all, or that it is the most efficient way to generate trust. An alternative is this. We can choose to *see as* in a way that we cannot choose to *believe*. I can choose to see the duck-rabbit drawing as either a drawing of duck or of a rabbit (once I realize that it can be seen in both ways), although I cannot choose to see a real duck as a rabbit. Consider a more significant (and real) case. Various people saw part of a fence (on a beach in Sydney) as an apparition of the Virgin Mary. Knowing that this part of the fence could be seen in that way, I may well be able to see the image of the Virgin Mary, too, if I tried. But I could certainly not choose to believe that I really was seeing her in the way that the devout

believed they were. Similarly, while I cannot choose to *believe* that someone is trustworthy, I can choose to see someone in that light in circumstances in which the evidence is ambiguous, vague, or inadequate. If the
evidence is strong one way or the other, of course, that choice may not be
there, just as I cannot choose to see a real duck as a rabbit. The way to create trust, then, seems to be merely to choose to see others as trustworthy.
But this on its own will not do. We do not want a situation in which one
can at will simply switch between seeing someone as trustworthy or
untrustworthy. We want the real duck or the real rabbit, and not just the
ambiguous drawing. The way forward is to act *as if* someone is seen as trustworthy (see Gambetta, 1988, pp. 224–229). Suppose that A acts as if B is
trustworthy. B now has the opportunity of providing evidence that he is
(or is not) trustworthy. If he behaves in a trustworthy manner, then A is
beginning to build up evidence that B is trustworthy, and a belief to this
effect could develop. Similarly, B's behavior coheres with A seeing him as
trustworthy. If B continues to behave in this fashion, A will just see him
in this light and the issues of seeing him as untrustworthy will not arise—
it would require too much implausible explanation, just as it is not easy to
see a real duck as a real rabbit.

This procedure for generating trust is similar, at least in spirit, to the
idea of William James in *The Will to Believe* for developing religious belief
(James, 1979). He argues that many important decisions cannot be made on
the basis of logic and evidence alone. Sometimes we must "take a leap in
the dark." That is, we must make a decision based on less than certainty,
and this involves risk. We could be wrong. This he believes leads, or can
lead, to religious faith. The suggestion here has been that something similar can happen in the case of trust. Choosing to act *as if* I trust can lead to
trust. Trust can emerge when I choose to act as if I trust, that is, choose to
make myself vulnerable to others, and find that nothing ill happened to me.
If the online environment is such that it is conducive to people acting as if
they trust, genuine trust can emerge. Those online will *see* others online *as*
trustworthy. This is not purely an abstract suggestion. There is evidence
that virtual terms working on projects develop trust if they initially act as
if they trust:

> the teams who were most successful in the virtual environment were able
> to capitalize on "swift" trust . . . the members jumped into the project act-
> ing as though trust existed from the start, even though they had no evi-
> dence that their groupmates would carry their share of the load. Their ini-
> tial willingness to show trusting actions led swiftly to actual trust.
> (Wallace, 1999, p. 86)

If it works in one online environment, there is no reason to suppose that it
could not in others as well.

CONCLUSION

Trust is important online and, despite some difficulties for its development in that environment, it is possible. The "seeing as" account of trust proposed earlier helps to explain why it is possible in an apparently hostile environment. If trust is purely cognitive—that is, a matter of our beliefs and expectations about the actions of another—then it is more difficult to explain why someone would take risks with others online about whose reliability one has very little evidence. On the seeing as account this is easier to explain. Once I see people online as trustworthy, I tend to trust them unless I have good reason not to. The lack of cues in individual cases does not matter much. There could be a number of explanations why I initially saw people online as trustworthy rather than untrustworthy. It could have been because I live in a basically trusting society, and just transferred my general trust to the online environment. Or perhaps I began by hesitantly acting as if I trusted, and, when nothing untoward happened, became more confident and came to see others online as generally trustworthy.

On the surface, this explanation appears to fit chat groups and the like better than the e-commerce context, where there is a greater resistance to trusting behavior. This could be the result of a variety of reasons. Perhaps there is less offline trust of businesses than there is of people generally. Or perhaps it is because the e-commerce environment is so different from our normal experience. Normally when I buy goods I almost immediately have both the goods and a receipt in my hand, so not much trust is necessary. Online purchasing requires more trust. Will my goods arrive? Will they be what I thought I ordered? Will my credit card number be safe? How will the information about my buying habits be used? These factors are likely to make the development of trusting behavior a slower process. There is, however, nothing inherent in the situation that would stop me from seeing online business as trustworthy.

This chapter began with the Aristotelian point that friendship is a central component in the good life, or in human flourishing, along with the claim that trust is important in friendship. Together these imply that trust is important in human flourishing. Given the role that the online world now plays for many people, trust is just as important in that world as it is in the offline, if we are to gain full advantage of that environment and if it is to contribute to human flourishing. There are, of course, dangers in trusting those about whom we know little online, and the activities of pedophiles and others show that care is required with respect to whom we see as trustworthy. But this is true in our everyday lives offline as well. Perhaps with respect to trust, the on and offline worlds are not so different.

REFERENCES

Alpern, Kenneth D. 1933. Aristotle on the Friendships of Utility and Pleasure, *Journal of the History of Philosophy* 21: 303–315.

Aristotle. 1941. *Nicomachean Ethics*, in McKeon, Richard (Ed.), *The Basic Works of Aristotle*. New York: Random House, pp. 927—1112.

Baier, Annette C. 1986. Trust and Antitrust, *Ethics* 96: 231–260.

———. 1994. "Trust and Its Vulnerabilities," in Baier, Annette, C., *Moral Prejudices: Essays on Ethics*. Cambridge: Harvard University Press, pp. 130–151.

Becker, Lawrence C. 1996. Trust as Noncognitive Security about Motives, *Ethics* 107: 43–61.

Camp, L. Jean. 2000. *Trust and Risk in Internet Commerce*. Cambridge: MIT Press.

Cassell, Justine, and Timothy Bickmore. 2000. External Manifestations of Trustworthiness in the Interface, *Communications of the ACM* 43 (December): 50–56.

Cheskin. 1999. eCommerce trust study, Cheskin Research and Studio Archtype/Sapient, http://www.cheskin.com/think/studies/ecomtrust.html.

Cocking, Dean, and Steve Matthews. 2000. Unreal Friends, *Ethics and Information Technology* 2: 223–231.

Coleman, James Samuel. 1990. *Foundations of Social Theory*. Cambridge: Harvard University Press.

Cooper, John M. 1977. Aristotle on the Forms of Friendship, *Review of Metaphysics* 30: 619–648.

———. 1980. "Aristotle on Friendship," in Rorty, Amelie Oksenberg (Ed.), *Essays on Aristotle's Ethics*. Berkeley: University of California Press, pp. 301–340.

Dasgupta, Partha. 1988. "Trust as a Commodity," in Gambetta, Diego (Ed.), *Trust: Making and Breaking Cooperative Relations*. New York: Blackwell.

Deuel, Nancy R. 1996. "Passionate Response to Virtual Reality," in Herring, Susan C. (Ed.), *Computer-Mediated Communication: Linguist, Social and Cross-Cultural Perspectives*. Amsterdam: John Benjamins Publishing, pp. 129–146.

Dreyfus, Hubert L. 2001. *On the Internet*. London: Routledge.

Dunne, Steve. 2001. The Short Life of Kaycee Nicole. *The Guardian*, May 26, pp. 26–27.

Fukuyama, Frances. 1995. *Trust: The Social Virtues and the Creation of Prosperity*. London: Penguin Books.

Gambetta, Diego. 1988. "Can We Trust Trust?," in Gambetta, Diego (Ed.), *Trust: Making and Breaking Cooperative Relations*. New York: Blackwell, pp. 213–237.

Govier, Trudy. 1997. *Social Trust and Human Communities*. Montreal: McGill-Queen's University Press.

Holton, Richard. 1994. Deciding to Trust, Coming to Believe, *Australasian Journal of Philosophy* 72: 63–76.

ICAC. 2001. *eCorruption: eCrime Vulnerabilities in the NSW Public Sector*, Sydney: Independent Commission Against Corruption.

James, William. 1979. *The Will to Believe and Other Popular Essays*. Cambridge: Harvard University Press.

Jones, Karen. 1996. Trust as an Affective Attitude, *Ethics* 107: 4–25.

Kiesler, Sara, and Robert Kraut. 1999. Internet Use and Ties That Bind, *American Psychologist* September: 783–784.

Kuhn, Thomas, S. 1970. *The Structure of Scientific Revolutions*, second edition. Chicago: University of Chicago Press.

Lagerspertz, Olli. 1998. *The Tacit Demand*. Dordrecht: Kluwer.

Nissenbaum, Helen. 2001. Securing Trust Online: Wisdom or Oxymoron?, *Boston University Law Review* 81: 101–131.

Parks, Malcolm R., and Kory Floyd. 1996. Making Friends in Cyberspace, *Journal of Communication* 46: 80–97.

Putnam, Robert D. 1994. *Making Democracy Work: Civic Traditions in Modern Italy*. Princeton: Princeton University Press.

Quine, W. V. 1970. *Philosophy of Logic*. Englewood Cliffs, NJ: Prentice-Hall.

Ratnasingam, Pauline. 2000. The Influence of Power on Trading Partner Trust in Electronic Commerce, *Internet Research: Electronic Networking Applications and Policy* 10: 56–62.

Reid, Elizabeth. 1998. "The Self and the Internet: Variations on the Illusion of the Self," in Gackenback, Jayne (Ed.), *Psychology and the Internet: Intrapersonal, Interpersonal, and Transpersonal Implications*. San Diego: Academic Press, pp. 29–42.

Rempel, John K., Michael Ross, and John G. Holmes. 2001. Trust and Communicated Attributions in Close Relationships, *Journal of Personality and Social Psychology* 81: 57–64.

Schneiderman, Fred, B. (Ed.). 1999. *Trust in Cyberspace*. Washington, DC: National Academic Press.

Sokolowski, Robert. 2001. Friendship and Moral Action in Aristotle, *Journal of Value Inquiry* 35: 355–369.

Thomas, Laurence. 1987. Friendship, *Synthese* 72: 217–236.

Updike, John. 1987. *Trust Me: Short Stories*. New York: Knopf.

van der Woning, Randall. 2001. "The End of the Whole Mess," http://vanderwoning.com/mess.shtml/blog.shtml.

van Gelder, Lindsay. 1991. "The Strange Case of the Electronic Lover," in Dunlop, C., and R. Kling (Eds.), *Computerization and Controversy*. Boston: Academic Press, pp. 364–375.

Wallace, Patricia. 1999. *The Psychology of the Internet*. Cambridge: Cambridge University Press.

WebTrust. 2002. www.cpawebtrust.com.

Weckert, John. 2002. "Trust, Corruption, and Surveillance in the Electronic Workplace," in Brunnstein, Klaus, and Jacques Berleur (Eds.), *Human Choice and Computers*. Boston: Kluwer. (Proceedings of 17th IFIP World Computer Congress, Montreal.)

PART II

SIX

Should We Let Computers Get Under Our Skin?

JAMES H. MOOR

Being connected with the passions also, the moral virtues must belong to our composite nature; and the virtues of our composite nature are human; so, therefore, are the life and the happiness which correspond to these.

—Aristotle

Being a human was ok, I even enjoyed some of it. But being a Cyborg has a lot more to offer.

—Kevin Warwick

THE CASE FOR BECOMING A CYBORG

ARISTOTLE SUGGESTS THAT human nature is fixed. Our human intellectual and moral virtues depend on our having this nature. If we changed our nature, we would change our virtues (excellences). Aristotle believed that if a friend became a god, for example, friendship with that person would cease because a god has a different nature than a human being. In the wake of evolutionary theory and modern genetics, the claim that human nature is fixed is not very plausible, but Aristotle's belief that shifting human nature might well alter moral virtue remains defensible. In today's scientifically changing world we need to confront this issue: if we change the kind of thing we are, what will be the consequences for ethics?

We will change ourselves genetically and we will change ourselves computationally as well. We will become cybernetic organisms—cyborgs—part human, part computer. The logical malleability of computers will allow us to go beyond what can be accomplished through genetic manipulation alone. The human body is the ultimate platform from which to launch new computer applications. It is likely that in the coming decades more and more computer hardware and software will be embedded in us. To what extent it should happen is the ultimate question, of course, but certainly there will be increasing pressure to produce cyborgs. Today the rationale and technology already coexist. First, we humans as creative creatures continually seek new ways to perform routine and not so routine tasks. Not infrequently our creative task solving involves the development of new tools. Second, the computer is the best master tool we have. The general-purpose computer is a meta-tool, a tool for making tools. If we have a task to do and we can express the task in terms of an appropriate algorithm to connect inputs to appropriate outputs, then in principle a computer can do it. In fact, even if we do not know an appropriate algorithm, computers using neural nets or genetic algorithms can sometimes evolve satisfactory computational structures for us. Third, considerable knowledge has been gained in recent years about interfaces between computers and living systems. We know that organic and inorganic structures can effectively interact at many levels—the organism level, the organ level, and the cell level. Someday nanomachines may interact in our bodies at the atomic level. Given that naturally curious humans love to find better solutions for problems, have a great master tool (the computer), and possess the perfect location (the human body) on which to store and operate the new devices, the gradual transformation of many humans into cyborgs, humans with computer parts, is all but certain.

Simply forbidding the implantation of computer chips because they are not natural, only artifacts, is not a plausible policy. This overly broad approach would not only prevent the use of beneficial computer implants but would rule out beneficial noncomputer implants such as artificial hip joints and dental crowns. Still, the thought of becoming a cyborg may seem rather repulsive. Who would want to have computer parts implanted? To become part computer? The idea of having a computer implanted may seem unnatural, possibly even grotesque, or at least something that undermines human dignity. But such a negative reaction is not defensible on close examination. In fact, the transformation of humans into cyborgs has been taking place with no loss of dignity for years, although we do not commonly think of it in those terms.

For example, hundreds of thousands of people have cardiac pacemakers and defibrillators implanted to maintain regular heartbeats and heart rhythms (Lu, Anderson, and Steinhaus, 1995, Pinski and Trohman, 2000). Such implants not only promote life but also the quality of life. Totally implantable pacemakers have been in use since 1960, and programmable pacemakers were developed in the mid-1970s. The newest pacemakers can communicate via phone and the Internet. A patient needs only to wave a wand over his chest to pick up signals from the generator and then plug the wand into the phone line to send his physician an update on how the device and patient are doing. It would be hard to raise a principled objection against such beneficial devices. Implanting computerized cardiac devices is no more unnatural than putting other products of technology, like medicines or processed food, into our bodies. Given the alternatives for the cardiac patient, these vital, portable computer implants considerably enhance human dignity, not reduce it (Ocampo, 2000).

A similar case can be made for the benefits of implanting computer chips for vision. There are various projects under way to develop bionic eyes that will restore some level of vision to blind patients. Some approaches put chips on or under the retina and others connect computer chips to other parts of the visual system. In 2002, a Canadian farmer, who had lost his sight eighteen years earlier, had a bionic implant. A digital camera mounted on his glasses sent an image to a computer worn on his belt. The image was processed and sent to electrodes implanted in his visual cortex. His vision was not fully restored, but he was not totally blind anymore. He was able to see well enough to navigate through rooms and even drive a car to a limited extent (Gupta and Petersen, 2002).

Some diseases, such as retinitis pigmentosa or age-related macular degeneration, damage the rods and cones in retinas but leave the rest of their visual wiring, the ganglia cells that process information from the rods and cones and the optic nerve, intact. The various visual bionics under development hold great promise for bypassing the damaged areas of the visual system and restoring vision to the patient. In the United States, over a million people are legally blind and worldwide millions more. These cutting-edge bionic implants will offer enormous benefit.

More examples of beneficial computer implants can be marshaled, but I believe the case for the benefits of some computer implants is established. The debate is not whether humans should ever become cyborgs because in some cases, particularly where beneficial implants help overcome severe disabilities, justification for becoming a cyborg is clear. The transformation of some humans into cyborgs will continue to happen and it should. People who wish to have such helpful computer implants should be allowed to have them.

But how far should the conversion of humans into cyborgs go? What are the ethical boundaries? Could we find ourselves in a position that we would want to get away from computer implants but couldn't? Could the implants be used to track us? Reduce our autonomy? Give us freakish powers? In this chapter I want to explore some potential ethical pitfalls of computer implants as well as the impact that computer implants might have on ethical theory itself.

THERAPY VERSUS ENHANCEMENT

The therapy versus enhancement distinction suggests a basis for a policy that would limit unnecessary computer implants. Given that the human body has natural functions, it might be argued that implanting chips in the body is acceptable as long as such implants maintain or restore the body's natural functions. In this spirit, consider the remarks of Michael Dertrouzos, a director of the MIT Laboratory for Computer Science, regarding the possibility of implants connected to the brain:

> Even if it would someday be possible to convey such higher-level information to the brain—and that is a huge technical "if"—we should not do it. Bringing light impulses to the visual cortex of a blind person would justify such an intrusion, but unnecessarily tapping into the brain is a violation of our bodies, of nature, and for many, of God's design. (Dertrouzos, 1997, p. 77)

The distinction between therapeutic applications and enhancing applications offers a criterion for limiting computer implants. Under this policy, pacemakers, defibrillators, and bionic eyes that maintain and restore natural bodily functions are acceptable. But giving patients additional pairs of robotic arms or infrared vision would be prohibited. It would endorse the use of a chip that reduced dyslexia but would forbid the implanting of a deep blue chip for superior chess play. It would permit a chip implant to assist the memory of Alzheimer's patients but would not license the implanting of a miniature digital camera that would record and play back what the implantee had just seen and heard. In a later book Dertrouzos stresses his point again, "Few people would implant a chip into their brain for less than life-and-death reasons. We have wisely set a high threshold for tampering with the core of our being, not just because of fear, but because of natural, moral, and spiritual beliefs" (Dertrouzos, 2001, p. 46).

Of course, even therapeutic applications raise ethical questions if they are not safe and effective or the patient has not given informed consent. But, let us assume safety, effectiveness, and informed consent. Does the therapy/enhancement distinction give a proper limit to computer implants? Although this policy generally avoids unethical implants, I believe it is too conservative and cannot be defended.

First Objection: Unclear Distinction

The line between therapy and enhancement is not always agreed on. Consider the example of cochlear implants (Spelman, 1999). A microphone is worn behind the ear and a mircrocomputer filters and analyzes the sound from the microphone, converting the sound into digital signals. These signals are sent by radio waves to a receiver implanted under the skin, then via a wire to electrodes embedded in the cochlea in the patient's ear, which in turn stimulate nerves that carry sound to the brain. When cochlear implants became available in 1985, they could help approximately 35 percent of patients; today they can improve hearing in about 80 percent.

Receiving a cochlear implant, a bionic ear, may seem obviously therapeutic. However, within the deaf community the issue of whether to get a cochlear implant has been controversial. Some deaf individuals have questioned whether these implants are desirable or even therapeutic. Some challenge the standard assumption of the medical community that deafness is a disability that can be "fixed" by having a cochlear implant. At the heart of the debate is the importance and normalcy of the deaf culture. Within the deaf community many find solidarity with others who are deaf and share a common language of signing. Therefore, some in the deaf community believe the acquisition of hearing through cochlear implants needlessly threatens to undermine an adequately functioning culture. These views are held strongly as illustrated by the fact that one member of the deaf community found her tires slashed when she refused to speak out against cochlear implants (Yaffe, 1999).

Some in the deaf community believe that deafness is a disability, but they maintain that it is not worth correcting given the damaged caused to the deaf community. But another position is that deafness is not a disability at all given the availability and success of sign language within the community. Much of the debate about cochlear implants turns on whether one takes the absence of hearing as a disability. If it is, then having a cochlear implant is therapeutic, and, if it is not, then having a cochlear implant is an enhancement.

There are many things that we cannot do, yet we do not classify them as disabilities. We cannot digest steel and we cannot breathe underwater without special equipment. It would be strange for someone, other than superman, to claim he had a disability because he could not leap tall buildings in a single bound. These sorts of actions are in the realm of inabilities, not disabilities. A disability is a lack of normal ability in reference to a class of individuals. Adults living today are disabled if they do not understand some language, but they are not disabled if they do not understand an extinct language. Those strongly opposed to cochlear implants might argue that within the deaf culture there is normal functioning with full use of language that happens to be a sign language, not an oral one. If the members of the deaf culture are picked as the reference class, then hearing should be regarded as an inability, not a disability. Given this standard, a cochlear implant would not be therapeutic and might be regarded as unnecessary and possibly detrimental.

My purpose here is not to argue for or against cochlear implants. Rather, it is to point out that the distinction between therapy and enhancement is not as straightforward as might be assumed. The decision about getting a cochlear implant is a personal choice and sometimes a difficult one that requires careful consideration of all the consequences. Families of deaf children may find themselves choosing between communities and are sometimes sharply divided within themselves on this issue. The decision can be agonizing because if the implant is to be most effective it must be implanted early in the deaf child's life, preferably before language development occurs.

The cochlear implant debate illustrates that the lack of agreement on what counts as a disability and what does not. However, even if there were agreement on what counts as therapy and what constitutes enhancement, implanted chips can offer a bit of both. For example, an implanted defibrillator can monitor a heart and deliver a shock within 30 seconds after life-threatening irregularities in rhythm are detected. The defibrillator restores normal heart function, but it does so through an enhancing functionality that people without defibrillators do not have. Or, consider an Alzheimer's patient who has a chip embedded that allows her to be located by others and perhaps even guides her back by global positioning satellites. Is this chip therapeutic or enhancing? Suppose a paralyzed patient has a chip implanted that allows him to control the lights in his room by shifting his neural patterns. Is this implant therapeutic or enhancing?

SECOND OBJECTION: LIMITATION OF FREEDOM

The second argument against the policy of allowing therapeutic but not enhancing implants is that it arbitrarily limits personal freedom. As long as the implantee and others are not being harmed by the implant, what is the objection to allowing it? In other matters we routinely allow, if not encourage, people to have enhancements. Generally speaking, education enhances as does exercise and a good diet. They enhance the body and the mind and we encourage all of them. Freedom is a core good and we properly allow people the freedom to exercise it. People, at least in a liberal state, are at liberty to have cosmetic surgery, belly-button rings, and tattoos. Enhancement is what many of us strive for much of the time. As a simple illustration, consider laser eye surgery guided by computer that can enhance vision beyond the normal 20/20. It would seem perverse to insist that a patient should not have the freedom to correct her vision to a better than normal 20/15 but had to stop at 20/20. Similarly, it seems perverse not to give people freedom to enhance themselves in other ways, including the implantation of computer chips if they wish.

In 1998, Kevin Warwick, a cybernetics professor from the University of Reading in the United Kingdom, had a chip implanted that permitted sensors in his laboratory to detect his location and motion. In March 2002, he had a much more sophisticated computer implant (Warwick, 2002). An array with 100 spikes was implanted in Warwick's wrist to connect his median nerve with a computer. The median nerve travels along the arm and contains both sensory neurons that detect pressure and temperature and motor neurons that connect the spinal cord with muscle groups in the hand. The spikes of the array were implanted in these sensory and motor neurons in the median nerve. Wires from the array traveled up Warwick's arm and surface through a skin puncture in his forearm. The wires were connected to a gauntlet, a transmitting/receiving device, located externally on Warwick's arm. The gauntlet sent information about neural firing to an external computer. The computer, properly calibrated, distinguished neural impulses when Warwick's left hand was open from when it was closed. This provided sufficient binary information for Warwick to guide miniature robots, manipulate a robotic hand, light up specially wired jewelry, and steer an adapted wheelchair.

Warwick could feel the impulse if the information flow was reversed and the computer sent a signal to the gauntlet that transferred it to the implant in his median nerve. In an interesting experiment Warwick wore a baseball cap with an ultrasonic transmitter and receiver. Ultrasonic impulses were sent out from the cap and bounced back quickly if objects were close. In this situation a rapid series of pulses were sent to the computer, to the gauntlet, and to his median nerve. If objects were farther away, the pulses were less rapid. This gave Warwick an extrasensory input. When blindfolded, but hooked up to the ultrasonic device, he could guide himself around his laboratory using bat-like echolocation. In another experiment, his wife, Irena, who had a simpler neural connection installed, and he could exchange binary information back and forth from one nervous system to the other via the Internet. Warwick has raised the possibility that one day more sophisticated information and possibly emotional responses could be communicated from nervous system to nervous system via the Internet.

Warwick's reports on his body image were interesting. Warwick makes it quite clear that having the implant under his skin was important as compared with simply putting on wearable computing that can easily be removed. "From the very start, I regarded the array and wires as being a part of me. Having it extracted, I knew, would be like losing part of my body, almost an amputation" (Warwick, 2002, p. 292). But he also had some sense of his body's being extended by the machine attachments like the robotic hand. "The articulated hand felt like a part of me, yet, because it was remote, in another sense it didn't" (Warwick, 2002, pp. 233–234).

Warwick acknowledges the potential risks, but believes the eventual benefits of computer implant enhancements outweigh these risks. Ethically, should Warwick enhance himself with computer implants? Some believe not. Langdon Winter suggests that such experiments are "profoundly amoral" (Vogel, 2002, p. 1020). Although becoming a cyborg may eventually raise questions about human nature, it is hard to see how the experiments that Warwick performed are beyond straightforward moral judgment. If he is not causing harm to others and not violating any particular duties, why should he not have the freedom to do it? His wife is at some risk of harm, but she freely gave her informed consent. Both his implant procedure and her procedure passed hospital ethics committee evaluation. The experiments may strike some as grotesque, scientifically ill defined, or grandstanding, but such judgments, assuming they were correct, would still not make the experiments amoral or immoral.

THE BORG ARGUMENT

The fear remains that allowing freedom of enhancement through computer chip implants will take us down a slippery slope to some very undesirable results. To imagine a worst case scenario, consider the Borg from the science fiction series *Star Trek*. The Borg is a collection of cyborgs that travels through space in a large cube that has the ability to assimilate new species that it encounters. The Borg's menacing conduct is indicated by its foreboding mottoes: "Resistance is futile" and "We will assimilate you." The inhabitants of the Borg have numerous unattractive appliances attached to them, possess no personal autonomy, and are controlled by the directives of a collective consciousness. The inhabitants of the Borg do not have individual lives worth living, at least not as intelligent creatures. They neither examine their lives nor personally flourish. And so, the argument runs, we do not want to end up like the inhabitants of the Borg. How do we prevent sliding down the slope to such an existence once we give people the freedom to implant chips?

Slippery slope arguments are not very convincing, particularly if the slope is rather long and stopping along it seems possible. There is considerable slope between allowing people the freedom to implant chips and becoming a Borg culture. But can we easily brake on the slope? I believe we can, but the Borg argument has some force. A Borg culture in which people become slave cyborgs is not something that sane people would choose for themselves. However, other mechanisms might push us toward such a state. Here are two.

The Sleepwalking Scenario. We might inadvertently fall into a Borg-like state if we are not careful. Imagine that people for good reasons decide to have chips implanted in order to communicate with their children or do their jobs better or receive the latest music and sports information or have medication automatically released. Eventually, almost everyone is hooked up to the Web internally and wirelessly. It is the way life is conducted. Babies are given chips as routinely as vaccinations. Such interconnections are useful in organizing our lives. Gradually, for practical, not evil, motives the Web/human system begins to take on a life of its own, coordinating people's activities by sending information tantamount to instructions for where to be and when to be there. Under such a condition the population might look better than the inhabitants of the *Star Trek* Borg, but its behavior might have an uncanny similarity.

The Totalitarian State Scenario. The Borg culture might come into existence through the directives of a dictator of a totalitarian state. Dictators want to control their population. What better way than putting their subjects to work with implants that track their locations and force their labor? Neither the sleepwalking scenario nor the totalitarian state scenario is likely to happen in the immediate future, but these developments are real possibilities. We have yet to produce an Orwellian 1984 society, but that is probably due to a shortage of the right kind of information technology. That technological shortcoming is rapidly being overcome and a Borg culture is something to be on guard against.

FREEDOM WITH RESPONSIBILITY

In general, I am advocating a policy of responsible freedom. People should have the freedom to implant computer chips in themselves, including implants for enhancements. As with all our actions, we should be alert if harm or the risk of harm is a factor. If harm or the risk of harm would occur to either the person being implanted or to others, we need to consider whether the action is justified. Harm does not automatically curtail freedom of action, but it does require justification. Exercising such freedom requires evaluating consequences and formulating relevant policies that can be advocated impartially and publicly so that anyone is permitted to follow them in similar circumstances (Moor, 1999).

Harm can result in many ways when implanting computer chips, but there are three general areas of major concern, three ethical hot spots, to which we should be particularly sensitive in the coming age of cyborgs. These areas are privacy, control, and fairness. Some computer implants will enhance privacy or control or fairness. Some will undermine them.

PRIVACY

In May 2002, Jeff and Leslie Jacobs and their son, Derek, were the first to have VeriChips implanted in their arms. These chips, little bigger than a grain of rice, store six lines of text. Information is read from the chip by a handheld computer. Such medical information could be lifesaving in giving emergency physicians information about allergies and special medical needs before they administered treatment. In the case of the Jacobs, the chips contain phone numbers and information about previous medications. The U.S. Federal Food and Drug Administration (FDA) ruled a month earlier that it did not regard the chip as a medical device and would not regulate it.

The chip is not very useful unless the implantee is at a hospital that has the appropriate handheld computer reader, but the technology is likely to spread because it is relatively inexpensive. The chip itself is dormant, but when the right radio frequency energy passes through the skin it activates the chip, which in turn emits a radio signal containing an identification number. This number can be sent to an FDA secure data storage site via telephone or the Internet. Given our flourishing Information Age, the demand for implanted chips to store personal, medical, and financial information as well as any information whatsoever is likely to increase.

Implanted chips can be more sophisticated than memory chips. VeriChip is the product of Applied Digital Solutions (ADS) that has for several years been working on another product called the "Digital Angel." The Digital Angel is a tracking device that uses Global Positioning System (GPS) technology. The Digital Angel technology potentially can be used to track almost anyone or anything from children, convicts, and cats to lost hikers and lost luggage. ADS has a bold vision of what the chip might be able to do. According to one early projection, the future chip, if implanted, will be powered by a piezoelectric device that converts energy from normal bodily movements into electricity. The chip will send information to receivers connected to various networks. In addition, the device will be able to collect information about the possessor's body, such as temperature and blood pressure. Blood oxygen and glucose level detection are promised as well. Its designers propose that pulse detection will be based on infrared radiation naturally emitted from the bloodstream. In this vision of the future, solid state accelerometers and gyroscopes will allow the Digital Angel to sense the posture and gait of the possessor to detect sudden falls. EKG and EEG detection are claimed to be in the works. If this information gathering comes to fruition, the objective is to transmit the information to receivers that make it available on the Internet through Web-enabled desktop, laptop, or wireless devices. Depending on its configuration, a Digital Angel device could be turned on or off by the possessor or the possessor's body or remotely by radio signal. The device would not need to be on and transmitting at all times, but would have the ability to turn on automatically if it sensed, for example, a heart attack or was sent an instruction to do so.

Digital Angel is the brainchild of Peter Zhou, who is enthusiastic about the future of implanted chip technology. Despite Zhou's enthusiasm, critics have expressed concerns. Civil rights groups compared the use of implanting these chips to Nazi tattooing and some Christians compared the implanting of the chips to the mark of the beast mentioned in the Bible. Thus far, ADS has brought out the first generation of the Digital Angel as a product to be worn as a wristband or carried. Its initial capability is limited to establishing the location of its possessor.

Regardless of the current stage of development of this implant, the concept of a chip that actively gathers data about its owner as well as sending and receiving information is technologically feasible and such chips will come onto the market for particular uses at some point. Potential uses are plentiful. A person who suffers from arrhythmia could be assisted when the chip monitoring her pulse notifies medical authorities of her location and her condition. A firearm could be programmed to fire only when the chip identifies its user as the proper owner. Herds of animals, not to mention millions of pets, could be tracked so that no animal is lost. Every soldier in a battle unit could be monitored for his or her location and health status. A kidnapped child possessing such a chip could be located and checked for life signs. Such a chip could serve as an ID for business and other human interactions. A potential customer could be positively identified biometrically through transmissions from the chip. Her transaction then would be charged automatically to or deducted from her account based on information passed along by the chip.

A world with implanted personal data chips will generate an enormous flow of personal information in novel ways that will require new protection plans for the privacy of individuals. New policies will need to be created to safeguard the collection of all the up-to-the minute information about people's health, location, financial condition, and other matters transmitted and received by these chips. It is not that personal privacy cannot in principle be protected with the use of such chips. The concern is that the technology will be developed and deployed without establishing privacy protection.

CONTROL

Another ethical hot spot in which implanted chips can provide enormous benefits but put us at risk is control. Respect for the agency of others is a hallmark of ethics. Implanted computer chips hold great promise for both giving and taking away human agency.

In the United States over a million patients suffer from Parkinson's disease, a degenerative neurological disorder that causes them to shake uncontrollably. Another two million suffer from essential tremor that causes similar violent shaking. The shaking is so debilitating that these patients often have trouble working, eating, and simply getting dressed. In the past the drug L-dopa has been given to Parkinson's patients, though its effectiveness wanes over time. Less than half of the patients with essential tremor are improved with medication. Sometimes patients undergo surgery to destroy parts of their brains that cause the shaking, but this procedure is not reversible and not always effective.

An alternative for these patients is to have a chip implanted. Physicians implant an electrode in a patient's thalamus and run a wire under the scalp to the patient's collarbone where a pulse generator is implanted. This device sends electrical signals customized for each patient to the electrode in the thalamus. A constant stream of electrical shocks blocks the tremors. The device is effective in stopping the shaking in both Parkinson's patients and essential tremor patients. The procedure is reversible and the device can be turned on and off by the patient.

The results of such an implant are nothing short of spectacular. A Parkinson's patient whose hands are shaking violently can run a magnet over his chest, activating the pulse generator, and within a few seconds his hands become steady. With another swipe of the magnet, the device is turned off, and his hands will begin to shake again. In one case a typical Parkinson's patient, who had lost her mobility and whose medications made her arms and legs move out of control, could sit down and play complex pieces on the piano after her implant was installed (Freudenheim, 1997).

This Deep Brain Stimulation technique using the pulse generator is now being used for a variety of other medical conditions—even for psychiatric conditions such as obsessive-compulsive disorder. One seriously ill patient had repetitive thoughts for hours and would wash his hands seventy times per day. After having a chip implant he stopped his compulsive hand washing and returned to work (Carmichael, 2002).

What is striking about these examples of implants is that they restore agency to the patients. Patients regain control of their lives. The sinister side is the threat that computer implants might be used to remove agency. Chips might be developed to induce uncontrollable shaking, to cause obsessive-compulsive disorder.

Consider the recent development of a ratbot. Three electrodes were placed in a rat's brain: two in the somatosensory cortical where the rat's brain processes touch from its right and left whiskers, and one in the medial forebrain bundle where the rat processes pleasure. When one of the two electrodes in the sensory region is stimulated, the rat experiences an apparent touch. If it turns in the direction of its right or left whisker depending on which side is stimulated, it is electrically rewarded in its pleasure center. With this setup and some radio controls to send the signals, researchers were able to guide the rat. Using a laptop, researchers maneuvered the rat through a difficult three-dimensional maze that included ladders, filing cabinets, and thin wooden boards. As one researcher appropriately remarked, "I certainly don't think it would be a good idea to put these in primates, or especially in humans" (Cook, 2002).

Rat brains are not human brains, but humans do have pleasure centers in their brains and one can easily imagine the use of implants to control humans. Could such a device be offered to help people stop smoking or lose weight? The military and the penal system might consider using the technology to produce loyal troops and obedient prisoners. Computer implants can potentially elevate human agency or severely reduce it. Continual vigilance regarding the deployment of such devices is necessary to ensure that respect for human agency is maintained.

FAIRNESS

A final ethical hot spot to consider is fairness. Implanted chips can tip the scales of justice in various ways. For example, implanted chips can encourage fairness by giving those with disabilities more power to interact in the world. Consider the case of Johnny Ray, who suffered a brainstem stroke in 1997. He has locked-in syndrome and no muscle control. Although he is cognitively intact, he is totally paralyzed and cannot make a motion. Researchers have inserted a subcranial cortical implant. Parts of the implant in the motor cortex are surrounded with tissue culture to encourage brain cells to grow toward the contacts. The patient is asked to think about distinctive conditions such as hot versus cold. The corresponding brain outputs are captured, amplified, and used to control an external device such as a cursor on a computer screen. "By reproducing the same brain pattern, Ray eventually was able to move the cursor at will to choose screen icons, spell, and even generate musical tones" (Hockenberry, 2001, p. 96).

When computer implants improve access and interactive capabilities for those who are disadvantaged, fairness is served. But there are easily imagined situations in which future implants might give the implantee unfair advantages. Just imagine a grandmaster chess chip that contained book openings and generated excellent chess moves. Suppose it were developed, giving its owner superior ability in playing chess. Presumably, such chips would need to be banned in championship play just as steroids are outlawed in Olympic competition. Chip implants that facilitated an athlete's coordination might be banned for similar reasons.

Fairness will be an ongoing concern as chip implants get better and more useful. Eventually, a chip implant divide will emerge: those who have chip implants versus those who do not (Macguire and McGee, 1999). Parents, as parents always do, will want to give their children the best abilities and opportunities possible. Those who can afford chip implants and chip upgrades will have a distinct advantage over those who cannot.

VIEWING THE DISTANT FUTURE

Thus far I have been considering the matter of computer implants in light of common morality in the short run. I have been focusing on ethical concerns for and against implanting chips in the near future. Now I wish to consider the possible implications of computer implants on metaphysical issues and ethical theory in the long run.

The possibility of enhancing humans through computer implants raises the question of what human nature could and should be. Traditionally, essentialist philosophers like Aristotle maintain that humans have a fixed nature. Some existentialist philosophers like Sartre argue that existence precedes essence and that human nature is radically free. We can change our essence by making different choices. In an era of increasing understanding of genetics and neurology, neither position seems quite right. Human nature does not appear to be irrevocably fixed or completely open. Computer implants offer us an opportunity to adjust at least some of our nature. Our essence as humans may not be radically open, but, if we are clever enough in developing implants, we can, if we choose, significantly change our nature from what it is now.

Accurate prediction of what computer implants will be available in the distant future is, of course, impossible. But let's speculate a bit. With implants we can change our internal functioning in ways that are not possible, using variations of our genetic code. We might enhance our sense of sight to access parts of the electromagnetic spectrum far beyond what any humans or other animals can. Similarly, our sense of hearing could be radically extended. Artificial devices for touch, taste, and smell already exist and these senses could be great enhanced. We could develop new senses. We might continue to experiment with implants for echolocation, for example, and discover at least in part what it is like to be a bat.

Communicating with other humans may be more direct than ever before. We could have sensors installed in our bodies that would let us know if our loved ones were in danger. We could lock and unlock doors, turn appliances on and off, and adjust the heat in our houses through computers that monitor neural patterns. And our cognition could be greatly enhanced with better memory and more accurate recall (Eisenberg, 2002). Perhaps education and physical conditioning could be done by downloads, not tedious schooling and training. Improving our abilities to create music or make inferences might be possible. Although all of this is speculation, nothing seems to preclude these possibilities. However the future develops, it seems likely that human nature as we currently conceive it could be modified.

Martha Nussbaum, defending an Aristotelean position, has argued against such aspirations.

> what my argument urges us to reject as incoherent is the aspiration to leave behind altogether the constitutive conditions of our humanity, and to seek for a life that is really the life of another sort of being—as if it were higher and better life for *us*. It asks us to bound our aspirations by recalling that there are some very general conditions of human existence that are also necessary conditions for the values that we know, love, and appropriately pursue. (Nussbaum, 1990, p. 379)

Of course, everything depends on what constitutes the conditions of our humanity. The example she uses to illustrate the point is mortality. She cites Odysseus's decision to choose the life of a mortal human being who returns to his marriage to a mortal woman although Calypso has offered him immortality and agelessness, a life of no fatigue, and no cessation of calm pleasure if only he would remain on the island with her. Nussbaum grants that we strive for excellence within our capabilities, but we should not strive to change those constitutive conditions.

Aiming for immortality may be aiming a little high, but why shouldn't we change our nature if we have good reasons to believe we would be better off with an improved nature? There is the danger that if some changed and others did not there could be a division of the species or at least significant new groupings within it. Today we have Human Nature version 1.0, but why not use implants to move to Human Nature 2.0, especially if the latter gives us longer life, more happiness, and increased freedom of action? And if Human Nature 2.0 is acceptable, why not Human Nature 3.0 in which some of the traditional abilities of Human Nature 1.0 are given up and replaced with new ones. The judgment to move to Human Nature 3.0 is made from the vantage of Human Nature 2.0 that understands the importance of some modifications differently than Human Nature 1.0. We might through this process bootstrap ourselves into a condition in which Human Nature 17.3 was quite different from Human Nature 1.0.

Such a transition in human nature could have a serious impact on the application of ethical theories. First, there is the moral scope issue. By "moral scope" I mean what kind of entities are regarded as moral agents and what kind as moral patients. We usually count normally functioning adult humans as moral agents. We assign them duties and hold them accountable. But other less sophisticated entities are sometimes treated as moral patients—that is, entities deserving moral protection, such as small children, fetuses, animals, and the environment. For many, moral patients are thought to merit less protection than moral agents. It is better to kill a tree than take a human life. Would humans of nature 17.3 regard humans 1.0 as full-fledged moral agents or as merely moral patients or as entities outside the scope of moral protection altogether?

Another difficulty raised for ethical theory if human nature were transformed is the creation of new values and the assignment of new weights to old values. Now, although there is variation in how much weight we give to various values, there is a shared structure of human experience in which these values play a role. Other humans experience pain and pleasure as we do. When other humans speak of excruciating pain, we know the experience they are having, even if we haven't suffered exactly that kind of pain ourselves, and we know it is something to be avoided if possible. But if human nature is divergent, the understanding and sympathy factors so important in ethics may begin to wane. How values are weighted may differ enormously. In this regard consider J. S. Mill's test to establish that some states are better than others. Mill imagined that a human had only to try both states and would know which is better. As Mill put it in his very famous comparison, "It is better to be a human being dissatisfied than a pig satisfied; better to be Socrates dissatisfied than a fool satisfied. And if the fool, or the pig, are of a different opinion, it is because they only know their own side of the question. The other party to the comparison knows both sides" (Mill, 1979, p. 10). But, assuming radical differences in human nature, we, who come with original equipment (i.e., Human Nature 1.0), may find ourselves in the role of the pig or the fool. Indeed, if the differences are significant enough, then no party may be able to experience both states and compare them.

And some of the consequences of computer implants might be truly bizarre and a challenge for ethical theory. Imagine that with the right implants some humans contribute wirelessly to a group mind. Unlike the Borg scenario, each individual thinks and acts freely on his or her own but part of the brain is used by a group mind that is connected through a computer implant. Different parts of the brains of different individuals might make different contributions. The actions of the group person might be carried out through some computerized device connected to the network. Such a collective might be treated ethically as a group person in terms of responsibility—not simply in the sense that it is a group made out of individuals who cooperate, say, as the members of a corporation do, but as a group that is made up closely interacting parts in the way the parts of the brain make up a normal individual person. Within such a group there might not be any easy assignment of responsibility and no particular individual who was in charge anymore than there is a homunculus guiding the activity of an individual brain. If this strange configuration of brain parts and computer implants were to develop, our accountability procedures would likely require adjustment.

CONCLUSION

Are there good reasons to limit the evolution of human nature with computer implants? Of course, there are good reasons to limit some kinds of implants. It would be ethically unacceptable to implant a chip that would do nothing other than put someone in intense pain. And there are good reasons to be extremely cautious in changing human nature that has been shaped by the merciless forces of evolution. Human nature is not arbitrary. Out of a history of seven million years of hominid evolution, we, Homo sapiens, are the ones who are left. But limits and caution do not preclude carefully considered advancement. We advance ourselves in many ways. Computer implants are only one of the latest methods of development.

Simply put, ethical theory and computer implants may affect each other. On the one hand, our common morality allows us to assess the use of computer implants. It can instruct us about when and when not to implant and how and how not to use computer implants. On the other hand, the implantation of computer chips may gradually change human nature enough that ethical theories will need to be adjusted. Aristotle was right to emphasize the close dependence of ethics on human nature. What is less clear is whether we should pursue a path that leads to transformation of this nature. Ethically speaking, there may be no nonquestion-begging way of judging the proper direction for the evolution of human nature. At the very least, the development of chip implants will put pressure on our ethical considerations. The concept of life may be understood less in organic terms and more in functional terms as our bodies contain more inorganic computerized parts. Replacement parts may become easier to obtain and hence some severe disabilities may be considered much less harmful. Some new abilities may become essential in order to flourish. Distinctions between mental acts and physical acts may begin to blur as our minds directly influence and are influenced by physical objects around us. Our responsibility standards may shift if we regularly obtain information via daily Internet downloads into implanted memory chips or group identity gains precedence over individual identity.

Whatever our cyborg future will hold, it is coming. Many of us born human will die cyborgs. The question we must reevaluate continually is not whether we should become cyborgs, but rather what sort of cyborgs should we become?

NOTE

I wish to thank the many people at the Computing and Philosophy Conference at Carnegie Mellon University, the Department of Philosophy at Dartmouth College, the Department of Philosophy at the University of Edinburgh, and the Centre for Applied Philosophy and Public Policy in Canberra, Melbourne, and Wagga Wagga, Australia, for many excellent suggestions. Special thanks to Neil Levy, Robert Sparrow, Christie Thomas, and John Weckert, and to my presidential scholars Christopher Moore and Jordyne Wu.

REFERENCES

Carmichael, M. 2002. Healthy Shocks to the Head, Newsweek, June 24, 56–57.

Cook, G. 2002. Scientists Produce 'Ratbot'—First Radio-controlled Animal, The Boston Globe, pp. A1 and A24.

Dertrouzos, M. L. 1997. What Will Be: How the New World of Information Will Change Our Lives, New York: HarperCollins.

———. 2001. The Unfinished Revolution: Human-Centered Computers and What They Can Do for Us. New York: HarperCollins.

Eisenberg, A. 2002. A Chip That Mimics Neurons, Firing Up the Memory, *The New York Times*, June 20.

Freudenheim, M. 1997. New Technique Offers Promise in Treating Parkinson's Disease, *The New York Times*, October 28.

Gupta, S., and Petersen, K. 2002. Could Bionic Eye End Blindness? http://www.cnn.com/2002/HEALTH/06/13/bionic.eye/index.html.

Hockenberry, J. 2001. The Next Brainiac, *Wired* 9: 94–105.

Lu, R., J. Anderson, and B. Steinhaus. 1995. The Evolution of the Implanted Pacemaker's Window to the World, *Biomedical Sciences Instrumentation* 31: 241–246.

MacguireJr, G. Q., and E. M. McGee. 1999. Implantable Brain Chips, *Hastings Center Report* 29: 7–13.

Mill, J. S. 1979. *Utilitarianism*. Indianapolis: Hackett.

Moor, J. H. 1999. Just Consequentialism and Computing, *Ethics and Information Technology* 1: 65–69.

Nussbaum, M.C. 1990. *Love's Knowledge: Essays on Philosophy and Literature*. Oxford: Oxford University Press.

Ocampo, C. M. 2000. Living with an Implantable Cardoverter Defibrillator, *Nursing Clinics of North America* 35: 1019–1030.

Pinski, S. L., and R. G. Trohman. 2000. Permanent Pacing via Implantable Defibrillators, *Pacing and Clinical Electrophysiology* 23: 1667–1682.

Spelman, F. A. 1999. The Past, Present, and Future of Cochlear Prostheses, *IEEE Engineering in Medicine and Biology* May/June: 27–33.

Vogel, G. 2002. Part Man, Part Computer: Researchers Test the Limits, *Science* 295: 1020.

Warwick, K. 2002. *I, Cyborg*. London: Century.

Yaffe, S. 1999. To Hear or Not to Hear. *Toronto Sun*, March 7.

SEVEN

Hackers and the Contested Ontology of Cyberspace

HELEN NISSENBAUM

INFORMATION TECHNOLOGY is an arena of rapid change where much is unsettled. The technology itself has evolved at a striking pace and in its heels has affected individual lives, societies, and political, social, and economic institutions. Moreover, as a series of public struggles over design and policy have demonstrated, these agents are far from unanimous in how they would judge and shape these social and technological changes. People, communities, and institutions jostle to promote their own visions, controversial policies, and competing technologies and technological standards, seeking the dominance of their own interests and values. Much of the contestation is explicit, public, and vocal: the fate of Napster, the digital divide, the promise (or lack) of proposed technical standards (e.g., P3P, PICS), the fair allocation of domain names, and many more.

This chapter brings to light a form of contestation and one of settling disputes that is much quieter, almost invisible. And the reason for its stealthy quality is that, on the face of it, these disputes are not explicitly about the way things ought to be, but about what there is, the nature of the things that inhabit both the world online and a world increasingly ordered through information technology. Nevertheless, because the result of such ontological or conceptual disputation is, or can be, ultimately normative, it is important to recognize its power and remain vigilant to its presence. One of the richest cases to illustrate this point is that of hackers, a category that has undergone radical transformation over a period of four decades.

HACKERS: BACKGROUND

Hackers were never part of the mainstream establishment, but their current reputation as villains of cyberspace is a far cry from decades past when, first and foremost, they were seen as ardent if quirky programmers, capable of brilliant, if unorthodox, feats of machine manipulation. True, their dedication bordered on fanaticism and their living habits appeared unsavory. But the shift in popular conception of hackers as deviants and criminals is worth examining not only because it affects hackers themselves and the extraordinary culture that has grown around them—fascinating as a subject in its own right[1]—but because it reflects shifts in the development, governance, and meaning of the new information technologies. I will argue that these shifts should not only be studied, but questioned and resisted.

In *Hackers: Heroes of the Computer Revolution* (1984), Steven Levy traces the roots of evolving hacker communities to the Massachusetts Institute of Technology in the late 1950s. Here, core members of the Tech Model Railroad Club "discovered" computers first as a tool for enhancing their beloved model railroads and then as objects of passion in their own right. These early hackers turned their considerable creative energies to the task of building and programming MIT's early mainframes in uneasy but relatively peaceful coexistence with formal employees of the university's technical and academic staff. In parallel, hacker communities flourished in other academic locales, particularly Stanford and Carnegie Mellon, spilling over into nearby cities of Cambridge, Palo Alto, and Berkeley.

Formidable programmers, the hackers (almost always young men) produced and debugged code at an astonishing rate. They helped develop hardware and software for existing functionalities and invented, sometimes as playful challenges, many novel algorithms and applications that were incorporated into subsequent generations of computers. These novel functions not only extended recreational capabilities of computing and information technology—gaming, virtual reality, and digitized music—but also increased practical capabilities such as control of robots and processing speed. Obsessive work leavened with inspired creativity also yielded a host of basic system subroutines and utilities that improved operating capacities and efficiency, steered the field of computing in novel directions, and became a fundamental part of what we experience—the ubiquitous windows interface, for example—every time we sit in front of a computer. (See Raymond, 2000, for other examples of hacker contributions.)

Levy and others who have written about this early hacker period (see, e.g., Hafner and Markoff, 1991; Sterling, 1992; and Thomas, 2002) describe legendary hacking binges—days and nights with little or no sleep—leading to products that surprised and sometimes annoyed colleagues in mainstream academic and research positions. The "pure hack" did not respect conventional methods or theory-driven, top-down programming prescriptions. To hack was to find a way, any way that worked, to make something happen, solve the problem, invent the next thrill. There was a bravado associated with being a hacker, an identity worn as a badge of honor. The unconventional lifestyle did not seem to put off adherents, even though it could be pretty unwholesome: a disregard for patterns of night and day, a diet of junk food, inattention to personal appearance and hygiene, the virtual absence of any life outside of hacking. Neither did hackers come off as very "nice" people; they did little to nourish conventional interpersonal skills and were not particularly tolerant of aspiring hackers with lesser skills or insufficient dedication.

It was not only the single-minded attachment to their craft that defined these early hackers but their espousal of an ideology informally called the "hacker ethic." This creed included several elements: commitment to total and free access to computers and information, belief in the immense powers of computers to improve people's lives and create art and beauty, mistrust of centralized authority, a disdain for obstacles erected against free access to computing, and an insistence that hackers be evaluated by no other criteria than technical virtuosity and accomplishment (by hacking alone and not "bogus" criteria such as degrees, age, race, or position).[2] In other words, the culture of hacking incorporated political and moral values as well as technical ends.

In the early decades—1960s and 1970s—although hackers' antics and political ideology frequently led to skirmishes with the authorities (e.g., administrators at MIT), hackers were generally tolerated with grudging admiration. Even the Defense Advanced Research Projects Agency (DARPA), the funding agency in the United States widely credited for sponsoring invention of the Internet,[3] not only turned a blind eye to unofficial hacker activities but indirectly sponsored some of them. For example, research it funded at MIT's Artificial Intelligence Laboratory was reported online in 1972 in HAKMEM, as a catalog of "hacks" (ftp://publications.ai.mit.edu/ai-publications/pdf/AIM-239.pdf). This report is prefaced, tongue-in-cheek, as follows: "Here is some little known data which may be of interest to computer hackers. The items and examples are so sketchy that to decipher them may require more sincerity and curiosity than a non-hacker can muster."[4] Eric Raymond, prolific philosopher of the Open Source movement, suggests that for DARPA, "the extra overhead was a small price to pay for attracting an entire generation of bright young people into the computing field" (Raymond, section 2, "The Early Hackers").

HEROES TO HOOLIGANS

Nowadays, when we hear about hackers it is usually as antisocial, possibly dangerous individuals who attack systems, damage other people's computers, compromise the integrity of stored information, create and distribute viruses and other harmful code, invade privacy, and even threaten national security. They flout the law by cracking into communications networks and copying and distributing copyrighted software and other intellectual works, caring nothing for the norms of common morality. They stay up all night and take on strange and menacing names like Legion of Doom, Acid Freak, The Knights of Shadow, Scorpion, Terminus, Cult of the Dead Cow, and The Marauder. To top it off, the essential credo of old-style hackerdom, creative brilliance above all, has given way to a culture of "script kiddies" or "copy-cats," who merely mimic the technical ingenuity of a few creative hackers to further antisocial and often selfish ends.

In interoffice memoranda, government advisories, and stories in the popular media and trade press, systems administrators and security experts stress the need to protect vulnerable systems and users against hackers, peppering their rhetoric with cautionary tales (all of them true): the hacker "Maxim," who threatened to post 300,000 stolen credit-card numbers on the Internet unless the online music-retailer CDUniverse paid him $100,000; master-hacker-addict Kevin Mitnick, at one point the most wanted hacker in the world, who gained access to corporate trade secrets worth millions; the loss of a ship at sea when a hacker brought down the weather forecasting system for the English Channel, and so on. And usually we are reminded of the millions of dollars each of these attacks cost in equipment, lost time, and productivity; the distribution of damaging viruses and works such as Klez, Nimda, Melissa, and ILOVEYOU; denial-of-service attacks on Yahoo!, America OnLine, and more. Each story is a reminder of the damage done, the millions of dollars lost in equipment, time, and productivity, and our disturbing vulnerability.

ACCOUNTING FOR THE SHIFT

What accounts for the transformation in our conception of hackers from Levy's "heroes of the computer revolution" to white-collar criminals and ter-rorists of the Information Age? One straightforward speculation is that hack-ers themselves have changed. They no longer discriminate in their targets; they victimize not only centralized bureaucracies, carefully chosen for their obstruction of the "hacker ethic," but also unsuspecting users and consumers of the digital media. Having cut themselves adrift from their idealistic moor-ings, they are no better than other common criminals, intruders, vandals, and thieves. We see them as villains now because they now are villains. Another speculation points not to a change in hackers themselves but to a change, largely, in us. Because our standards and values have changed, what we used to admire or tolerate we now deplore. Value shifts like these are not unprece-dented; consider the cases—more significant, obviously—of slavery, racism, sexism, sexual mores, and corporal punishment.

These suggestions hold some truth, but they form a dualism that begs for synthesis. My own account seeks such middle ground by reading the transformation against the backdrop of a shifting social context. Before considering this account, however, we should review two other accounts that have drawn contextual phenomena into their stories. One, offered by Deborah Halbert, hypothesizes that the shift in our evaluation of hackers is the result of a conscious movement by mainstream voices of governmental and private authority to demonize and portray hackers as abnormal, deviant, bullies, who victimize the rest of ordered society (Halbert, 1997). Hackers are presented as the new enemy of the Information Age, an age in which old enemies (e.g., the Soviet Union) have dissipated and the world order has shifted. Mainstream media, law, and government focus on the destructive acts of hacking in an effort to construct a new enemy and justify systematic lines of action, such as very public indictments of particular hackers (e.g., Kevin Mitnick, Robert Morris, and Craig Neidorf).

Demonizing hackers serves two ends important to government and established private powers. One is to control the definition of normalcy in the new world order of computer-mediated action and transaction; the good citizen is everything the hacker is not. According to Halbert, "It is the role of the deviant to mark the boundaries of legitimate behavior. Hackers, constructed as deviants, help define appropriate behavior and appropriate identities for all American citizens, especially in a computer age where ethical guidelines are still ambiguous" (p. 362). A second end is the justification of further expenditures in security, vigilance, and punishment. To the extent that established powers can persuade us of the severity and urgency of hacker threats, they are likely to elicit support for security measures, including governmental vigilance over the Internet, greater financial investment in safeguarding computer systems and information, and tougher sanctions on hackers.

In a similar vein, Andrew Ross[5] portrays the changing moral status of hacker as a cultural regrouping with hackers pitted against the corporate and government mainstream (Ross, 1991). He suggests that in entrenching the association between hackers and viruses, mainstream culture linked the hacker counterculture with sickness and disease, particularly with such stigmatized diseases as AIDS. According to Ross, making this link helped mainstream forces to generate equivalent hysteria in the casual user and moral indignation in the legislature. At the same time, software vendors benefited from public distrust of unauthorized copies of computer programs. In the process, "a deviant social class or group has been defined and categorized as 'enemies of the state' in order to help rationalize a general law-and-order clampdown on free and open information exchange" (Ross, 1991, p. 81).

Like the explanations proposed by Halbert and Ross, my own account brings into the foreground various contextual and historical factors, though it does so from a different vantage point, some greater specificity, and with the benefit of a larger temporal arc. The core thesis is that changes in the popular conception of hacking have as much to do with changes in specific background conditions and changes in the meaning and status of the new digital media and the powerful interests vested in them as with hacking itself. Supplementing this thesis is a proposal about the mechanism by which this shift has been achieved—namely, mediated through a manipulation of the ontology of cyberspace, rather than through only direct influence on policy and prescription.

HISTORICAL CONTEXT

It is generally acknowledged by observers and scholars of information technology that many of its significant developments were incubated in a collaboration between the military establishment (particularly through its funding agencies) and institutions of academic research, rapidly diffusing out into general use from these specialized and closely knit communities. (See, e.g., Abbate, 1999; Hafner and Lyon, 1996; Rosenzweig, 2003). Writers like John Perry Barlow, Howard Rheingold, and Nicholas Negroponte chronicled rapid popular adoption of the technology through deeply optimistic interpretive frames. Writing in the 1980s and mid-1990s, they elaborated a mythology of cyberspace—the Internet and World Wide Web—new frontiers, where great freedoms and opportunities lay, where brave (if sometimes bizarre) cowboys and "homesteaders" would create a space distinct from conventional physical space embodying these ideals of liberty and plenty. Their work both echoed and nurtured the earlier hacker ideals.[6]

But this was only half the story; the other half is a story of normalization. Technologies of information quickly passed from early obscurity and mythological idealism into the mainstream of everyday experience and the early demographics of cyberspace populated by the exotic constellation of camgirls, BBS (electronic bulletin boards), avatars (graphical icons representing characters in online games and other exchanges), ISPs (Internet Service Providers), chat rooms, portals, MUDs (multiuser dungeons/domains/ dimensions—online computer-managed games or structured social experience involving many players, bearing some resemblance to the game "Dungeons and Dragons"), MOOs (multiuser object-oriented settings, a further variation of MUDs), and hackers expanded to include familiar transplants—collective and individual—from physically bounded space. Local retailers, global corporations, credit-card companies, traditional media corporations, governments (local, state, and federal), grandmothers, preachers, and lonely hearts sought their fortunes online. Pragmatic economic visions (from the likes of Vice President Al Gore) competed with the romantic mythologies of futurists as cyberspace became increasingly domesticated, encompassing the mundane and being encompassed by it. These familiar presences, in turn, brought along familiar practices and modes of interaction and associated norms and institutions.

By far the most vigorous and important of these transplants was the commercial marketplace and supporting institution of private property. Indeed, private property leached into and became central to all the multiple layerings of the online world, from physical infrastructure on up. Global telecommunications corporations took over from government agencies possession and oversight of the fiber-optic cables, airwaves, and switches. Commercial Internet service providers (such as AOL) and others, including cable and phone companies, became dominant providers of popular online access. Even ubiquitous, open, nonproprietary protocols, like TCP/IP, the fundamental building blocks of the Internet and Web, are threatened with replacement by proprietary standard. (For a discussion of this issue, see Sandvig, 2002.)

The property metaphor has also crept into the informal culture of the Web. Increasingly conceived as spaces *belonging* to people and organizations, Web sites may be visited and viewed, but largely under the terms defined by Web site owners: wander but do not touch (unless authorized), link but do not deep-link (see Elkin-Koren, 2001),[7] receive cookies as a condition of entry. The weight of property claims in computerized environments has also tipped the balance against other claims, for example, in the case of electronic surveillance in the workplace (employers reading employee e-mail and keeping track of their Web surfing). A survey of one thousand adults, reported by the Angus Reid Group in May 2000, found that three of four workers believe employers are within their rights to monitor employee e-mail and Internet use at work, a dramatic turnaround from a few years before. More surprising than the result itself, however, was the robust acceptance by most survey subjects that employers' ownership over computer resources gave them the right to monitor (Friedman, 2000).

Owners of content, long a dominant force in more established media, are increasingly demanding in their property claims over software, images, music, movies, and other intellectual works in digital electronic form, exploiting existing laws and sponsoring new ones, such as the controversial Digital Millennium Copyright Act (DMCA) in the United States, tailored for the online environment. They lobby for international treaties that would protect their interests beyond and across national boundaries. Scholars of intellectual property law in new media, like James Boyle and Yochai Benkler, frame this progression as a second enclosure movement, in which the enclosure, this time, is not of land and physical property but of the creations of the intellect and the digital networks across which it travels.

In other arenas besides property, computerized networks have undergone changes due to efforts at restrictive regulation: online speech, online gambling, the assignment of domain names, access itself, to name a few.

Taken together, they have contributed to the transformation of a relatively intimate, mildly anarchistic environment to one governed by institutionally imposed order. Larry Lessig has described this transformation, with some nostalgia, as the passage from Net95—the open online world that readily evinced Barlow's new frontier—to the enclosed, gated, regulated world of Net01 (Lessig, 1999, p. 27).

It may be obvious how this sea change strands hackers. While the exotic personae of cyberspace can be tolerated as long as they play by the rules of the new order, hackers are fundamentally inimical to it. The credo of their early years, which included a commitment to free flow of information, unrestricted access to computer resources, and the idea of computer technology as an instrument of the public good, runs counter to these rules. For corporate and government agents, this remnant of the old anarchy constitutes an unsettling threat.

SOCIAL ONTOLOGY:
THE CONSTRUCTION OF SOCIAL REALITY

Before returning to the question of hackers, I would like to introduce a vocabulary drawn from John Searle's work about the nature and sources of the entities and facts that constitute social life, or what we might call a social ontology. Although the details of Searle's substantive picture fall outside the core purposes of this chapter, he generates a vocabulary that is useful for framing our discussion of hackers. According to Searle, it is useful to posit a social ontology, including social entities and facts, in addition to a natural ontology of natural entities and facts.[8] A social ontology, which could include, for example, money, marriage, property, and government, is defined by conventions, practices, and institutions of social life. These sets of rules, which may vary enormously in their constitution as well as the degree to which they are explicitly codified, define a great variety of institutions, with each defining, in turn, sets of entities with particular status and functionality: a lump of metal attains the status of money and takes on particular functions, a person attains the status of president of the United States of America and fulfills a variety of functions that this role incurs, a ball swishing through a basketball hoop attains the status of a goal and functions to increase one team's score.

In terms of Searle's vocabulary, we would express the decades-long developments as the emergence or construction of a social reality online, a variety of social institutions, both quirky and conventional, and not always in easy coexistence. Each defines populations of social agents such as "Webcam girls," BBS operators, Web surfers, Web masters, Web site owners, content owners, consumers, vendors, security agents, and so on. Beyond more or less explicitly defined roles, accorded status and function within these institutions, others evolve in natural or even subversive ways in a manner not unique to cyberspace. As in marriage, where we have not only husbands and wives, but also honeymoons, marriage therapists, and adulterers; and in property we have not only owners, buyers, sellers, and realtors, but thieves, trespassers; and so on, in contemporary, thickly institutionalized cyberspace, beyond the social agents mentioned previously, we also have hackers. I will argue that the status of hackers in the social ontology of cyberspace is as agents who willfully defy the rules; as adulterers are to marriage, thieves to property, so hackers are to the set of interlinked institutions that have colonized the online world.

HACKERS AS BAD ACTORS OF CYBERSPACE

From the late 1950s through the mid-1980s, to be a hacker was to participate in a set of activities with a single-minded passion, to possess a set of skills, to hold a certain set of beliefs, and to hold *to* a set of norms. Although there was no single, identifiable organization representing hackers and no formal entry requirements, there was a scattered "association" of hackers, a sense of solidarity among comrades, a loosely networked group, and, especially when numbers were small enough, a sense that to be a hacker was to be vetted by a cohort of cultural peers (Sterling, 1992, Part 2). As with any natural category,[9] it is possible to wonder whether one or another of these properties was essential to it, but, details aside, many would have agreed that the cluster or properties picked out a readily identifiable category, or at least one identifiable by members and knowledgeable colleagues and observers.

With the growing importance of institutions online, however, and the emergence of a social ontology defined by them, hackers have taken on new significance, not as a self-identified group or subculture, but as bad actors in the new social reality. Cast as the "bad guys" of computerized and computer-mediated social reality, they are sociopaths, thieves, opportunists, trespassers, vandals, Peeping Toms, and terrorists. More than stirring negative public relations, these labels transform social meaning, refashioning the concept of hacking into one imbued with negative content. Our language is full of normative terms: "murder" when we mean an unlawful, wicked, premeditated killing; "theft" when we mean the wrongful taking of something one does not own; "weed" when we mean wild and unwanted plant. Words like these constrain what a speaker can say without stumbling into awkward inconsistencies; they foreclose certain moral discussions. To ask whether murder is wrong is odd, for by conceding that a killing is a murder we have already passed moral judgment. In some cases, terms such as murder usefully enable expressive precision—in courts of law or in strong personal judgments: "As far as I'm concerned factory owners who dump toxins into drinking water are murderers." But in others, affixing a moral label can stunt exploratory deliberation, as it does, I believe, in the case of hacking.

If hackers are thieves, vandals, and terrorists, it makes no sense to ask whether hacking is good or bad, whether we are for it or against it.

What I am trying to suggest is that normative disputes can be settled in at least two ways. One is to tackle disagreements head on, debating whether a given act, decision, or policy is good or bad, acceptable or unacceptable, and so forth. But normative points can also be scored an insidious way by, somehow, meddling with an ontology or conceptual schemata. Conceptual schemas carve the world into perceptible and intelligible chunks. Concepts determine ontology by individuating constitutive entities, defining what there is in our world and what, therefore, we can readily talk about. If the conception of hacker as transgressor dominates, our capacity to ask in a meaningful way whether hacking is bad, or good, or morally neutral is limited. To call a hacker good becomes virtually oxymoronic.

In their book on classification and standardization, G. Bowker and S. L. Star explore this capacity of schemes of classification to serve not only epistemological ends—organizing the world into useful chunks—but also political ones. Political ends may be served when: (1) Overly inclusive categories merge differences, causing a variety of entities to seem to be of one kind and, by consequence, deserving of a common treatment; (2) a distinctive set of marginal entities are made to disappear in a scheme that lumps them together with a dominant set (e.g., as described by Bowker and Star, the Nursing Interventions Classification was careful to include explicit categories for frequently overlooked nursing functions like providing spiritual support and cheering up patients through humor); (3) borders are drawn in politically charged ways (e.g., when a fetus is to count as a person); and (4) important commonalities are missed when a meaningful aggregate is disaggregated into several parts (e.g., finally recognizing a variety of activities as belonging together in the single category of "sexual harassment"). (See Bowker and Star, 1997, especially chapter 7.)

James Boyle brings to light another case in which categorization carried political clout (Boyle, 1997). According to Boyle, significant political progress in the effort to protect the environment politically was made when proponents succeeded in classifying together in the single category of environmentalism the set of diverse concerns of nature lovers, hikers, opponents of pollution, campers, birdwatchers, conservationists, and hunters: "In one very real sense, the environmental movement invented the environment so that farmers, consumers, hunters and birdwatchers could all discover themselves as environmentalists" (Boyle, 1997, p. 113). When these previously disparate groups were able to see themselves as having something in common—the environment—they could consolidate diverse streams of energy and activism (pp. 108–109).

Behind such conceptual shifts must be a diverse range of causes about which I can only here speculate. Boyle's account suggests that intellectual enlightenment was a key to the shift, namely, the discovery that two new analytic frameworks, ecology, on the one hand, and welfare economics, on the other, could be applied, in common, to apparently disparate concerns of the various interest groups. Looking for the epistemological mechanism behind the establishment of social facts, Searle posits collective assent, or "collective intentionality" (p. 97), which occurs when "sufficient numbers of members of the relevant community continue to recognize and accept the existence of such facts" (p. 117). In a similar vein, Bowker and Star stress community agency when they identify naturalization (as articulated in the field of science and technology studies) as the key mechanism by which a community ceases to think of a particular entity as artificially constructed and accepts it as an element of the natural or untheorized environment.

Although a comprehensive and systematic account of what moves collective assent (or naturalization) is, again, beyond my scope here, we will draw on conventional wisdom about institutional agents that, historically, have been implicated in shaping and changing collective conceptions of reality, namely, public policy, the courts, and, of course, the media. Focusing on activity within the United States, we see Congress addressing the hacker "problem" with the 1986 Computer Fraud and Abuse Act that was followed by continuous refinements and increasingly harsh punishments, culminating in the 1998 Digital Millennium Copyright Act. Law enforcement agencies enforced these newly rigorous rules in well-publicized sting operations of the 1980s, which Bruce Sterling calls "hacker crackdowns," police and FBI agents arrested hackers and "Phreaks" (hackers who break into telecommunications networks), confiscated equipment, and pursued public indictments of infamous hackers such as Kevin Mitnick, Robert Morris, and Craid Neidorf. Hacker arrests and incarcerations have become commonplace.

Courts have demonstrated a willingness to cooperate in such crackdowns by handing down guilty verdicts and imposing stiff punishments, from fines to jail sentences. In highly visible and expressive cases, courts shut down Shawn Fanning's Napster and prohibited publication of DeCSS, a program that decrypts DVD disks for Linux machines, in Eric Corley's *2600 Magazine* (known as a magazine for hackers). Some observers believe that the pendulum has swung too far, as, for example, the National Association of Criminal Defense Lawyers, which has argued that sentences for hackers are now disproportionately harsh (Lemos, 2003).

Finally, the media has played a critical role in bringing the matter of hacking to public attention by presenting and framing countless stories, including some already mentioned, about hackers sending destructive viruses, initiating denial of service, breaking into highly sensitive utilities of military systems, and distributing pirated software and other electronic property. According to Eric Raymond, this trend can be traced back as early as 1984, when the mainstream press began covering episodes of unauthorized break-ins into computer systems and "journalists began to misapply the term 'hacker' to refer to computer vandals, an abuse which sadly continues to this day." (See Raymond, 2000, Section 5.) Samples drawn from the print media illustrate this trend:

- *The New York Times*, June 13, 1999: "Computer hackers attacked the United States Senate's main Web site on Friday, the second such electronic assault on the high profile Internet page in just over two weeks." Later in the same article, "In an obvious taunt directed at the F.B.I.—which is conducting a national crackdown on computer hackers—they wrote on part of the page: "Yon can stop one, but you cannot stop all."
- *The Buffalo News*, June 29, 1999 headline: "Web Site of U.S. Army is invaded by Hackers."
- *The Boston Herald*, August 1, 1999: "It was the kind of threat for which computer hackers are famous, a declaration of war dripping with the risk-free bravado so common on the anonymous Internet. The warning, which appeared on a hacked Web page of the U.S. Interior Department in late May, promised unrelenting attacks against government computers to avenge an FBI roundup of hackers associated with the group Global Hell."
- LA Times.com, November 7, 2000: "A 20 year-old hacker who seized control of sensitive computer programs at the Jet Propulsion Laboratory in Pasadena and at Stanford University pleased guilty to federal charges Monday." http://www.latimes.com/cgi-bin/print.cgi.
- *Time* magazine (Canadian edition) May 22, 2000, headline: "School for Hackers: The Love Bug's Manila birthplace is just one of many Third World virus breeding grounds" suggests that De Guzman, who is suspected of unleashing the virus, is an example of a growing force of hackers in the "Third World." Law enforcement officials warn that "small cells of hackers—some at colleges, others in contact only electronically—pose an unprecedented threat to the computer systems of the industrialized world."
- *The San Jose Mercury News*, July 10, 2002: "Security Flaw Afflicts Popular Technology for Encrypting E-mail: The flaw allows a hacker to send a specially coded e-mail—which would appear as a blank message followed by an error warning—and effectively seize control of the victim's computer. The hacker could then install spy-software to record keystrokes, steal financial records, or copy a person's secret unlocking keys to unscramble their sensitive emails."
- CNET News.com, July 15, 2002, headline: "House Oks Life Sentences for Hackers: The House of Representatives on Monday overwhelmingly approved a bill that would allow for life prison sentences for malicious computer hackers. . . . The CyberSecurity Enhancement Act had been written before September 11 terrorist attacks last year, but the events spurred legislators toward Monday evening's near-unanimous vote."

- *The New York Times*, January 17, 2003, headline: "Increase in Electronic Attacks Leads to Warning on Iraqi Hackers and U.S. Safety."
- *The New York Times*, August 12, 2002, headline: "Hacker Obtains Shuttle Design Files, Baffling NASA. Cybercrime investigators for the National Aeronautics and Space Administration are trying to figure out how 43 megabytes of sensitive design data about planned space vehicles got into the hands of a hacker."
- *The Washington Post*, February 19, 2003, headline: "8 Million Credit Accounts Exposed; FBI to Investigate Hacking of Database. A hacker broke into a computer database containing roughly 8 million Visa MasterCard and American Express credit card numbers earlier this month, prompting an FBI investigation into one of the largest intrusions of its kind."

A steady stream of media reports in which vandals, burglars, thieves, terrorists, and trespassers are labeled as hackers does more than shift our focus, it establishes a new prototype.[10] The more times people hear of hackers in these terms the more they are led to see these hackers not as exceptions but as the rule. A category shift occurs not as a result of revised formal definitions, or at the edges where boundaries are carved, but at the center where the *typical* hacker is drawn. The accumulation of stories constructs the prototype of a newly defined category.

We do not have to posit a massive conspiracy to understand why the media have followed this path. As Todd Gitlin has argued, established institutions, compared with opposition movements, exert a formidable influence in how the mass media construe reality (Gitlin, 1990). Besides the obvious advantages of wealth and power, established institutions are able to nominate official spokespersons who present a coordinated, authoritative account of these institutions' positions and perspectives. By contrast, opposition movements typically lack such mechanisms. Although a sense of solidarity binds many hacker-comrades together, and a dispersed, loosely associated network of small bands convene around electronic discussion groups (such as Slashdot.com), magazines (such as *2600: The Hacker Quarterly*), and even annual conferences (such as Defcon), yielding what Bruce Sterling called a "digital underground," there are no formal entry requirements and no organizations or individuals who stand for or can legitimately claim to represent *the* hacker perspective. In such circumstances, as Gitlin would predict, even when it is not explicitly manipulated by establishment voices, media presentation of hackers falls prey to serendipity and the media's taste for celebrity and melodrama (Gitlin, 1990).

TELEOLOGY

It remains to ask why established institutions would promote this particular transformation in the social ontology of the online world. For law enforcement and security agencies, including national security agencies, hackers represent anarchy and disobedience, and for corporate agents they exemplify stubborn resistance to the imposed order of private property, borders, and restricted access. Hackers are not readily "tamed"; they explicitly eschew the rules of centralized authorities. This is a bad enough threat. How much worse if the rest of us were to identify with hackers and their "ethic"? The seventy million people who downloaded Napster and the even greater numbers who ignore the threats of established authorities and subscribe to file-sharing services such as Aimster, KaZaA, and others are a corporate executive's nightmare not only because of the direct impact on the record industry's profitability and power but because they signal a normative seepage, the beginnings of shifting loyalties and commitment.

Searle highlights the capacity of collective intentionality to sustain as well as break down institutional structures, in some instances, overpowering direct force itself. Pointing to the cases of the 1992 riots in Los Angeles and the dissolution of the Soviet Union, Searle speculates that the turning points in each occurred when protesters (rioters and dissidents, respectively) induced sufficient sympathy among large portions of their respective collectives and no longer could be relegated to the status of deviants. At this point, police could no longer sustain authority over them. When collective intentionality deserts prevailing institutional norms, when there is massive identification with radically dissident voices, then the very institutions themselves risk dissolution. Although, ideally, such upheaval would become a staging ground for productive public examination of issues, norms, and policies, this has not occurred in the case of hacking. Instead, established institutions have tried to increase the distance between hackers and the rest of us by means of an ontological transformation that reconceives hackers as deviants and hence fair targets for repression and punitive action. Such efforts seem to have gained considerable public acceptance in the wake of the September 11, 2001, terrorist attacks on the World Trade Center, at least in the short term.

Albert Hirschman's exit and voice provide an interesting framework for expressing the clash between hackers and established powers (Hirschman, 1990). Hirschman posits exit and voice as two of the ways people (consumers, members, clients, etc.) can try to shape business institutions, political and religious organizations, and other forms of organized community. Dissatisfaction is expressed through exit when customers cease buying a product, members leave a church, participants resign from an organization, and parents remove their children from a school. Voice, according to Hirschman, involves, "any attempt at all to change, rather than to escape from, an objectionable state of affairs, whether through individual or collective petition to the management directly in charge, through appeal to a higher authority with the intention of forcing a change in management, or through various types of actions and protests, including those that are meant to mobilize public opinion" (Hirschman, 1990, p. 30).

Although the ideal response to deterioration in the quality of a product or service is for organizations or corporations to heed the messages of exit and voice, managers, according to Hirschman, tend to prefer to shun efforts to change, preferring to "act as they wish, unmolested as far as possible by either desertions or complaints of members" (Hirschman, 1990, p. 93). At the same time they seek ways to make themselves less vulnerable to either forms of dissidence, devising mechanisms for defusing the power of voice and exit, focusing on ways to "strip the members-customers of the weapons which they can wield" (p. 124). The possibilities that Hirschman discusses include playing collusive games with competitors to diminish the effects of exit, making exit exceedingly difficult, "domesticating" voice, even silencing it altogether by excommunication or expulsion.

Institutional responses to hackers are well illuminated by Hirschman's framework as we can see in the case of Napster, for example. The story is familiar: in 1999, Shawn Fanning, a freshman at Northeastern University, grew dissatisfied with the poor accessibility of music online. He *exited* the constraints of the music industry by hacking an alternative system of distributing music based on peer-to-peer file sharing. To date, the music industry has responded precisely as Hirschman's theory would predict, not by heeding the message of dissatisfaction but seeking what Hirschman would call excommunication and expulsion. In this case, it involved prosecuting Fanning in a court of law, signaling to one and all that exit from their system would be exceedingly costly. Their move is equivalent to pushing the protesters to the margins of good society where they can be dealt with as deviants. Another case is open source software, which can also be read as exit from commercialized, closed code. To date, we have witnessed two types of reactions. One, led by Microsoft, aggressively tries to quash it (make exit difficult), famously calling the Open Source movement a 'cancer'. Others have tried to domesticate it by portraying the hackers of open source not as dissidents but as workers who can be folded into their system of property and control. (See Wayner, 2000.)

THE VALUE OF HACKING

Hirschman's framework is not purely descriptive, but conveys a strong normative message as well. The tactics employed by managers to avoid facing up to the substantive complaints of dissidents and deserters are shortsighted and unwise, most likely leading to the long-term decline of the organizations (firms, states, etc.) they represent. This lesson is, I contend, worth heeding in the case of hackers. Although the ontological transformation of hackers from heroes to hooligans, in the short term, might suppress uncomfortable and inconvenient disruptions, the long-term effects are less clear, especially for society at large. Long-term outcomes of the various blocking strategies are worth studying. To this end, I conclude by considering some consequences of giving way to the reformation of the concept of hacking from earlier meanings of fanatical programmer and adherent of the hacker ethic to destructive deviant, a common criminal, or even a terrorist.

The finding I wish to stress is this: although shifting the meaning of hacking does not immediately cause those identified with the earlier hacker ideology actually to disappear, it causes them *effectively* to disappear into what Bowker and Star call the marginal residual—namely, atypical members of a category that do not fit salient characterizations. Lodged at the margins, these hackers lose their robust identity and with that goes recognition of their ideas, ideals, and ideologies that constitute an alternative vision for a networked society. The following cases illustrate valuable contributions these hackers have made to society and, by inference, what we stand to lose as they are pushed into the margins.

Most significant, perhaps, are the remarkable technical contributions self-identified hackers have made outside the framework of the commercial marketplace. Many scoffed when Richard Stallman and his followers in the Free Software movement, quintessential hackers in the old sense, insisted that software should be free—"as in speech," Stallman regularly quips, "not beer"—but the enormous body of free software, including Linux, poses a formidable challenge to glib truisms about intellectual property and innovation. Eric Raymond, referring to the origins of the phenomenal Open Source movement, notes that "the hacker culture, defying repeated predictions of its demise, was just beginning to remake the commercial software world in its own image." (See also Wayner, 2000.) Hacker ideology also inspired such luminaries as Tim Berners-Lee, dubbed "the inventor of the World Wide Web." In his account of constructing a remarkable global information system, he has situated his efforts within the purview of projects and ideologies of such early hackers as Ted Nelson (Berners-Lee and Fischetti, 1999). Contributions that hackers have made to social welfare extend beyond free code to include access to technology and information; Raymond writes, "many of the hackers of the 1980s and early 1990s launched Internet Service Providers selling or giving access to the masses" (Raymond, 2000, Section 7).

Hackers have also contributed in the political arena, supporting causes of liberty and individual autonomy in policies involving information technology. In 1994–1995, for example, they were part of the concerted opposition to the Clinton administration's misguided Clipper proposal, which would have limited individual access to strong encryption. In 1996, they joined the broad coalition opposing, and ultimately defeating, the Communications Decency Act, on grounds that it would lead to unacceptable censorship of the Internet.

Hackers have also contributed to efforts against political oppression, devising ingenious forms of political protest. In a historic case in 1998, "hacktivists" supporting Mexican Zapatista rebels developed Floodnet, a coordinated bombardment of client requests that temporarily shut down the Web site of Mexican president Ernesto Zedillo. The attack was carefully planned and controlled in the tradition of peaceful civil disobedience not to destroy, but, as described by Ricardo Dominguez, one of its leaders, "To create a disturbance that becomes symbolic, so a certain community can gain a voice in the media" (Ricardo Dominguez quoted in Romano, 1999).[11] More recently, hackers have focused attention on the growing presence of video surveillance technologies in private and public spaces. The hacktivist group Institute for Applied Autonomy, for example, charts routes of least surveillance through Manhattan streets, and an anonymous Web site at http://rtmark.com/cctv/ offers advice on how to disable surveillance cameras. The journalist Stuart Millar has characterized hacktivism as a "highly politicized underground movement using direct action in Cyberspace to attack globalization and corporate domination of the Internet," and, as such, an ideological heir to the great protest movements of the nineteenth and twentieth centuries (Millar, 2001).[12]

If there is something political tying together these descendents of early hackers it is protest—protest against encroaching systems of total order where control is complete and dissent dangerous. These hackers defy the tendencies of established powers to overreach and exploit without accountability. With their specialized skills, they resist private enclosure and work to preserve open and popular access to online resources, which they consider a boon to humanity. Ornery and irreverent, they represent a degree of freedom, an escape hatch from a system that threatens to become overbearing. In societies striving to be liberal and democratic, this is a significant part of the value of hacking and an important reason to resist obfuscation of the category.

It is important to note, however, that sustaining the positive meaning of hackers does not require denying or turning a blind eye to those who turn their skills and know-how to stealing information or money, damaging and vandalizing information or systems, or placing critical systems at risk of malfunction. We deplore these actions, just as we would deplore any actions that deliberately harm others. Nevertheless, the problematic consequence of viewing these actors as prototypical hackers is that it marginalizes the remainder; they are "left dark" (Bowker and Star, 1999, p. 321) without a robust presence in the social ontology of cyberspace.

CONCLUSION

Recognizing, as others have done before, the transformation in the way hackers are viewed, I have argued that it is not merely a matter of a change in evaluative judgments of hackers and hacking, but in the very meaning of the terms. Hacking is now imbued with normative meaning whose core refers to harmful and menacing acts and, as a result, it is virtually impossible to speak of, let alone identify, the hackers who engage in activities of significant social value. Because the old hackers eschewed centralization of authority and invasive property boundaries, the ontological shift is convenient for those who seek to establish control in the new order and economy of cyberspace. Not only does it vilify early hackers by association with evil hackers, but it becomes virtually impossible even to see them, for we have lost the vocabulary with which to identify them. As a collateral loss, it is harder to deliberate over the conflicting substantive principles.

Concepts carve the world into meaningful chunks and serve particular ends, whether they are explicitly crafted, as the case of the International Classification of Diseases (Bowker and Star, 1999), or emerge naturally as the meaning of everyday language. As Searle remarks, "social reality is created by us for our purposes and seems as readily intelligible to us as those purposes themselves" (Searle, 1995, p. 4). In the extreme, the evolution of appropriate conceptual schema may even be seen to serve the flourishing of a species, as some have suggested in the case of vervet monkeys, for example, that are able to warn troop members about the presence of predators with special "words" conveying something about the nature of these predators—whether airborne (an eagle) or terrestrial (a snake) (Cheney and Seyfarth, 1990).[13]

In this sense, our concepts are teleological, not only shaping our thoughts and utterances, but facilitating, making awkward, or even depriving us of the facility to think and talk about certain things. In some cases, such as the vervets' refined conception of predators, these conceptual schema serve shared or common ends within a community of agents, thinkers, and speakers. But this is not universally true of all conceptual and classification schema, which, in ways discussed earlier, may favor some members' interests at the expense of others as I have argued to be the case as established institutions of cyberspace have enlisted the concept of hacking in their quest for order and control. The recognition of contested ends is partly what impassions Bowker and Star's book when they declare: "One of this book's central arguments is that classification systems are often sites of political and social struggles, but these sites are difficult to approach. Politically and socially charged agendas are often first presented as purely technical and they are difficult even to see" (Bowker and Star, 1999, p. 196).

I have argued that we are not all well served by the transformation of "hacker" into a category that includes only at its edges those who espouse the hacker ideology (or "hacker ethic"). These hackers have much to offer individual users of cyberspace and ultimately to contribute to the public good. Nevertheless, to many of the institutions invested in strong property rights and traditional ordering, even these hackers constitute a threat. They challenge institutional strongholds and are sufficiently skilled at manipulating the underlying technologies to meet their ideological commitments. All the better if this irksome group and its causes would fade from public conscious-ness into the margins of a larger category typified by vandals, terrorists, and criminals. All the better for the institutions if they can craft an enemy in common with individual users and consumers so as to subordinate *all* who might challenge them.

Computers and the Internet have extended our modes of association, action, expression, and access to information and have conjured into exis-tence many wondrous entities and interactions. The precise nature of these entities is not always understood and questions about them arise that have implications for policy and values—questions like: What is a border in cyber-space? Where are the edges of a hypertext document? What is it to be an owner of something online? What is public; what is private? What is identity online; what are identities? Is virtual friendship, friendship, virtual war, war, virtual sex, sex? Like the question about hacking, these ontological questions have normative implications. The general thesis of this chapter, with impli-cations beyond hacking, is that questions like these, about what there is online, can be seminal to basic concerns about what ought to be.[14]

NOTES

This chapter has incubated over long period, originating with Jeroen van den Hoven's invitation to a July 2000 Conference on Social Ontology, Erasmus Univer-sity, Rotterdam. Versions were also presented at Carnegie Mellon and at the Institute for Advanced Study, Princeton, and a short version was prepared for *Dissent* magazine. Along the way, I received invaluable research assistance and editorial and substantive advice from Robert Cavalier, Brian Cogan, Debra Keates, Eben Moglen, Maxine Phillips, Greg Pomerantz, James Rule, Michael Walzer, audiences at the various venues where the paper was presented, and editors and anonymous reviewers of the journal *New Media and Society*.

Reprinted with permission from *New Media and Society* 6 (2): 61–83. Copyright 2004 SAGE Publications.

1. See, e.g., interesting work by Douglas Thomas (2002).

2. See Levy, especially chapter 2.

3. See, e.g., historical accounts in Rosenzweig and Hafner and Lyons.

4. Thanks to Greg Pomerantz for directing me to this delightful document.

5. An anonymous reviewer helpfully drew my attention to this work.

6. For example, Barlow's, "Coming into the Country," Rheingold's *The Virtual Community: Homesteading on the Electronic Frontier*, Negroponte's *Being Digital*.

7. To deep-link is to bypass the front page of a Web site, linking directly to desired content on another page within it—for example, bypassing the *New York*

Times front page and linking directly to a particular story. Owners of commercial Web sites fear the loss of revenues from advertisements or their front-page portals and argue that deep-linking constitutes a copyright violation.

8. Some readers have claimed this to be an unconventional usage of "ontology."

9. Here I depart from Searle's usage. Searle uses natural ontology as a contrast with social ontology. I am invoking more standard usage here, referring to natural categories as contrasted with artificially constructed categories and classification schema.

10. One of the fundamental questions asked by cognitive scientists is how people categorize or conceptualize their worlds. Eleanor Rosch rose to prominence in the field by articulating "prototype theory" as a compelling answer to this question. George Lakoff, Mark Johnson, John Taylor, and others have developed and extended this theory into neighboring fields such as linguistics. In addition to developing the theory, Rosch and others have generated a formidable body of confirming experimental results. For my purposes, it is sufficient to note about prototype theory that it offers an alternative view of categorization to the Aristotelian idea that members of a category share a common set of necessary and sufficient, or defining, properties. Instead, Rosch argues that most, if not all, natural categories have fuzzy borders and, typically, no set of properties that all members would share in common. She suggests that, for these categories, we hold a prototype in mind and move from the prototype to other members of the category by analogy.

11. See also http://www.eco.utexas.edu/Homepages/Faculty/Cleaver/chiapas95. html and http://www.eco.utexas.edu/Homepages/Faculty/Cleaver/chiapas95.html for further documentation of this case.

12. And still there are those driven simply for the love of the pure hack, such as Robin Malda, one of the founders of Slashdot, who writes on his home page: "The Internet: What can I say? I'm an addict. The 'net for me was the point for computers. . . ." http://cmdrTaco.net/rob.html.

13. I thank Dan Rubenstein for pointing me to this reference.

14. Said in respectful disagreement with G. E. Moore's naturalistic fallacy.

REFERENCES

Abbate, J. 1999. *Inventing the Internet.* Cambridge: MIT Press.

Barlow, J. P. 1991. Coming into the Country, *Communication of the ACM* 34, 3: 12–21.

Berners-Lee, T. with M. Fischetti. 1999. *Weaving the Web: The Original Design and Ultimate Destiny of the World Wide Web by Its Inventor.* San Francisco: HarperCollins.

Bowker, G. C., and S. L. Star. 1999. *Sorting Things Out: Classification and Its Consequences.* Cambridge: MIT Press.

Boyle, J. 1997. A Politics of Intellectual Property: Environmentalism for the Net, *Duke Law Journal* 47: 87–116.

Cheney, D. L., and R. M. Seyfarth. 1990. *How Monkeys See the World : Inside the Mind of Another Species.* Chicago: University of Chicago Press.

Elkin-Koren, N. 2001. Let the Crawlers Crawl: On Virtual Gatekeepers and the Right to Exclude Indexing, *Dayton Law Review* 26: 180.

Friedman, S. 2000. Most Workers Don't Mind Workplace Online Monitoring-Poll, *Newsbytes* URL (consulted May 3 2000) http://www.newsbytes.com/pubNews/00/148466.html.

Gltlin T. 1990) *The Whole World Is Watching: Mass Media in the Making and Unmaking of the New Left*. Berkeley: University of California Press.

Hafner. K., and M. Lyon. 1996. *Where Wizards Stay up Late: The Origins of the Internet*. New York: Touchstone Books.

Hafner, K., and J. Markoff. 1991. *Cyberpunk: Outlaws and Hackers on the Computer Frontiers*. New York: Simon and Schuster.

Halbert, D. 1997. Discourses of Danger and the Computer Hacker, *The Information Society* 13: 361–374.

Himanen, P. 2001. *The Hacker Ethic and the Spirit of the Information Age*. New York: Random House.

Hirschman, A. 1990. *Exit, Voice and Loyalty: Responses to Decline in Firms, Organizations, and States*. Cambridge: Harvard University Press.

Lakoff, G., and M. Johnson. 1980. *Metaphors We Live By*. Chicago: University of Chicago Press.

Lane, T. 1997. Web Cookies: Their Reason, Nature, and Security, June 1997 *BITS: Computing and Communications News* (consulted April 16, 2001) http://www.apt.lanl.gov/projects/ia/library/bits/bits0697.html.

Lemos, R. 2003. Lawyers: Hackers Sentenced Too Harshly, *CNet News.com* (consulted February 20, 2003).

Lessig, L. 1999. *Code and Other Laws of Cyberspace*. New York: Basic Books.

Levy, S. 1984. *Hackers: Heroes of the Computer Revolution*. New York: Doubleday.

———, and B. Stone. 2000. Hunting the Hackers, *Newsweek*, February 21.

Markoff. J. 1993. Keeping Things Safe and Orderly in the Neighborhoods of Cyberspace, *The New York Times*, October 24.

Millar, S. 2001. Hackers: The Political Heroes of Cyberspace, *The Guardian*, March 8.

Negroponte, N. 1995. *Being Digital*. New York: Knopf.

Raymond, E. 2000. A Brief History of Hackerdom, November 17, revision 1.24 URL (consulted November 17) http://catb.org/~esr/writings/hacker-history/.

Rheingold, H. 1993. *The Virtual Community: Homesteading on the Electronic Frontier*. New York: HarperCollins.

Romano, M. 1999. The Politics and Hacking, *Spin*, November 1999: 168–174.

Rosenzweig, R. 2003. "How Will the Net's History Be Written? Historians and the Internet," in M. Price and H. Nissenbaum (Eds.), *Internet and the Academy*. New York: Peter Lang.

Ross, A. 1991. *Strange Weather: Culture, Science and Technology in the Age of Limits.* London: Verso, pp. 75–100.

Sandvig, C. 2002, November 23. Communication Infrastructure and Innovation: The Internet as the End-to-End Network that Isn't, paper presented at the American Association for the Advancement of Science Research Symposium with the Next Generation of Leaders in Science and Technology Policy, Washington, DC. http://research.niftyc.org/Communication_Infrastructure_and_Innovation.pdf.

Schwartau, W. 2000. *Cybershock: Surviving Hackers, Phreakers, Identity Thieves, Internet Terrorists, and Weapons of Mass Disruption.* New York: Thunders Mouth Press.

Searle, J. 1995. *The Construction of Social Reality.* New York: Free Press.

Sterling, B. 1992. *The Hacker Crackdown.* New York: Bantam.

Taylor, J. R. 1995. *Linguistic Categorization: Prototypes in Linguistic Theory,* second edition. Oxford: Clarendon Press.

Thomas, D. 2002. *Hacker Culture.* Minneapolis: University of Minnesota Press.

Wayner, P. 2000. *Free for All: How Linux and the Free Software Movement Undercut the High-Tech Titans.* New York: HarperBusiness.

EIGHT

Moral Imperatives for Life in an Intercultural Global Village

CHARLES ESS

DURING THE 1980s AND 1990s in the Western world, much of the moral imperative for the development and distribution of computer-mediated communication (CMC) technologies such as the Internet and the Web derived from Marshall McLuhan's utopian vision of an "electronic global village." This wired village presumed that these technologies were accessible, culturally neutral, and communicatively transparent to all the peoples of the world: as such, CMC would facilitate the realization of ostensibly universal ethical and political values—equality, freedom of expression, democratic governance, and, of course, economic prosperity as the result of radically free and global trade.

As the events of September 11, 2001, made tragically clear, however, Western—specifically American—visions of the Good, the True, and the Beautiful are not always as manifestly universal in their scope and validity as their proponents tend to assume. On the contrary, Western emphases on material prosperity through capitalism and free trade are seen—with considerable justification—to have enormous human and social costs, beginning with *increasing* problems of maldistribution of important social and economic resources, as the gaps between rich and poor grow both within the United States and between the developed and developing nations. A particular reflection of these gaps is the "digital divide," the split between the *information* haves and have-nots.[1] At a still deeper level, contemporary Western models are called into question as continuing forms of colonization, that is, the imposition, through subtle and gross forms of force and coercion, of economic and political arrangements that both contradict and override the traditions, values, practices—indeed, the very identity—of diverse peoples and nations.[2]

As Benjamin Barber put it, globalization and the ongoing expansion of Western models and power appear to offer the world's peoples a Manichean choice between a McWorld and violent confrontation in the name of preserving cultural identity (1992, 1995). Globalization—facilitated in part precisely through contemporary information technologies—seems to move intractably toward a homogenous McWorld, a global consumer culture whose lingua franca is English and in which trade, as the only shared cultural activity, overrides all significant cultural and linguistic differences. Not surprisingly, Barber argues, in the face of this threat we thus see "jihad" arise— efforts to defend local identity and autonomy, efforts that can become notoriously violent in the name of cultural survival.[3]

In this light, we must then ask whether the lovely visions of an electronic global village, in which CMC technologies would foster greater global understanding and thereby greater peace—especially as they facilitate free expression, democratic polity, and economic prosperity—are simply the newest ideological veneer of Western colonialism. In fact, in the 1980s and 1990s, as CMC technologies were deployed among an ever-wider range of peoples and traditions—including non-Western and indigenous peoples—these technologies evoked a range of diverse responses, including outright rejection and radical modification in order to preserve local cultural identities and practices. These responses make clear that, indeed, the optimistic vision of "wiring the world" with Western-designed CMC technologies runs the risk of serving as the ideological justification for yet another form of cultural imperialism, a "computer-mediated colonization" that serves the power and interests of the West. Paradoxically, the icon of an electronic global village, precisely in its pretense to global validity, re-presents the danger of imposing specifically Western values and practices on multiple peoples and nations whose deepest cultural values and communicative preferences are often quite different from those embedded in and fostered by Western CMC technologies.

Our enthusiasm for these technologies and the ostensible gains they promise, in short, threatens simply to serve as yet another form of McWorld—one that runs the very real danger of only further feeding reaction, including violent reaction, against its sponsors in the name of preserving cultural identity. But I will argue that we are not left simply with the choice between a homogenous McWorld and a fragmented plurality of disconnected cultures and peoples. Rather, precisely by our becoming aware of the values and communicative preferences favored by Western CMC technologies, and how these often conflict with the communicative preferences and values of diverse cultures, we will see models for middle grounds emerge—ones that conjoin global connectivity with a plurality of local cultural identities.

To see how this is so, I begin by focusing on the specific claim—popularized through McLuhanesque icons of an "electronic global village"—that "wiring the world" with computer-mediated communications (CMC) technologies such as the Internet and the World Wide Web will inevitably result in greater democracy, equality, individual freedom, and economic prosperity. I refine and test this claim by first turning to Habermas's conceptions of communicative reason, the ideal speech situation, and the public sphere as a philosophically more robust theory of democracy—one that endorses communitarian and pluralist understandings of democracy, in contrast with plebiscite and libertarian views. I then review significant ways in which Habermas's conceptions are modified to meet postmodernist and feminist critiques, so as to defend especially a notion of "partial publics" (*Teilöffentlichkeiten*) as a praxis-informed conception that may be realizable on the Internet.

I then test this conception from a global perspective—that is, in light of efforts to implement computer-mediated communication (CMC) technologies in diverse cultural settings. These lessons from praxis provide both examples and counterexamples of a (partial) public sphere as instantiated via the Internet and the Web. These examples illustrate, moreover, that CMC technologies embed Western cultural values and communicative preferences. This means that well-meaning efforts to "wire the world" in the name of an ostensibly universal/cosmopolitan vision of electronic democracy, paradoxically enough, emerge as a form of computer-mediated colonization, that is, an imposition of a specific set of cultural values and communicative preferences on diverse cultures. At the same time, however, additional examples from praxis demonstrate that diverse cultures can resist and reshape Western technologies: indeed, paradigm cases emerge of best practices for realizing Habermasian notions of democracy and pluralism—first, by taking up Michael Walzer's concepts of "thick" and "thin" cultures, and attending to the *social context of use* (i.e., the larger complex of community values, as reflected in an educational process intended to preserve and enhance those values in the use of computing technologies).

In light of both theory and praxis, an electronic global village incorporating Habermas's conception of partial publics is possible. But the conditions of its possibility include both attention to the social context of use as well as a (re)new(ed) theoretical attention to *embodiment*—attention apparent in a recent renaissance of interest in hermeneutics and phenomenology, as well as postmodern feminism. Building on the work of Cees Hamelink and others, I argue that a moral imperative emerges here for a Socratic education that attends to diverse cultural values and communicative preferences on the model of Renaissance women and men who are fluent in and can comfortably negotiate among multiple cultures and communication styles. Such Socratically educated Renaissance women and men are required first of all as an antidote to the otherwise prevailing tendency of a commercialized Internet to create "cultural tourists" and "cultural consumers"—"the Borg with a smiling face"—who thereby sustain a computer-mediated colonization. In Habermasian terms, moreover, such an education fulfills the requirements for empathic *perspective-taking* and *solidarity* with one's dialogical partners and sister/fellow *cosmo-politans* (world citizens). In Aristotelian terms, finally, such education aims toward *phronesis*, the prudence or practical wisdom necessary to everyday judgment in ethics, politics, and human contentment.[4]

A computer ethics shaped by these theoretical and praxis-oriented insights—including models drawn from the ancient, Medieval, and Renaissance worlds—thus finds resources in diverse ethical and cultural traditions to bring to bear on contemporary problems, rather than starting de novo. At the same time, this form of computer ethics emphasizes the need to design and implement CMC technologies in ways that sustain and enhance diverse cultural values—in part by requiring that users of a genuinely worldwide Web develop a cultural and communicative literacy that allows them to comfortably negotiate among a diversity of culturally distinct moral communities. Finally, by emphasizing a moral imperative to sustain diverse cultural values and communicative preferences (i.e., beyond those approaches that stress ethics as needed to control harmful behaviors facilitated by CMC), a computer ethics oriented toward culture and communication would work as a form of virtue ethics (Western) that also moves toward becoming "exemplary persons" (*junzi*—Confucian)—and as a (Western) ethics of care that deeply resonates with Confucian emphases on care and responsibility for the whole human community and natural order. Such a "glocalized" ethics—that is, ethics that conjoin local ethical traditions with a global pluralism that goes beyond the local and its attendant risks of dogmatic ethnocentrism—provides a middle ground that may escape the otherwise Manichean choice between a homogenized McWorld and fragmented plurality. Rather, the *humane beings* shaped by such a glocalized education and ethos could then take up CMC technologies as a means toward greater human excellence, perhaps on new scales and levels.

WILL CMC TECHNOLOGIES INEVITABLY DEMOCRATIZE AN ELECTRONIC "GLOBAL VILLAGE"?

The claim is frequently made that CMC technologies "democratize"—meaning, generally, that these technologies will flatten local and global hierarchies (including those of corporate culture) as they bring about a greater freedom and equality. While popular literatures tend to assume that "democracy" means libertarian and plebiscite forms (i.e., emphasizing individual freedom *from* the constraints of communities and a notion of a direct "one person, one vote" rule by simple majority), in the scholarly literature communitarian and pluralist forms of democracy are defended by theorists who draw on Habermas's theory of communicative reason, the ideal speech situation, discourse communities, and a public sphere that realizes the freedom, equality, and critical rationality required for democracy (see Harrison and Falvey, 2001, for a comprehensive overview of the literatures of democracy in CMC, as well as Ess, 1996, pp. 198–212, and Hamelink, 2000, pp. 165–185). For postmodern and feminist critics, however, Habermas is simply another expression of a modern Enlightenment conception of rationality that, despite its intentions to liberate both the individual and society, paradoxically—indeed, dialectically (see Horkheimer and Adorno, 1972)—leads instead to a totalizing/instrumental conception of reason that only conspires to objectify and enslave humanity in ruthlessly efficient, technologically facilitated totalitarian regimes (see Poster, 1997, pp. 206–210, for a representative overview of postmodern criticisms of Habermas). Habermas has responded to these critiques by first arguing that postmodernism rests on an epistemological and ethical relativism that contradicts its own clear value preferences, including its own insistence on liberation and democracy. He has also incorporated especially feminist notions of solidarity and perspective-taking into his conception of communicative reason in order to more clearly differentiate communicative reason from the forms of modern/instrumental reason targeted by feminists and postmodernists.[5]

More recent debate between Habermas and critics such as Niklas Luhmann has further sharpened the theoretical and practical limitations of Habermas's conception of democracy and the public sphere. For example, Barbara Becker and Josef Wehner echo postmodern analyses of the fragmenting and decentering effects of CMC (see especially Jones, 2001) as they observe that the interactive communications characteristic of the Internet amount to special interest groups—that is, small groups of people bound together only by a common interest but otherwise scattered geographically and culturally and not necessarily connected (or interested) in any larger, more commonly shared universe of discourse concerning pressing political issues, and so on. In addition, Becker and Wehner see several significant obstacles to electronic democracy, whether in the form of libertarian "electronic town halls" or a Habermasian public sphere, beginning with the massive maldistribution of the economic resources and infrastructure required to participate in either. They further take up Bourdieu's notion of cultural capital (1984) to point out that not everyone has the level of education needed to participate meaningfully in Internet exchanges. (In other terms, these are central factors contributing to the digital divide.) Finally, the information superhighway threatens to drown us in an information flood: "Through networking, more and more participants have a voice; but because of the increasing number of participants, there is less and less time to listen" (2001, p. 79). In the face of these difficulties, Becker and Wehner take up Habermas's conception of *Teilöffentlichkeiten* (partial

publics)—including professional organizations, university clubs, special interest groups, and so on—as loci of discourses that contribute to a larger democratic process in modern societies. Over against the antidemocratic impacts and
potentials of CMC, they see this Habermasian notion as describing an important way in which CMC technologies may sustain (within limits) a "civil society" as part of a larger democratic process. Such partial publics can be viewed
as something of a theoretical compromise between a full-fledged public sphere
on the Internet and its complete absence in the celebrated postmodernist
fragmentation and decentering (cf. Jones's conceptions of "micropolis" and
"compunity," 2001, pp. 56–57; Holmes, 2000).[6]

HABERMASIAN THEORY IN LIGHT OF PRAXIS

In their comprehensive review of the literature on CMC and democracy,
Harrison and Falvey (2001) find widely divergent results regarding the question as to whether CMC technologies in fact further some form of democratic communicative action. Some positive examples can be found—including
Harrison and Stephen's study of some forty community networks that fulfilled
their intentions of providing equal access to information by offering free
access to the network, including, in some cases, equipment in public places
for utilizing network resources (1998). By the same token, if we now turn to
what happens in praxis—that is, what occurs when CMC technologies are
deployed in specific settings—we find that there are both *examples* and *counterexamples* to a Habermasian conception of a public sphere online, as well as
significant middle grounds.[7]

EXAMPLES

CMC researchers have documented a number of discourse groups that fulfill
the Habermasian description of partial publics, including NGOs' use of the
Internet to organize and coordinate their activities (e.g., in Uganda: see
McConnell, 1998; a men's discussion group: see Rutter and Smith, 1998).
Ethnic communities—including emigré Chinese communities (Joo-Young
Jung, 2000) and diaspora Russians (Sapienza, 1999)—also use the Internet
and the Web to sustain connections with friends and family who are geographically dispersed. Insofar as these uses entail the creation of an electronic
partial public that sustains shared discussion of community issues, they are
consistent with Becker and Wehner's argument that the Internet supports
partial publics.[8]

COUNTEREXAMPLES

At the same time, however, counterexamples to the democratization thesis
abound. Anthropological, feminist, and postmodern authors provide exam-

ples of CMC technologies serving authoritarian ends and preserving cultural hierarchies of power, status, privilege, and so on.

At one end of the spectrum of possible responses to CMC technologies, the eKiribati, a nation in the Solomon Islands, has rejected the introduction of the Internet into their communities—in part, precisely because of its putative claims to opening up and leveling communication among participants. Because of cultural traditions that include an acceptance of secrecy and limited access to specific kinds of information, the eKiribati see the ostensive democratization potential of the Internet as a threat to this element of their cultural identity (Sofield, 2000).[9]

Louise Postma (2001) has further documented the ways in which indigenous peoples in South Africa conform to the prevailing cultural capital (Bourdieu, 1984) of the European culture that defines 'learning centers.' The norms of the dominant culture are appropriated by learning center users and used *against* their original cultural norms and values, including *epistemological* preferences for orality and performance as primary modes of communication. Using Friere's terms, the technologies thus support a *situational empowerment*—one that comes from conformity to prevailing norms and values—rather than a *critical empowerment,* one that sustains and enhances diverse modes of individual and group styles, values, acts, and so on. In particular, the learning centers foster *individual* excellence over group achievement—a preference that is distinctively Western (2001, p. 326). This finding is consistent with other research, beginning with Hofstede (1980, 1983, 1984, 1991) and Hofstede and Bond (1988), that highlights the contrast—and potential conflicts—between Western emphases on the individual vis-à-vis Eastern and traditional emphases on the community. Where CMC technologies foster individualism—precisely as they are touted as ways of achieving *individual* excellence and achievement—then they are understandably perceived in more community-oriented cultures as a threat to a most basic cultural norm.

Sunny Yoon (1996, 2001) has documented a number of ways in which cultural and commercial factors work in the context of South Korea *against* any potential democratization effects—including any electronic "public sphere" envisioned along Habermasian lines. Rather, the Internet and the Web, especially as shaped by the forces of commercialization, can work instead as controlling mechanisms for capital and power.

Yoon's analysis relies on both Foucault (see Yoon, 1996) and Bourdieu's notion of *Habitus* (1977). *Habitus* highlights the role of individual will power and choice as manifested in individuals' everyday practices: these in turn build up the larger society and history in an "orchestra effect." In addition, Bourdieu describes "cultural capital"—including symbolic and institutional power such as language and education as constituting a *meconnaissance* ("misconsciousness"), a kind of false consciousness that legitimates existing authorities.

Through a quantitative analysis, Yoon demonstrates that rather than encouraging use of the Internet as a medium of participatory communication, the way Korean newspapers report on the Internet contributes to the commercialization of the Net: such commercialization further contributes to the Korean "digital divide," that is, unequal access to and distribution of information resources.[10] Through interviews with young Koreans ("Gen-Xers"), Yoon then shows that as use of the Internet shapes educational rules and linguistic habits, it thus exercises symbolic or positive power—including symbolic violence in Bourdieu's sense. Specifically, Internet use leads Korean students to accept the significance of English as the lingua franca of the Internet without question. Language thereby becomes a cultural capital that exercises "symbolic power over the cultural have-nots in the virtual world system," a cultural capital that induces a "voluntary subjugation" (2001, p. 257).[11]

Finally, Yoon's informants make it clear that individuals take up the Internet not because of its democratizing potentials but, on the contrary, because it increases their status, and, in Hofstede's terms, their power distance over others. In particular, because teachers, principals, and parents rely on their students and children to accomplish computer-related tasks (e.g., designing Web pages), young people acquire a remarkable new power over their elders, one that directly contradicts the traditional Confucian sense of obedience to and respect for these traditional authority figures. This finding is not only consistent with other research in those countries shaped by the Confucian tradition:[12] it further makes clear that what may look like democratization in Western cultural contexts (as the Internet opens up communication and empowers individuals) can, in other cultural contexts, work in directly antidemocratic ways, as the Internet simply transfers hierarchical power and status from one group to another.

MIDDLE GROUNDS

Finally, there are some significant examples of CMC technologies leading to at least a partial fulfillment of hopes for democracy and equality in cultural contexts previously marked by more centralized and hierarchical forms of government. To begin with, Michael Dahan (1999) has documented ways in which the introduction of the Internet, along with several other important cultural and political developments, helped Israel shift toward greater openness and democracy. Indeed, Dahan has undertaken an ambitious experiment to use the Internet to foster greater openness—indeed, friendship—among Palestinians and Israelis. This experiment exceeded his best expectations, as Israelis and Palestinians, after months of communication via the Internet, came together for a first face-to-face meeting that solidified sensibilities of respect and friendship initially fostered online. This experience, unfortunately, culminated just prior to the most recent outbreak of violence between Israelis and Palestinians, leaving its future very uncertain (Dahan, 2001).

Deborah Wheeler (2001) tests the democratization promise with an ethnographic study of Kuwaiti women and their use of the Internet—with decidedly mixed results. On the one hand, these new technologies appear to have a liberating impact for younger women—for example, as they allow women to converse "unescorted" with men in chat rooms, and to meet and choose mates on their own (rather than agree to the cultural norm of arranged marriages). On the other hand, the cultural restrictions against women speaking openly are directly mirrored in distinctively male and female uses of the Internet and the Web. As she observes, new communication technologies—despite the (deterministic) assumptions of Western CMC enthusiasts who believe that "wiring the world" will automatically issue in greater communicative openness and democracy—do not automatically liberate us from the distinctive cultural values that define specific societies (2001, p. 202).

As a final but also exemplary instance of such middle grounds, we can consider Hongladarom's analyses of Thai USENET newsgroups and online chat groups (2000, 2001). Hongladarom first documents how a Thai newsgroup established modes of communication—including the question of whether Thai should be the official language of the newsgroup—that reinforced local cultural identity and community. In Michael Walzer's terms (1994), Hongladarom refers to this as a manifestation of "thick culture," that is, a worldview both deep and broad enough to define basic beliefs, values, communication preferences, and so on that vary—sometimes markedly—from culture to culture. At the same time, however, participating in a local newsgroup did not prevent Thais from also taking up the communication abilities of an umbrella "cosmopolitan culture" (2001, p. 317) or, in Walzer's terms, a "thin culture." This thin culture is marked by a shared lingua franca—English and its pidgens—that makes for functional but limited communication (e.g., as when airline pilots globally use English). Again, despite the deterministic view that CMC technologies, as embedding Western cultural values, will thus inevitably reshape "target" cultures along the lines of democracy, individualism, and so on, Hongladarom finds that a global Internet culture as "thin" is not necessarily able to override local "thick culture" and its attendant practices.[13] Rather, individuals seem able to maneuver within and between both a thick local culture and a thin global culture.[14]

A HABERMASIAN/DEMOCRATIC ELECTRONIC GLOBAL VILLAGE? THE (RE)TURN TO EMBODIMENT

These theoretical considerations and practical examples drawn from a variety of cultures suggest that an electronic global village—especially if such a village is to be democratic in ways at least partially informed by Habermas's conception of partial publics and is to preserve and enhance diverse cultural identities—is possible. But this survey also makes it clear that realizing this possibility rests on at least two conditions. First, especially regarding Hongladarom's example of the discussion concerning the language to be used in the Thai chat room, realizing a Habermasian partial public and its associated forms of democratic discourse requires *conscious attention to the social context of use, including education.* This same point is made, as we saw (note 14), in Sy's example (2001) of consciously appropriating Borgmann's notion of focal things and practices (1984), and the focus in the UNIMAS/Barrio project on the prevailing social preferences of the Kelabit (Harris et al., 2001). Finally, the necessity of attention to *social context of use* is further consistent with the analyses provided by Postma and Yoon as well as the comprehensive survey undertaken by Harrison and Falvey (2001).

Indeed, several writers have argued recently that the kind of education required for undertaking the attention to fundamental values defining cultural worldviews and for making the choices regarding the implementation of CMC in diverse settings that will avoid cultural homogenization is precisely a *Socratic* education that stresses critical thinking regarding one's own beliefs as well as those of others. Most broadly, such an education will prepare people for what Cees Hamelink has described as the "'culture of dialogue' that the democratic process requires" (2000, p. 184; cf. Dreyfus 2001).

Second, this attention to social context of use also means a (re)new(ed) attention to the role of *embodiment* in our epistemologies and ontologies, our ethics and our politics. That is, earlier optimism regarding the inevitable march of a computer-mediated democracy as facilitated by wiring the world with the CMC technologies of the Web and the Internet rested in part on a view of the self in cyberspace as somehow radically disconnected from the body at the terminal—where this body was subject to and carrier of specific histories, traditions, and cultural shapings. Especially in light of the *cultural* differences between the West, the Middle East, Asia, and indigenous peoples—to assume that wiring the world will automatically move CMC users to more egalitarian and democratic modes of engagement requires us to assume that the self in cyberspace must be radically divorced from its life as an embodied member of a culture that may stress more hierarchical and less democratic modes of engagement. (Two of the best known proponents of this Cartesian—indeed, Gnostic dualism—are the early Donna Haraway [1990] and John Perry Barlow [1996]: both argue that liberation and equality promised by cyberspace will be found only by a radical rejection of the embodied self in a world Barlow contemptuously called "meatspace." Here Barlow borrows directly from William Gibson's *Neuromancer* [1984], a science fiction novel of enormous influence on our notions of cyberspace—first of all, as *Neuromancer* introduces this term.[15]) By contrast, the results from praxis make clear that while Western CMC technologies in fact embed and foster specific Western values and communication preferences, both Western and non-Western users of these technologies are not simply reshaped to conform to those values and preferences. On the contrary, as the examples described of the Thai coffeehouse, the UNIMAS/Barrio project, and the Filippino "cyberbarangay" suggest, individuals and groups may *both* take up CMC technologies ("thin" culture) and remain well anchored in their distinctive cultural preferences and values ("thick" culture). But this means that CMC users still enmeshed in their distinctive "thick culture" are *embodied* users—selves ultimately interwoven with a specific body in a specific history, community, and culture.[16]

These middle grounds between individuals and groups as either (1) entirely unaffected or (2) entirely reshaped by the cultural values and communicative preferences embedded in Western CMC technologies, moreover, cohere with other indications that we are turning from the more polarized notions of modernists versus postmodernists, cyberhells versus cyberheavens, and so on that tended to dominate 1990s discourse and literature. In particular, there is a clear turn *from* a Cartesian (indeed, Gnostic or "cybergnostic") dualism underlying not only cyborg enthusiasm of the early Donna Haraway but also "Ectopians" such as Hans Morovec (1988) who hope to find liberation for a disembodied mind in cyberspace *to* a focus on *embodiment* as analyzed from hermeneutical, phenomenological, and/or feminist perspectives.

A primary example of this turn is the work of Barbara Becker (1997, 2000, 2001, 2002). Becker seeks to conjoin Luhmann, Hayles, Habermas, and others in her phenomenological account of embodied existence. Becker points out that postmodern theories (constructivism, deconstruction, and Luhmann's system theory) and the deconstructive feminist theory of Judith Butler jointly emphasize "the discursive and cultural construction of body, sex and nature" (2001, p. 69)—an approach that further parallels current approaches in artificial intelligence and Haraway's hopes for liberation in cyberspace. But in Becker's view, all these theories run the risk of overlooking the particular *materiality* of bodies, subjects, and nature by reducing them to exclusively textual, discursive, or medial constructions. She counters these theories of disembodied selves with her own conception of *responsivity*, that is, a cooperation between body and mind, subject and object, nature and culture.[17]

In particular, despite the cyberfeminism of early Donna Haraway, Becker argues that while we must acknowledge

> the undoubtedly discursive construction of body and identity, the own sense [*EigenSinn*] of materiality cannot totally be reduced to an effect of social practices and narratives. The materiality of the body implies its own generative power and creates its own emphases apart from all discursive and technical

domination. Accordingly the body is not an empty space of social attributions but it participates in the process of creating atmospheres and open
spaces of meaning beyond explicit communication and cultural formations.
Considering this, materiality and in particular bodies have to be regarded as
actors in the process of constituting sociality instead of treating them as passive instances. (2001, p. 58f.)

To denote this sense of a material body active in shaping its social existence,
Becker uses the neologism *LeibSubject*, "BodySubject," in explicit contrast
with a radical split between *Geist* and *Leib*, mind and body. This split, it
should be clear, underlies postmodern conceptions of a *Geist* liberated from
Leib in cyberspace. By contrast, Becker develops a rich account of how the
self as a *LeibSubject* exists in the threshold (*Schwelle*) of interaction between
Geist and *KörperLeib*, between one BodySubject and an "Other" (*Fremde*),
between self as BodySubject and an environment (*Umwelt*).[18]

Not only is there an inexorable connection between body and self:
Becker expands on Heidegger to develop a notion of "being-toward-the-
world" (*Zur-Welt-Sein*)—and thereby to speak of the BodySubject as embedded in the world (*Welteinbettung*). In this light, "cybernauts," while appearing
to pursue a postmodern overcoming of all traditional viewpoints, in fact simply "reestablish the traditional vision of domination" of the material/bodily
worlds thematic of modernity since Descartes. Like Descartes, they can do so,
finally, only by committing to a radical dualism that separates the self (*etre
raisonnable*) from body (*etre sensible*) so as to make the latter something inferior and to be mastered—or, as Haraway and Morovec would have it, escaped.
But if Becker's account of self as a "BodySubject" is correct, such escape is
illusory at best and threatens instead to disconnect us from existence as
embodied beings inextricably interwoven with a larger environment
(*Umwelt*), including a society that shapes our sense of self through language
and ritual.[19]

Becker's work coheres with other recent phenomenologically grounded
analyses—most notably, by Albert Borgmann (1999) and Hubert Dreyfus
(2001). Dreyfus is especially useful here because his account of how we learn
as *embodied* creatures is immediately conjoined with an explicitly Aristotelian
understanding of learning as oriented toward the development of *phronesis*,
the excellence or virtue of practical wisdom or judgment that is central to our
lives as ethical and political creatures.[20] Most briefly: the *practice* of the habits
and skills necessary for acquiring *phronesis* as a kind of lived wisdom requires
a lifetime of engagement with one another as embodied beings—in part, as
Dreyfus argues, because acquiring and practicing the highest levels of knowledge and skill, including *phronesis*, require long apprenticeship in real-world,
embodied settings: as informed by and applied to the nearly infinite variability of the fine-grained details that mark out each real-world context as dif-

ferent from others in ethically relevant ways—these knowledges, habits, and wisdom go far beyond the sort of general, conceptual knowledge that can be taught and applied in (current) online settings. As we will see more fully by way of conclusion, moreover, this (re)turn to *embodiment* and *phronesis* is a hopeful sign for a *global* ethics that will include Eastern perspectives. Briefly, such *nondual* conceptions of humanity not only allow us to recover more classical and traditional conceptions of being human—and thereby important ethical and political resources for how we should guide our lives: at the same time, these nondual conceptions, oriented toward human excellence or *virtue* ethics and bringing to the foreground the role of *care* (e.g., in perspective-taking and solidarity) more directly cohere with Eastern conceptions.

THE INTERNET AND OUR MORAL LIFE: THE EDUCATIONAL IMPERATIVE

Taken together, these two conditions—attention to social context of use, including an appropriate Socratic–Aristotelian education, and a renewed appreciation for the central significance of embodiment in shaping our knowledge of the world, our engagement with one another as members of distinctive cultures, and so on—point to a moral imperative in education. On the one hand, the prevailing values and practices of "surfing the Web" are shaped largely by a commercially driven culture that emphasizes consumption. Especially as the Internet and the Web make it increasingly easy to encounter culturally distinctive "Others" (i.e., as more and more cultures and peoples produce Web-based resources as a way of making themselves known, of advertising their products for sale, etc.), the bias in a commercializing Web and Internet is thus toward becoming "cultural consumers" and "cultural tourists" as diverse cultural resources are commodified for consumption. For the cultural consumer and tourist, the "Other" is merely another consumable resource—an object to be taken in, if desired, and/or rejected according to one's whim or taste. In this way, a commercialized Web and Internet tend to shape us into a consumer version of the Borg—the *Star Trek* creatures who relentlessly consume all biological and cultural resources and homogenize them into a single "culture" of complete submission to "hive-mind." Such consumerist drones may be perfectly suited to helping economies hum along; in all likelihood, however, they will fail to embody the habits, values, skills, and goals of which excellent human beings (East or West), *phronesis*, and democracies are made.

By contrast, I have argued that we are well guided in our thinking about the Internet and the Web by the historical examples of the Middle Ages and the Renaissance (2000). As Mehl (2000) and others have pointed out, our time—including the technologies of the Web and the Internet—resembles the Medieval and Renaissance experience of cultural flows, for example, the mixtures of Jewish, Christian, and Muslim philosophy and science, further spiced with a rich infusion of Chinese technology and invention, that issue into what we now call the natural sciences. At the same time, the dramatically expanding knowledge of "Others" for the Renaissance human beings—from the recovered worldviews of the Greeks and Romans to increasing understanding of Asia, the Muslim world, and the peoples of the New World—led not only to colonization and warfare but also precisely to the crucial *humanist* and *cosmopolitan* sensibilities that emphasized *both* immersion into the richness of diverse cultures and the possibility of coming to understand at least some elements shared by all human beings. Hence, we can complement Cees Hamelink's account of the necessity of a *Socratic* education for a global ethic with the further recognition that a Renaissance humanism is at least in part an expression of the Socratic project. As the allegory of the cave makes especially clear, this education is about moving beyond the prevailing beliefs, values, and assumptions of our native culture to a larger perspective that helps us recognize the strengths and limits of a given cultural worldview. In anthropological terms, education of this sort is a move beyond our ethnocentrism—a move facilitated not only by philosophical analyses of worldviews, but most especially by the experience of living as an embodied being in a culture and linguistic world different from our own. Both philosophy and experience in other cultures thus lead to a form of cultural humility—one that recognizes that every view is at best partial, but that a more complete understanding of both ourselves and others may be reached by becoming familiar with a variety of cultures and philosophies, rather than remaining dogmatically content with just one.

Indeed, it would seem that a Socratic-Renaissance education is marked precisely by a recognition of the central importance of *embodiment*. As is well known, the Renaissance is centrally marked by a return to classical models of philosophy, art, and literature—a turn that not only recalls attention to classical virtue ethics in Socrates, Plato, and Aristotle, but also to an especially Greek affirmation and celebration of the *body*, in contrast with what Nietzsche has called "the metaphysics of the hangman," that is, the tendency toward dualism, especially in orthodox Christianity, that denigrates body in particular and this life in general for the sake of an otherworldly reward (1988, p. 500). The emphasis in Renaissance humanism on immersion in "other" languages and cultures—in particular, through travel—clearly presumes that such education is for Greek-like, *embodied* minds.[21] Analogously, Dreyfus's critique of distance learning vis-à-vis the highest goals of liberal learning—precisely the habits, skills, and *phronesis* of embodied human beings—makes explicit the connection between Socratic-Renaissance education as one that is not only oriented toward the skills of rational dialogue, but also the Aristotelian virtue of *phronesis*, as both the goal and condition of the good life for *embodied* human beings.

In short, to realize a Habermasian form of democracy requires a Socratic–Aristotelian education that emphasizes critical thinking and dialogue among *embodied* human beings as essential conditions of democracy. The Renaissance model also calls for educating human beings to be familiar with the languages, values, beliefs, and practices of multiple cultures—thus moving us beyond our own cultural skins so that we can inhabit the lifeworld of genuinely different cultures and peoples. A Socratic–Aristotelian education is thus called for that emphasizes critical thinking and dialogue—but also a deep engagement with "other" cultures, languages, and worldviews as a way of helping us move out of our particular cultural cave to a more considered position of appreciation for diverse cultures and a correlative epistemological humility regarding any single claim or worldview. Doing so, finally, aims precisely at the development of *phronesis*, the practical wisdom or judgment, required of human beings, not only for the sake of ethical virtue and political justice, but finally for enjoying a genuinely good life as embodied beings in community with one another.

Such an education is clearly an antidote to the consumerist bias of the Web and the Net, which instead encourage us to view the Other as a customer and/or exploitable resource. In this second direction, we can further note that such a Socratic–Aristotelian–Renaissance education fulfills the Habermasian/feminist requirements for perspective-taking and solidarity. That is, especially as we become more and more familiar with the values and communicative preferences that define distinctive cultures—rather than feeling compelled to overrun those cultures and redefine them along the lines of our own communicative preferences and values (a "hegemonic cultural monologue"), we are better prepared to engage in a genuine *dialogue* that instantiates communication between two (or more) distinct partners whose identity is preserved and enriched through the exchange.[22] This involves us, as both Hongladarom (2001) and Jones (2001) emphasize, in Carey's notion of communication as *ritual*, a mode of communication that helps individuals cohere as a community, in part as such communication engages not simply an intellectual exchange of ideas, but a multisensory/emotive experience, such as that shaped by ritual, theater, spectacle, and so on. To say it another way: such an education, as it focuses centrally on the role of living and knowing as an *embodied* creature in a world of multiple cultures and peoples, and on moving in more just and democratic directions, will consist of the theory and praxis of making the world more and more a place in which both our minds and bodies are at home.[23]

This last formulation, finally, suggests a strong connection between this largely Western approach to developing a computer ethics and at least one distinctively Eastern framework—namely, Confucian ethics.[24] To begin with, the terms used to describe personhood (*ren*) and a person's thoughts and feelings (*xin*) defy the Gnostic/Cartesian emphasis on a radical mind–body split. First, *ren* is one's entire person: one's cultivated cognitive, aesthetic, moral, and religious sensibilities as they are expressed in one's ritualized roles and relationships. It is one's "field of selves," the sum of significant relationships, that constitute one as a resolutely social person. *Ren* is not only mental, but physical as well: one's posture and comportment, gestures and bodily communication. (Ames and Rosemont, 1998, p. 49)

Similarly, Ames and Rosemont render *xin* as "heart-and-mind," despite the Western mind–body dichotomy, to make the point that "there are no altogether disembodied thoughts for Confucious, nor any raw feelings altogether lacking (what in English would be called) 'cognitive content'" (1998, p. 56). In these ways, then, there is a strong resonance between these classical Chinese conceptions and those emerging in Western efforts to overcome the various problems of a radical mind–body split—including its CMC-related forms (the "cybergnosticism" of early Haraway and Perry)—for example, what Hayles labels a "posthuman" (i.e., post-Cartesian) self, and what Becker (2001) simply calls the "BodySubject."

In fact, on the basis of what Tu Wei-Ming terms our "embodied humanity" (1999, p. 30), Confucian ethics conjoins in Western terms (1) a Socratic virtue ethics with (2) an ethics of care that resonates with both feminist and environmental ethics. First, just as both Socratic and Aristotelian virtue ethics emphasize the primary importance of developing those habits *(ethos)* that allow us to become "virtuous" (i.e., from *arete*, "excellence") human beings (see Aristotle, *Nichomachean Ethics*, esp. Book II, pp. 1103a14–26), so Confucian ethics likewise emphasizes the life goal of becoming a *junzi*, an exemplary person, one who, as *ren* and *xin* (see earlier), thus *embodies* humane excellence (Ames and Rosemont, 1998, p. 62f.). As Tu Wei-Ming makes clear, moreover, the Confucian emphasis on *embodied* humanity is at the same time an emphasis on the self as a *relational* (rather than atomistic) self—that is, one inextricably interrelated with community, nature, and heaven *(tian)* (1999, p. 33). This means, second, that the primary Confucian ethos of filial piety, "as an authentic manifestation of embodied love," and as refracted through these moments of interrelationship, thus issues in a primary posture of *gratitude* and *thanksgiving* "to those to whom we owe our subsistence, development, education, well-being, life, and existence," namely, "Heaven, Earth, Ruler, Parents, and Teachers" (1999, p. 34). Analogous to Western ethics of care for both the human and ecological communities, this Confucian ethos thus entails a sense of fidelity and fiduciary responsibility to a community that begins in family and ultimately encompasses the world (1999, p. 35).

Finally, the Confucian emphasis on an embodied self as inextricably interrelated through family, community, Earth, and heaven, thereby issues in an ethos that is at once local and global. As embodied centers of relationships, we are "a concrete living person," persons who are "embedded in our sociality" (Tu, 1999, p. 35). This means that "our ethnicity, gender, language, land, class, and faith are constitutive elements of who we really are." But because this self is interrelational, the twin duties of filial piety and self-cultivation (becoming fully human/e) issue in "respect for the teacher, loyalty to nation, caring for the suffering of others, sympathy with the myriad things and veneration for Heaven, Earth, sages, and worthies" that go beyond ethnocentrism and simply local loyalties (Tu, 1999, p. 36). Rather, while clearly rooted in the embodied and thus local self and community, such an ethos at the same time issues in the "universal human aspirations" of "mutuality with community, harmony with nature, and continuous communication with Heaven." Just as a Socratic-Renaissance education for embodied human beings seeks to conjoin a more universal global ethic with respect for (and rootedness in) local ethical traditions, so Confucian ethics, on this showing, is likewise a "glocalized" ethics—that is, an ethics that encompasses the local traditions and values of embodied persons as thus members of specific ethical and political communities, while at the same time passes beyond these (and their risks of dogmatic ethnocentrism) to a more universal view that stresses care and responsibility for the whole human community and the natural order.

Taken in these directions, a Socratic education in critical thinking and dialogical skills, coupled with Aristotelian and Confucian ethics and a Renaissance immersion in multiple cultures, languages, and lifeworlds, might serve as a more genuinely global ethics—one required for use of the Internet and the Web as technologies with a global reach. Such a locally rooted and globally oriented computer ethics would help us realize some of the best possibilities of the Internet and the Web, as these technologies open up genuinely global cultural flows—flows that, as the Middle Ages and the Renaissance have demonstrated, further reveal new combinations and ways of being fully human. At the same time, by increasing the urgency for developing such an ethics and facilitating its development precisely through its global reach, the Internet would become both motivator and means toward greater human excellence, perhaps on new scales and levels.

NOTES

An earlier version of this chapter appeared in *Ethics and Information Technology* IV (1) (February 2002): 11–22. I am grateful to the editor, Jeroen van den Hoven, for kind permission to reprint portions of my earlier article here. I would also like to express my deep appreciation to Henry Rosemont, Jr., Hans-Georg Moeller, and the participants in three conferences: "Information Technologies and the Universities of Asia," Bangkok, Thailand, April 3–5, 2002; the 13th Symposium ("Ethik Ost und West: Ethics East and West," June 4–8, 2001); and 14th Symposium ("Tod Ost und West: Death East and West," May 20–24, 2002) of the Académie du Midi/Institut für Philosophie. If my suggestions for a global ethic, especially one cohering with Eastern worldviews and traditions, have any merit, it is due in large measure to their acute criticism and generous wisdom as I first explored these coherencies in these contexts.

1. Although the available literature, including Web pages, on the digital divide is now overwhelming (a Google search on "digital divide" results in over 549,000 Web pages), the interested reader can usefully begin with the September 2000 report by the Pew Internet and American Life Project, "Who's Not Online?" (http://www.pewinternet.org/reports/toc.asp?Report=21). A more recent analyses, "A NATION ONLINE: How Americans Are Expanding Their Use of the Internet" uses the most recent U.S. census data (http://www.ntia.doc.gov/ntiahome/dn/index.html).

Of course, analyses of the digital divide reflect political commitments. On the one hand, the Bush administration has argued that the digital divide is no longer a significant issue—a claim challenged by the Consumers Union in May 2002 (see http://www.consumerfed.org/DigitalDivideReport20020530.pdf). At the same time, the United Nations has been gearing up for its "World Summit on the Information Society" in November 2005 (see http://www.itu.int/wsis/).

From the standpoint developed in this chapter, however, the digital divide must be understood not simply as a matter of economic, material, and infrastructure disparities: it is also very much a matter of *culture* (see note 2).

2. It is arguable that the digital divide is not simply the result of extant economic, political, and infrastructure disparities; in addition, the digital divide is exacerbated precisely by *cultural* differences of the sort explored in this chapter. We will see in the analyses by Sofield (2000), Becker and Wehner (2001), Postma (2001), and Yoon (1996, 2001) that this divide reflects a split between those who possess the *cultural capital* (see Bourdieu) needed to access CMC technologies and those who do not possess this capital, either by way of their national and/or socioeconomic status, and/or because they *choose* (as in the case, e.g., of the eKiribati—Sofield, 2000), in the name of preserving distinctive cultural identity, not to engage in the current forms of CMC technologies precisely because they embed and foster specifically Western cultural values and communication preferences. In particular, Yoon (2001) makes clear how the commercialization of the Internet contributes to the Korean digital divide. (See also note 10, below.)

This view of the role of culture and the presence/absence of the specific sorts of cultural capital needed to successfully exploit CMC technologies is further supported by the global study of Maitland and Bauer (2001), who found that, along with infrastructure factors, the *cultural factors* of being able to use English and what Hofstede (1980, 1983) identified as "low power distance" (i.e., characteristic of those societies—including many Western societies—as less hierarchical than "high power distance" societies, that include many Eastern societies) as consistently contributing to *greater technology diffusion* in a given country/culture.

3. Barber points out that *jihad* in Islam denotes primarily an internal spiritual struggle. Only secondarily does it mean a "holy war"—and even then only a defensive war. It is but one more artifact of the long centuries of hostility between Islam and Christendom, and then between Islam and "the West," that *jihad* has come to mean the "evangelical" offensive war exemplified in Western journalistic usage of the term. Although Barber acknowledges that his use of the term is thus "rhetorical"—that use is offensive to Muslims first of all, as it reinforces the Western stereotype of Islam as a

war-like religion. Indeed, this use of the term should be offensive to people of all faiths, who recognize and value the deep interrelations between Judaism, Christianity, and Islam as the Abrahamic religions of the West: this stereotype turns on its head a religious emphasis shared among these traditions *and* the major religions of Asia (Hinduism, Buddhism, Confucianism) on practicing compassion toward all members of the human family and a correlative emphasis on resolving conflict through nonviolent means whenever possible (cf. Rosemont, 2001). In addition, anyone valuing logic should abhor the stereotype as it takes a very tiny number of "fundamentalists" to be representative of all Muslims. On both religious and philosophical grounds, the stereotype is false and misleading, and absolutely contradicts the spirit of dialogue intended here.

4. Aristotle defines *phronesis* as an excellence or virtue *(arete)*, consisting of "a truth-attaining rational quality, concerned with action in relation to the things that are good for human beings" *(Nichomachean Ethics* VI.v.6). Jaeger takes Aristotle to mean here "an habitual disposition of the mind to deliberate practically about everything concerning human weal and woe (1934, p. 83, referring to 1140b4 and 220). He further connects Aristotle to Socrates on this point: "To Socrates *phronesis* had meant the ethical power of reason, a sense modeled on the common usage that Aristotle restores to its rights in the *Nicomachean Ethics*" (1934, p. 83).

5. Habermas develops these concepts initially in his theory of communicative action in two volumes so titled (1984a, 1987a). Two additional essays necessary for understanding Habermas are "Discourse Ethics" (1990) and "Justice and Solidarity" (1989). In the latter, Habermas argues that the ideal speech situation requires not only the rules of discourse (as intending to guarantee free and equal participation in conversations) that will lead to consensus shaped solely by "the force of the better argument and no other force" (Nielsen, 1990, p. 104). To be the legitimate source of community norms—i.e., norms that all agree to follow—such consensus further requires a sense of *solidarity* between participants. Habermas defines solidarity as a concern for "the welfare of consociates who are intimately linked in an intersubjectively shared form of life and thus also to the maintenance of the integrity of this form of life itself" (p. 47, quoted in Ingram 1990, p. 149). Finally, this apparently empathic concern for others requires a *perspective-taking* in which "everybody is stimulated to adopt the perspective of all others in order that they might examine the acceptability of a solution according to the way every other person understands themselves and the world" (Nielsen, 1990, p. 98; cf. Benhabib, 1992, pp. 8–9).

By incorporating especially feminist emphases on the crucial role of emotion and empathy in shaping judgments and our inevitable entanglement with one another in the Webs of relationships that form human communities, Habermas both retains the Enlightenment focus on human freedom and rationality and emphasizes that these are necessarily intertwined with others in the community of communicative rationalities. Ingram discusses these reformulations in greater detail, especially in relation to Kant's conception of the human being as a moral autonomy and the correlative ethics (1990, pp. 145–146).

In addition, the requirement for solidarity means that Habermas's theory endorses a *communitarian* conception of democracy (cf. Abramson et al., 1988, p. 30). See Ess, 1996, pp. 212–216, and Hamelink, 2000, pp. 55–76, for more detailed discussion.

6. Two additional comments on Habermas are worth nothing here. On the one hand, Hans-Georg Möller sees a Habermasian set of discourse rules standing at the entrance of a German-language children's community *(Kindernetz)*—i.e., rules that participants must agree to in order to receive a log-on identity and password for the Web site, its chat rooms, and so on. From a Habermasian perspective, these rules are seen as ways of ensuring that personal identity will be protected so that discourse will be open, free of irrational forces, and so on. Drawing on the media theory of Niklas Luhmann, however, Möller argues that

> individuality in our post-modern society is gained through social exclusion. To be an individual means to be special, to be different from others. However, the patterns of "exclusive" individuality are supplied and validated only by communication, i.e. by society. Thus, individuality becomes para-doxical: Social agents gain their "individuality" not "by themselves," but by adopting one or, more often, several of the identities offered by social discourse. . . . It seems to be precisely this "pseudo-individuality"—and not the Habermasian one—which is enhanced by the new modes of electronic communication. (2000)

On the other hand, David Holmes, while recognizing the difficulties that lead Becker and Wehner to move to supporting partial public spheres, argues that

> it is also true that individuals are mobile across communicative mediums and continuously participate not in a pre-given public sphere, but in the process of constructing publicness across a range of mediums. It is less the case, I argue, that the contemporary public sphere is breaking down and becoming fragmented as is the fact that it is sustained across increasingly more complex, dynamic and global kinds of communication environments. (2000, p. 384f.)

7. Although the survey provided by Harrison and Falvey is the most comprehensive and useful known to me, it is also largely devoted to CMC research in a first-world, English-speaking context. My own work includes attention to a broader range of diverse cultural settings, including the Middle East, Asia, and indigenous peoples. As will become quickly apparent, the results of this larger survey are consistent with Harrison and Falvey's findings, and should be seen as a complimentary way of making their larger point.

8. I have also argued that the Australian decision to set limits on USENET newsgroups to the exchange of pornography and discussion of sex, including bestiality and child sex, is at least consistent with Habermasian requirements. Such a decision could be justified under Habermas's discourse ethic, given three conditions. One, the community of participants would have to openly discuss the issue and come to consensus on what norms their discourse communities would endorse. Two, such a discussion would require full participation *by all those affected* by any proposed norms, *including* women and children—not simply the predominantly male subscribers to the USENET groups in question. And, three, all participants—including precisely those interested in exchanging pornography, etc.—would be required to exercise solidarity

and perspective-taking, that is, the admittedly difficult task of attempting to put one-self in the place of "the Other," in this case, precisely the women and children who are objectified in pornography, who may live with unpleasant consequences of its con-sumption, etc. Under these conditions it is not hard to imagine that such a discussion might result in a consensus to prohibit such discourse and uses of the system *as public*, especially if it could be demonstrated that such discourse otherwise worked to *exclude* the voices of all members of a democratic community—most obviously, the voices of women who are offended, sometimes into silence and withdrawal, by pornography that degrades them (Ess, 1996, pp. 218–220).

This argument, finally, may be strengthened by the growing recognition in both empirical research and ethical reflection on the Internet and the Web that—whatever our expectations may be—communication in these media are more or less intrinsi-cally *public* (see Walther, 2002). That is, genuine *privacy*—and thereby adherence to the norms of a specified subgroup—is all but impossible to achieve, except through the intentional use of encryption software. If our communications on the Internet and the Web are thus intrinsically *public*, Habermasian and feminist perspective-taking would insist even more dramatically on the importance of our attending to the voices of women, children, and others (e.g., vulnerable and marginalized populations such as abuse survivors, gay, lesbian, bisexual and transgendered persons, etc.) in considering the communicative norms by which we should operate as participants in a public medium. As we will see in the conclusion, these emphases on perspective-taking and care will provide critical resonance with Confucian ethics, and thereby play a critical role in what I sketch out as a possible *global* ethics.

9. This rejection, moreover, is supported by an apparently opposite cultural value. While accepting a hierarchical structure of access to information (i.e., as reserved for only a few), the eKiribati insist on a near-perfect *equality* in terms of mate-rial possessions. To show that one has more than others—e.g., by driving a new car—is called "shining" and is severely sanctioned. Because access to the Internet also promises individuals the possibility of economic advancement over their neighbors—i.e., shining—this provides a second rationale for its exclusion from the islands (Sofield, 2000).

10. The role of journalism in shaping whether CMC technologies are taken up and in turn foster democratic or antidemocratic directions is not limited to Eastern contexts. See Willis (2000) for an analysis of how *Wired* magazine (perhaps *the* pre-mier print advocate of CMC technologies in the United States), contrary to its appar-ent ideological commitment to the now-familiar values of the electronic global village (including an explicitly Jeffersonian conception of democracy, equality, etc.), in fact represents a "corporatized Internet," one marked by restricted access for only the afflu-ent, primarily white male elites of the middle and upper-middle classes, as "participa-tion" in the Internet and an emerging "techno-lifestyle" are conceptualized and mod-eled as merely new modes of consumption.

11. In his analysis of the multiple cultural factors working against any kind of equal access to CMC technologies in India, Kenniston also documents how English reinforces current distribution patterns of "power, wealth, privilege, and access to desired resources" (2001, p. 283). At the same time, this situation becomes even more complicated as new software is developed that makes it increasingly easier to intro-

duce Chinese and Japanese characters into Web addresses, etc.—with the resulting prediction that Chinese may be the dominant language of the Internet by 2007.

12. Research by Abdat and Pervan (2000) and Rahmati (2000) make clear that a cluster of cultural values in South Asia—specifically: face-saving (Confucian), high uncertainty avoidance (low risk tolerance), high collectivism/low individualism, and high power distance—conflict with the cultural values embedded in Western CMC. These findings, moreover, correlate with Maitland and Bauer's demonstration that low uncertainty avoidance and gender empowerment are significant cultural factors *promoting* diffusion of IT (2001).

13. Hongladarom, referring to Walzer (1994, pp. 1–19), puts it this way:

Moral arguments are "thin" when they are shorn of their particular histories and other cultural embodiments which make them integral parts of a cultural entity. These are the parts that make the arguments "thick." To use Walzer's own example, when Americans watched Czechs carry placards bearing words like 'Truth' and 'Justice,' they could relate immediately to the situation and sympathized with the marchers. However, when the arguments are at the local level, as to which version of distributive justice should be in place, there might well be disagreements, and Americans may find themselves disagreeing with the particular conception of justice which is eventually adopted. The sympathetic feeling one feels across the Ocean is part of the "thin" morality, but the localized and contextualized working of those moral concepts is part of the "thick" (2001, p. 318).

In this way, a "thin" morality depends on something like Aristotle's *pros hen* and analogical equivocals—the use of terms in different but related ways—such that the different (and more univocal) meanings of terms (e.g., "justice" in a specific cultural context) thus partially defines the *difference* between cultures. (See Aristotle, *Metaphysics* 1003a33, and Burrell, 1973, p. 470).

14. Other recent reports from Malaysia (Harris et al., 2001), and the Phillipines (Sy, 2001) likewise suggest that such middle grounds—ones that preserve local identities while facilitating global connections—are possible. Harris et al (2001) is especially worth noting as an example of a project to introduce CMC technologies among the Kelabit of Borneo in ways that begin by paying conscious attention to the prevailing values, interests, and, in Ong's terms, overwhelmingly *oral* communication "technology" of this highland people. The project continually involves community members in decisions surrounding the design and implementation of Internet and Web access, so that whatever cultural values and preferences these technologies may embed and foster, they will *not* inadvertently overcome defining community norms and preferences. Similarly, Sy (2001) develops a notion of a "cyberbarangay" as an explicit response to Habermas's question, "How can the power of technical control be brought within the range of the consensus of acting and transacting citizens?" (1987b, p. 57, in Sy 2001, p. 297).

Sy is very clear about the many ways that introducing CMC technologies in the Philippines work as an electronic colonization of the Filippino lifeworld (see especially pp. 305–308). Yet he is optimistic that a Habermasian style of democracy and social practice can be realized in the Philippines, especially in conjunction with attention to using CMC venues such as Internet cafés to serve as places for both traditional and new "focal practices" (Albert Borgmann, 1984, p. 219), but this will require that IT be "brought to the fore of public deliberation free from domination and . . . become a technology of citizenship" (2001, p. 309f.).

15. In fact, early on, Gibson describes his main character, Case, after he had had his nervous system dramatically attacked so as to erase his virtuoso skills as a "cowboy," a hacker who worked by projecting his disembodied consciousness into cyberspace: "For Case, who'd lived for the bodiless exultation of cyberspace, it was the Fall. In the bars he'd frequented as a cowboy hotshot, the elite stance involved a certain relaxed contempt for the flesh. The body was meat. Case fell into the prison of his own flesh" (p. 6). This strikingly *theological* language—and its reference to the later, Augustinian reading of the second Genesis creation story that stresses precisely the *contempt* of sexuality and body—is perhaps not accidental. In a later episode, an Artificial Intelligence attempts to distract Case from his primary mission by constructing for him an alternative space, one inhabited by a former girlfriend. Echoing the role of Eve, as interpreted by Augustine, she becomes the temptress who occasions his fall:

There was a strength that ran in her, something he'd known in Night City and held there, been held by it, held for a while away from time and death. . . . It belonged, he knew—he remembered—as she pulled him down, to the meat, the flesh the cowboys mocked. It was a vast thing, beyond knowing, a sea of information coded in spiral and pheromone, infinite intricacy that only the body, in its strong blind way, could ever read. (*Neuromancer*, 1984, p. 239)

This intimation that the digitized domains of cyberspace may *not* be able to fully capture all there is to *body* anticipates, as we will see, the return to embodiment in more recent, "post-postmodern" literature and philosophy. In the meantime, it is worth noting that the 1990s postmodern contempt for body as "meat"—especially apparent in Barlow—is rooted in an explicitly *Christian* theology, namely, that of Augustine and his teaching of original sin. In this way, Nietzsche's critique of especially Christian dualisms as "the metaphysics of the hangman" thus directly applies to an important conceptual root of 1990s postmodern dualisms as well.

16. More recent research likewise documents the ability of people from diverse cultures to consciously weave together diverse cultural elements in a *hybridizing* process that conjoins thick/local culture with an emerging thin/global culture. For example, Piecowye documents how young women of the United Arab Emirates stand as examples of users who can consciously chose what elements of global cultures they wish to appropriate while they simultaneously insist on preserving their own cultural values and practices (2002). Similarly, Bickel finds that www.rawa.org, a Web site established by women in Afghanistan under the Taliban regime, serves as an example of what Ulf Hannerz calls "emergent, hybridizing Webs of meaning" (1992, p. 264, in Bickel, 2002) between centers and peripheries. Finally, Bucher, in his comparisons of German and Chinese Web pages, endorses the notion of "glocalization" (taken from Robertson, 1995), as indicating that "the main effect of global communication is not (yet) the evolution of a global public sphere but the connections between distant local cultures" (2002, p. 5).

17. Still more recently, Becker has explored the significance of the *skin* in our experience of body as the organ and site of our dynamic interaction with the larger world: "Marking and Crossing Borders: Bodies, Touch and Contact in Cyberspace," paper presented as part of the special session sponsored by the APA Committee on Philosophy and Computers, APA Central Meeting, Chicago, April 26, 2002. While this paper extends her analysis in important ways, I will not be able to refer to it extensively here.

18. She makes her argument in part by taking up Merleau-Ponty's notion of *chiasmus* in which "activity and passivity, creation and imitation balance one another in the intertwining of body-subject and environment. This not only entails the decentralization of the metaphysical "être raisonnable," but as well of the "être sensible." . . . Only in the emergent chiasmus does the decentered bodysubject unfold, elucidating the limits of control which it may gain about itself, others and the world" (2001, p. 69).

19. In particular, Becker offers an especially evocative description of how the inextricable interaction constituting the *LeibSubjekt* interacts with language:

> Und doch erkennen wir uns wieder in dem, was wir sagen und in der Art, wie wir etwas zum Ausdruck bringen. Rhythmus und Klang, Annäherung und Berührung, Gestik, Mimik und Bewegung: der Körperleib meldet sich auf unterschiedlichste Weise zu Wort und färbt auf diese Weise auch die Sprache, nicht nur die gesprochene, durch Tonfall, Redeweise und Klang, sondern auch die geschriebene Sprache, wie beispielsweise in der Poetik und in der Metaphorik.

> [And yet we recognize ourselves in what we say and how we say it. Rhythm and sound, gesture, mimicry and movement: the body becomes voice [meldet sich . . . zu Wort] in the most diverse ways and thus also colors its language—not only the spoken language (through tone, turn of phrase, and sound) but also the written language (e.g., in poetry and metaphor). (2002, p. 43)

In terms of the Innis/Ong schema, this interaction expresses the conjunction of orality (as spoken language tied, she makes clear, to body) and literacy (the written language of poetry and metaphor). Moreover, there is an intriguing resonance here between Becker's phenomenological account of the "BodySubject" and the collaborative/kinesthetic epistemologies of oral cultures; see Harris et al., 2001, and Postma, 2001.

20. For a more complete account of this turn toward embodiment, see Ess, 2002b. For a discussion of Borgmann, see Ess, 2002a.

21. Perhaps the most famous and moving affirmation of *this life* and embodiment comes from Homer's *Odyssey* (1961), as Odysseus seeks to flatter the shade of Agamemnon in Hades:

> Let me hear no smooth talk
> of death from you, Odysseus, light of councils.
> Better, I say, to break sod as a farm hand

> For some poor country man, on iron rations,
> Than lord it over all the exhausted dead.
> (Book 11, lines 542–546)

I would add here that Plato—at least as read from a Straussian beginning point—likewise contributes to this emphasis on the importance of embodiment.

That is, in contrast with the more standard readings—including Nietzsche's—that take Plato to be a (sometimes clumsy) dualist—on a more Straussian reading of Plato (especially in *The Republic* and *The Symposium*), Plato's conception of the *psyche* may be described as something of an emergent phenomenon—i.e., of an entity or set of processes (denoted as reason, spirit, and appetite) that, while clearly distinct from one another and from body, are nonetheless intimately interwoven with both one another and body. Briefly, Plato suggests this sort of *irreducible difference and connection* through the analogy of the line (*Republic*, Book VI, pp. 509d–511e/190–192), the allegory of the cave (*Republic*, Book VII, pp. 514a/193ff.), and, more broadly, through the use of the metaphor of the body itself as an organic entity—i.e., one whose individual and irreducibly distinct parts must function together in the proper relationship or *harmony* for the whole to achieve health and well-being (e.g., pp. 462a–462d/141f.). (*Republic* references are to the standard Stephanus pages, followed by page references to *The Republic of Plato* [1968]).

Plato exploits the structure of mathematical analogy—what we would call an arithmetical proportion—to demarcate the intellectual domain as irreducibly *different* from the domain of sense: at the same time, however, just as the shadows of a thing are thereby inextricably *connected* with the thing as their origin, so the domain of sense is inextricably *connected* with the intellectual domain (cf. *Republic*, Book IV, pp. 44a/124). By the same token, the *psyche* is both inextricably connected with the body, while simultaneously irreducibly different (Ess, 1983). This conjunction of connection *and* irreducible difference, moreover, as mapped onto the allegory of the cave suggests that while the psyche of the philosopher may be able to abstract itself from the cave of sense knowledge and body, the abstraction is not clearly an insistence on solely an *ontological* difference. On the contrary, the path up is the path down, and Socrates is clear that the philosopher must always return to the cave—i.e., to the domain of body, sense knowledge, and thereby the political life. Similarly, in Diotima's account of the erotic ladder of philosophy in the *Symposium*, the philosophical quest for Beauty itself begins with the sensory and beauty-in-bodies (pp. 210a–212a). While Beauty itself is clearly different from its multiple and imperfect manifestations in both souls and bodies, Beauty itself is at the same time inextricably interwoven with souls and bodies precisely as these manifest, however imperfectly, Beauty as such.

It is certainly true, of course, that Socrates, both in the *Republic* and *Phaedo*, discusses the immortality of the soul. In the *Republic*, however, as Bloom points out, this theme is taken up in the context of what is explicitly identified as a *mythos*—the myth of Er; the rhetorical function of the myth is not so much to elaborate a serious philosophical teaching as to illustrate an important teaching in terms that Socrates' audience can grasp (see *Republic*, Book X, pp. 614b/297ff.; Bloom's "Interpretive Essay," pp. 434ff.). Similarly, Socrates' discussion of the immortality of the soul in the *Phaedo* must be seriously qualified by the rhetorical recognition that this discussion takes place with two Pythagoreans—i.e., interlocutors already committed to the belief in the soul as immortal. On a Straussian reading, Socrates uses the discussion of the soul's immortality as a form of "salutary rhetoric," i.e., a dialogical device shaped more by the demands of his specific audience than by his own specific philosophical commitments (however far these may be discerned in the dialogues).

22. Indeed, this Habermasian/feminist approach—especially as it aims precisely toward a *global* computer ethics—is both consistent with and helpfully complemented by Floridi and Sanders'notion (this volume) of *ecopoiesis*, as it "recognizes the agent's responsibilities toward the environment (including present and future inhabitants) as its enlightened, creator steward or supervisor, not just as its virtuous user and consumer."

23. Beverly Bickel affirms this Renaissance emphasis on becoming a cosmopolitan precisely through embodied experience of and familiarity with multiple cultures—and with specific regard for the *democratizing* potentials of CMC: "The democratic potential of the Net for promoting 'civic pluralism' will partly rely on its being constructed by those capable of negotiating global differences, creating multiple, complex meanings and crossing boundaries" (2003).

24. Of course, similar comparisons with other nondualistic traditions could be made here, including Daoism (see Hans-Georg Möller, especially "Daoismus und Chan-Buddhismus [2001, pp. 180–184]), Buddhism (e.g., Erin McCarthy's discussion of Yuasa Yasuo's philosophy of the body, 2002), and Vedanta Hinduism (Deutsch, 1969).Moreover, it needs saying that there are real risks of attempting to establish such coherencies—but these risks are well known to anyone who has pursued comparative philosophy. Among the many difficulties (issues in translation, understanding historical and cultural contexts, etc.), Bina Gupta points out that "comparisons proceed smoothly as long as two systems display large similarities and clear differences—but the danger is that the comparative philosopher has, through interpretation, eliminated important differences." Despite these dangers, however, the only way to know if comparative philosophy might succeed is to try it—either piecemeal (Bina Gupta, "Comparative Philosophy: Problems, Assumptions, Possibilities," APA Central Conference, Chicago, April 27, 2002) or holistically (Yu and Bunnin, 2001).

In particular, these resonances *include* irreducible differences of their own. Jiyuan Yu develops a far more nuanced and careful comparison between Aristotelian virtue ethics and the Confucian notion of *ren* (1998). Professor Yu's conclusion is worth citing here:

while for Confucius, a complete notion of *ren* is a synthesis of *ren* as love and *ren* as conforming to *li*, for Aristotle a full notion of virtue comprises virtue as state of character as well as virtue as exercising practical rationality, and is an organic synthesis of them. It is the synthesis of these two determinations that determines the mean state. Virtue as mean in turn determines the nature of all other ethical virtues.

It is interesting to notice that with regard to the concept of virtue, neither Confucius's synthesis nor Aristotle's is fully respected historically. In the West, Aristotle's interplay between practical wisdom and ethical virtue has been separated since the Enlightenment. Philosophers contrast the authority of reason to tradition, and then try to establish universal and transcultural principles of morality in which virtue does not have any significant place. The current revival of virtue ethics is in a sense to "return" to Aristotle's combination between reason and virtue, although with significant alterations. Correspondingly, in the East, Confucian synthesis of ren as love and ren as returning to li is also severed in the later development of Confucianism. Ren as observing li comes to be more and more rigid and inflexible, and moves far from ren as love. Li was eventually accused in the May Fourth movement of "eating man." The basic spirit of the May Fourth movement is to set a sharp contrast between Chinese tradition and Western science and democracy, and then uphold the latter while rejecting the former. But the recent resurgence of Confucianism in East Asia emphasises the value of Chinese tradition and criticizes Western individualist morality. This sounds like a tendency to "return" to Confucius's notion of ren. If the comparison of this chapter is sound, we would like to suggest that while an Aristotelian revival would do well to borrow the Confucian insight of filial love, a Confucian revival could hardly be constructive without developing an Aristotelian function of rationality in weighing and reanimating the tradition.

That said, the project of seeking a coherent global ethic, while clearly ambitious, is at the same time a central impetus of Western philosophy since at least the Stoics, and as recently as Henry Rosemont Jr.s' lecture and book, *Rationality and Religious Experience* (2001). Most briefly, Professor Rosemont argues that we can find in the world's great religions a common focal point (my term—from Aristotle's *pros hen* or focal equivocal) that will fund a global ethic—one desperately needed in an era of globalization. Very briefly, Professor Rosemont characterizes this shared sensibility as "the sense that we are absolutely safe" (p. 31).

REFERENCES

Abdat, Sjarif, and Graham P. Pervan. 2000. "Reducing the Negative Effects of Power Distance during Asynchronous Pre-meeting without Using Anonymity in Indonesian Culture," in Fay Sudweeks and Charles Ess (Eds.), *Cultural Attitudes towards Technology and Communication*, Proceedings of the Second International Conference, Perth, Australia, July 12–15, 2000, 209–215.

Abramson, Jeffrey, Christopher Arterton, and Gary Orren. 1988. *The Electronic Commonwealth: The Impact of New Media Technologies on Democratic Politics.* New York: Basic Books.

Ames, Roger, and Henry Rosemont, Jr. 1998. *The Analects of Confucius: A Philosophical Translation.* New York: Ballantine Books.

Aristotle. 1968. *The Nichomachean Ethics.* Trans. H. Rackham. Cambridge: Harvard University Press.

Barber, Benjamin. 1992. Jihad vs. McWorld. *The Atlantic Monthly*, March: 53–63.

———. 1995. *Jihad versus McWorld.* New York: Times Books.

Barlow, John Perry. 1996. A Declaration of the Independence of Cyberspace. http://www.eff.org/pub/Censorship/Internet_censorship_bills /barlow_0296.declaration.

Bateson, Gregory. 1972. *Steps to an Ecology of Mind*. New York: Ballantine Books.

———. 1979. *Mind and Nature: A Necessary Unity*. New York: Bantam.

Becker, Barbara. 1997. "Virtuelle Identität: Die Technik, das Subjekt und das Imaginäre," in Barbara Becker and Michael Paetau (Eds.), *Virtualisierung des Sozialen: Die Informationsgesellschaft zwischen Fragmentierung und Globalisierung*. Frankfurt: Campus Verlag, pp. 163–184.

———. 2000. Cyborg, Agents and Transhumanists, *Leonardo* 33 (5): 361–365.

———. 2001. "Disappearance of Materiality," in Vera Lemecha and Reva Stone (Eds.), *The Multiple and the Mutable Subject*. Winnipeg: St. Norbert Arts Centre, pp. 58–77.

———. 2001. "Sinn und Sinnlichkeit: Anmerkungen zur Eigendynamik und Fremdheit des eigenen Leibes" [Sense and Sensibility: Remarks on the Distinctive Dynamics and Strangeness of One's Own Body], in L. Jäger (Ed.), *Mentalität und Medialität*. Munich: Fink Verlag, pp. 35–46.

———, and Josef Wehner. 2001. "Electronic Networks and Civil Society: Reflections on Structural Changes in the Public Sphere," in Charles Ess (Ed.), *Culture, Technology, Communication: Towards an Intercultural Global Village*. Albany: State University of New York Press, pp. 65–85.

Benhabib, Seyla. 1992. *Situating the Self: Gender, Community, and Postmodernism in Contemporary Ethics*. New York: Routledge.

Bickel, Beverly. 2002. "The Contested Construction of Knowledge: Afghan Women Asserting Leadership Via the Net," in Fay Sudweeks and Charles Ess (Eds.), *Proceedings: Cultural Attitudes Towards Communication and Technology 2002*. Murdoch, Western Australia: School of Information Technology, Murdoch University, pp. 153–180.

———. 2003. Weapons of Magic: Afghan Women Asserting Voice via the Net, *Journal of Computer-Mediated Communication* 8:2. http://www.ascusc.org/jcmc/vol8/issue2/bickel.html.

Bolter, Jay David. 2001. "Identity," in T. Swiss (Ed.), *Unspun*. New York: New York University Press, pp. 17–29. Available online at http://www.nyupress.nyu.edu/unspun/samplechap.html.

Borgmann, Albert. 1984. *Technology and the Character of Contemporary Life: A Philosophical Inquiry*. Chicago: University of Chicago Press.

———. 1999. *Holding onto Reality: The Nature of Information at the Turn of the Millennium*. Chicago: University of Chicago Press.

Bourdieu, Pierre. 1977. *Outline of a Theory of Practice*. Trans. R. Nice. Cambridge: Cambridge University Press.

———. 1984. *Distinction: A Social Critique of the Judgement of Taste*. Trans. R. Nice. Cambridge: Harvard University Press.

Bucher, Hans-Jürgen. 2002. "The Power of the Audience: Interculturality, Interactivity and Trust in Internet Communication," in Fay Sudweeks and Charles Ess

(Eds.), *Cultural Attitudes towards Technology and Communication 2002*, Proceedings of the Third International Conference on Cultural Attitudes towards Technology and Communication, Montréal, Canada, July 12–15, 2002, 3–14. Murdoch, WA: School of Information Technology, Murdoch University. Available online at http://www.it.murdoch.edu.au/catac/.

Burrell, David. 1973. *Analogy and Philosophical Language*. New Haven: Yale University Press.

Dahan, Michael. 1999. National Security and Democracy on the Internet in Israel. Computer-Mediated Culture, a special issue of *Javnost-the Public*, Fay Sudweeks and Charles Ess (Eds.), VI (4): 67–77.

———. 2001. Personal communication.

Deutsch, Eliot. 1969. *Advaita Vedanta: A Philosophical Reconstruction*. Honolulu: University of Hawaii Press.

Dreyfus, Hubert. 2001. *On the Internet*. New York: Routledge.

Ess, Charles. 1983. *Analogy in the Critical Works: Kant's Transcendental Philosophy as Analectical Thought*. Ann Arbor: University Microfilms International.

———. 1996. "The Political Computer: Democracy, CMC, and Habermas," in Charles Ess (Ed.), *Philosophical Perspectives on Computer-Mediated Communication*. Albany: State University of New York Press, pp. 197–230.

———. 2001. "What's Culture Got to Do with It? Cultural Collisions in the Electronic Global Village, Creative Interferences, and the Rise of Culturally-mediated Computing," in C. Ess (Ed.), *Culture, Technology, Communication: Towards an Intercultural Global Village*. Albany: State University of New York Press, pp. 1–50.

———. 2002a. Borgmann and the Borg: Consumerism vs. *Holding on to Reality*. A review essay on Albert Borgmann's *Holding on to Reality*, special issue of *Techne*, edited by Phil Mullins.

———. 2002b. "Philosophy of Computer-Mediated Communication," in Luciano Floridi (Ed.), *The Blackwell Guide to the Philosophy of Information and Computing*. Oxford: Blackwell.

———. 2003. "Are we there yet? Emerging Ethical Guidelines for Online Research," in Sarina Chen and Jon Hall (Eds.), *Online Social Research: Methods, Issues, and Ethics*. New York: Peter Lang.

Gibson, William. 1984. *Neuromancer*. New York: Ace Books.

Habermas, Jürgen. 1984. *The Theory of Communicative Action, Vol. 1: Reason and the Rationalization of Society*. Trans. Thomas McCarthy. Boston: Beacon Press.

———. 1987a. *The Theory of Communicative Action, Vol. II: Lifeworld and System: A Critique of Functionalist Reason*. Trans. Thomas McCarthy. Boston: Beacon Press.

———. 1987b. *Toward a Rational Society: Student Protest, Science, and Politics*. Trans. J. Shapiro. Cambridge: Polity.

———. 1989. Justice and Solidarity: On the Discussion Concerning Stage 6. *Philosophical Forum* 21, 12 (Fall/Winter): 32–52.

————. 1990. "Discourse Ethics: Notes on Philosophical Justification," in *Moral Consciousness and Communicative Action*. Cambridge: MIT Press, pp. 43–116.

Hamelink, Cees. 2000. *The Ethics of Cyberspace*. London: Sage.

Hannerz, Ulf. 1992. *Cultural Complexity: Studies in the Social Organization of Meaning*. New York: Columbia University Press.

Haraway, Donna. 1990. "A Cyborg Manifesto: Science, Technology, and Socialist-Feminism in the Late Twentieth Century," in Donna Haraway (Ed.), *Simians, Cyborgs, and Women: The Reinvention of Nature*. New York: Routledge, pp. 149–181.

Harris, R., P. Bala, P. Sonan, E. K. Guat Lien, and T. Trang. 2001. Challenges and Opportunities in Introducing Information and Communication Technologies to the Kelabit Community of North Central Borneo, *New Media and Society* 3 (September): 271–296.

Harrison, Teresa M., and Lisa Falvey. 2001. "Democracy and New Communication Technologies," in William B. Gudykunst (Ed.), *Communication Yearbook 25*. Hillsdale, NJ: Lawrence Erlbaum.

Hayles, Katherine. 1999. *How We Became Posthuman: Virtual Bodies in Cybernetics, Literature, and Informatics*. Chicago: University of Chicago Press.

Hofstede, Geert. 1980. *Culture's Consequences: International Differences in Work-related Values*. Beverly Hills: Sage.

————. 1983. National Cultures in Four Dimensions. *International Studies of Management and Organization* 13: 52–60.

————. 1984. The Cultural Relativity of the Quality of Life Concept, *Academy of Management Review* 9: 389–398.

————. 1991. *Cultures and Organizations: Software of the Mind*. London: McGraw-Hill.

————, and M. H. Bond. 1988. The Confucius Connection: From Cultural Roots to Economic Growth, *Organizational Dynamics* 16 (4): 5–21.

Holmes, D. 2000. "Technological Transformations of the Public Sphere," in F. Sudweeks and C. Ess (Eds.), *Second International Conference on Cultural Attitudes towards Technology and Communication 2000*. Murdoch, WA: School of Information Technology, Murdoch University, pp. 373–86. Available online at http://www.it.murdoch.edu.au/~sudweeks/catac00/.

Homer. 1961. *The Odyssey*. Trans. Robert Fitzgerald. New York: Vintage Books.

Hongladarom, Soraj. 2001. "Global Culture, Local Cultures and the Internet: The Thai Example," in C. Ess (Ed.), *Culture, Technology, Communication: Towards an Intercultural Global Village*. Albany: State University of New York Press, pp. 307–324.

————. 2000. Negotiating the Global and the Local: How Thai Culture Co-opts the Internet. *First Monday* 5:8. http://firstmonday.org/issues/issue5_8/hongladarom/index.html.

Horkheimer, Max, and Theodor W. Adorno. 1947/1972. *Dialectic of Enlightenment.* Trans. John Cumming. (*Dialektik der Aufklärung.* Amsterdam: Herder and Herder, 1947).

Ingram, David. 1990. *Critical Theory and Philosophy.* New York: Paragon House.

Jaeger, Werner. 1934. *Aristotle: Fundamentals of the History of His Development.* London: Oxford University Press.

Jones, Steve. 2001. "Understanding Micropolis and Compunity," in Charles Ess (Ed.), *Culture, Technology, Communication: Towards an Intercultural Global Village.* Albany: State University of New York Press, pp. 51–66.

Joo-Young Jung. 2000. Globalize or not?: The Internet and the Social Factors Shaping Globalization. Internet Research 1.0: The State of the Interdiscipline, First Conference of the Association of Internet Researchers, University of Kansas, Lawrence, September 16.

Keniston, Kenneth. 2001. "Language, Power, and Software," in Charles Ess (Ed.), *Culture, Technology, Communication: Towards an Intercultural Global Village.* Albany: State University of New York Press, pp. 281–306.

McCarty, Erin. 2002. Yuasa's Theory of the Body and Ethics, APA Central Conference, Chicago, April 25.

Maitland, Carleen, and Johannes Bauer. 2001. "Global Diffusion of Interactive Networks: The Impact of Culture," in Charles Ess (Ed.), *Culture, Technology, Communication: Towards an Intercultural Global Village.* Albany: State University of New York Press, pp. 87–128.

Mehl, James V. 2000. Drawing Parallels With the Renaissance: Late Modemism, Postmodernism, and the Possibility of Historical Layering, *The Midwest Quarterly: A Journal of Contemporary Thought* 41, 4 (Summer): 401–415.

Möller, Hans-Georg. 2000. The *Kindernetz:* Electronic Communication and the Paradox of Individuality. Computers and Philosophy Conference (CAP 2000), Carnegie Mellon University, Pittsburgh, August 11.

———. 2001. *In der Mitte des Kreises: Daoistisches Denken.* Frankfurt am Main: Insel.

Moravec, Hans. 1988. *Mind Children: The Future of Robot and Human Intelligence.* Cambridge: Harvard University Press.

Nielsen, Torben Hviid. 1990. Jürgen Habermas: Morality, Society, and Ethics: An Interview with Torben Hviid Nielsen, *Acta Sociologica* 33(2): 93–114.

Nietzsche, Frederich. 1988 [1954]. "Twilight of the Idols" *[Götzen-Dämmerung]* in *The Portable Nietzsche.* Trans. W. Kaufmann. New York: Penguin, pp. 463–563.

Piecowye, James. 2003. *Habitus* in Transition? CMC Use and Impacts among Young Women in the United Arab Emirates, *Journal of Computer-Mediated Communication* (8:2). http://www.ascusc.org/jcmc/vol8/issue2/piecowye.html.

Poster, Mark. 1997. "Cyberdemocracy: Internet and the Public Sphere," in David Porter (Ed.), *Internet Culture.* New York: Routledge, pp. 201–217.

Postma, Louise. 2001. A Theoretical Argumentation and Evaluation of South African Learners' Orientation towards and Perceptions of the Empowering Use of Information, *New Media and Society* 3 (3: September): 315–328.

Rahmati, Nasrin. 2000. "The Impact of Cultural Values on Computer Mediated Group Work," in Fay Sudweeks and Charles Ess (Eds.), *Cultural Attitudes towards Technology and Communication*, Proceedings of the Second International Conference, Perth, Australia, July 12–15, 2000. School of Information Technology, Murdoch University: Perth, Australia, pp. 257–274.

The Republic of Plato. 1968. Translated, with notes, an interpretive essay, and a new introduction by Allan Bloom. New York: Basic Books.

Robertson, Roland. 1995. "Glocalization: Time-space and Homogeneity-Heterogeneity," in Mike Featherstone, Scott Lash, and Roland Robertson (Eds.), *Global Modernities*. London: Sage, pp. 25–44.

Rosemont, Henry. 2001. *Rationality and Religious Experience: The Continuing Relevance of the World's Spiritual Traditions*. With a Commentary by Huston Smith. Chicago and La Salle: Open Court.

Rutter, Jason, and Greg Smith. 1998. "Addressivity and Sociability in 'Celtic Men,'" in Charles Ess and Fay Sudweeks (Eds.), *Proceedings: Cultural Attitudes Towards Communication and Technology '98*. Sydney: University of Sydney, pp. 152–157.

Sapienza, Filipp. 1999. "Communal Ethos on a Russian Émigré Web Site," in Fay Sudweeks and Charles Ess, guest editors, "Computer-Mediated Culture," a special issue of *Javnost—The Public* VI (4): 39–52.

Sofield, Thomas. 2000. "Outside the Net: Kiribati and the Knowledge Economy," in F. Sudweeks and C. Ess (Eds.), *Cultural Attitudes towards Technology and Communication*. Murdoch, WA: School of Information Technology, Murdoch University, pp. 3–26. Available online at http://www.it.murdoch.edu.au/~sudweeks/catac00/.

Suchman, Lucy. 1987. *Plans and Situated Actions: The Problem of Human-Machine Communication*. Cambridge and New York: Cambridge University Press.

Sy, Peter. 2001. Barangays of IT: Filipinizing Mediated Communication and Digital Power, *New Media and Society* 3 (3: September): 297–313.

Tu, Wei-Ming. 1999. "Humanity as Embodied Love: Exploring Filial Piety as a Global Ethical Perspective," in Marko Zlomislic and David Goicoechea (Eds.), *Jen Agape Tao with Tu Wei-Ming*. Binghampton: Institute of Global Cultural Studies, pp. 28–37.

Walther, Joe. 2002. Research Ethics in Internet-Enabled Research: Human Subjects Issues and Methodological Myopia, *Ethics and Information Technology* 4: 205–216. Available online at http://www.nyu.edu/projects/nissenbaum/ethics_wal_full.html.

Walzer, Michael. 1994. *Thick and Thin: Moral Argument at Home and Abroad*. Notre Dame, IN: University of Notre Dame Press.

Wheeler, Deborah. 2001. "New Technologies, Old Culture: A Look at Women, Gender, and the Internet in Kuwait," in Charles Ess (Ed.), *Culture, Technology, Communication: Towards an Intercultural Global Village*. Albany: State University of New York Press, pp. 187–212.

Willis, Ann. 2000. "Nerdy No More: A Case Study of Early Wired (1993–96)," in F. Sudweeks and C. Ess (Eds.), *Cultural Attitudes towards Technology and Communication*. School of Information Technology, Murdoch University, pp. 361–372. Available online at http://www. it.murdoch.edu.au/~sudweeks/catac00/.

Yoon, Sunny. 1996. "Power Online: A Poststructuralist Perspective on CMC," in Charles Ess (Ed.), *Philosophical Perspectives on Computer-Mediated Communication*. Albany: State University of New York Press, pp. 171–196.

———. 2001. "Internet Discourse and the Habitus of Korea's New Generation," in C. Ess (Ed.), *Culture, Technology, Communication: Towards an Intercultural Global Village*. Albany: State University of New York Press, pp. 241–260.

Yu, Ji-yuan. 1998. Virtue: Aristotle and Confucius, *Philosophy East and West* 48 (2): 323–347.

———, and Nicholas Bunnin. 2001. "Saving the Phenomena: An Aristotelian Method in Comparative Philosophy," in M. Bo (Ed.), *Two Roads to Wisdom?— Chinese Philosophy and Analytical Philosophy*. LaSalle, IL: Open Court, pp. 293–312.

NINE

Internet Ethics

The Constructionist Values
of *Homo Poieticus*

LUCIANO FLORIDI AND J. W. SANDERS

ETHICAL ISSUES ARE often discussed in terms of putative resolutions of hypothetical situations, such as "What should one do on finding a wallet in a restaurant restroom?" Research and educational purposes may promote increasingly dramatic scenarios (sometimes reaching unrealistic excesses[1]), with available courses of action more polarized and less easily identifiable as right or wrong. But the general approach remains substantially the same: the agent is confronted by a moral dilemma and asked to make a principled decision by choosing from a menu of alternatives. Moral action is triggered by a situation.

In "situated action ethics" (to borrow an expression from AI), such moral dilemma may give the false impression that the ethical discourse concerns primarily a posteriori reactions to problematic situations in which the agent unwillingly and unexpectedly finds herself. The agent is treated as a world user, a game player, a consumer of moral goods and evils, a browser,[2] a guest, or a customer who reacts to preestablished and largely unmodifiable conditions, scenarios, and choices. Only two temporal modes count: present and future. The past seems irrelevant ("How did the agent find herself in such predicament?"), unless the approach is further expanded by a casuistry analysis.

Ethics, however, is not only a question of dealing morally well with a given world. It is also one of constructing the world, improving its nature,

195

and shaping its development in the right way. This *proactive*[3] approach treats the agent as a world owner, a game designer or referee, a producer of moral goods and evils, a provider, a host, or a creator. The agent is supposed to be able to plan and initiate action responsibly, in anticipation of future events, in order to (try to) control their course by making something happen or preventing something from happening rather than waiting to respond *(react)* to a situation, once something has happened, or merely hoping that something positive will happen.

There are significant differences between reactive and proactive approaches. There is no space to explore them here, but one may mention, as a simple example, the moral responsibilities of a Webmaster as opposed to those of a user of a Web site. Yet differences should not be confused with incompatibilities. A mature moral agent is commonly expected to be both a morally good user and a morally good producer of the environment in which he operates, not least because situated action ethics can be confronted by lose–lose situations, in which all options may turn out to be morally unpleasant and every choice may amount to failure. A proactive approach may help to avoid unrecoverable situations. It certainly reduces the agent's reliance on moral luck. As a result, a large part of an ethical education consists in acquiring the kinds of traits, values, and intellectual skills that may enable the agent to switch successfully between a reactive and a proactive approach to the world.

All this is acknowledged by many ethical systems, albeit with different vocabulary, emphasis, and levels of explicitness. Some more conservative ethical theories prefer to concentrate on the reactive nature of the agent's behavior. For example, deontologism embeds a reactive bias insofar as it supports duties on demand. Another good example is the moral code implicit in the Ten Commandments, which is less proactive than that promoted in the New Testament. On a more secular level, the two versions of Asimov's laws of robotics provide a simple case of evolution. The 1940 version is more reactive than the 1985 version, whose new zeroth law includes a substantially proactive requirement: "A robot may not injure humanity, or, through inaction, allow humanity to come to harm" (see Clarke, 1993–1994, for a full analysis and further references).

Ethical theories that adopt a more proactive approach can be defined as *constructionist*. They are the ones that interest us here. One of the best examples of constructionist ethics is virtue ethics. The analysis of its scope and limits will introduce our discussion of a constructionist approach to cyberethics.

THE SCOPE AND LIMITS OF VIRTUE ETHICS
AS CONSTRUCTIONIST ETHICS

According to virtue ethics, an individual's principal ethical aim is to live the good life by becoming a certain kind of person. The constructionist stance is expressed by the desire to mold oneself. This goal is achieved by implementing or improving some characteristics, while eradicating or controlling others. The stance itself is presupposed: it is simply assumed as uncontroversial that one does wish to live the good life by becoming the best person one can. Some degree of personal malleability and capacity to choose critically provide further background preconditions. The key question "What kind of person should I be?" is (rightly, in our view) considered a reasonable and justified question. It grounds the question "What kind of life should I lead?" and immediately translates into "What kind of character should I construct? What kind of virtues should I develop? What sort of vices should I avoid or eradicate?" It is implicit that each agent strives to achieve that aim *as an individual*, with only incidental regard to the enveloping community.

Different brands of virtue ethics disagree on the specific virtues and values identifying a person as morally good. The disagreement, say between Aristotle, Paul of Tarsus, and Nietzsche, can be dramatic, not least because it is ultimately ontological, in that it regards the kind of entity that a human being should strive to become. In prototyping jargon, theories may disagree on the abstract specification of the model, not just on implementation details.

Despite their divergences, all brands of virtue ethics share the same subject-oriented kernel. This is not to say that they are all subjectivist, but rather, more precisely, that they are all concerned exclusively with the proper *construction* of the moral subject, whether a self-imposed task or an educational goal of a second party, like parents, teachers, or society in general. To adopt another technical expression, virtue ethics is intrinsically *egopoietic*. Its *sociopoietic* nature is merely a by-product, in the following sense. Egopoietic practices that lead to the ethical construction of the subject inevitably interact with, and influence, the ethical construction of the community inhabited by the subject. So, when the subjective microcosm and the sociopolitical macrocosm differ in scale but essentially not in nature or complexity, as one may assume in the idealized case of the Greek polis, egopoiesis can scale up to the role of general ethics and even political philosophy. Plato's *Republic* is an excellent example. Plato finds it unproblematic to move seamlessly between the construction of the ideal self and the construction of the ideal city-state. But so does the Mafia, whose code of conduct and "virtuous ethics" for the individual are based on the view that "the family" is its members.

Egopoiesis and sociopoiesis are interderivable only in sufficiently *simple* and *closed* societies, in which significant communal behavior is ultimately derivable from that of its constituent individuals. It is hard to specify "sufficiently" precisely, but some light can be cast here by trying to clarify what "simple" and "closed" mean.

On the one hand, "simple" refers to the "vertical" growth of a society, that is, to its degree of *autonomy*. A society is no longer sufficiently simple, but qualifies as increasingly *complex* when some of the major new variables that govern its development are internal forces, emerging holistically from the actions and decisions of its members, forces like unemployment or price inflation, for example, that are beyond the control of single human agents.

On the other hand, the threshold between a closed and an open society (no reference to Popper here) is to be identified in the level and relevance of interconnections and interactions between the society in question and other similar macroagents. A sufficiently open society is one in which some of the major new variables that govern its development are external forces influencing it from without. Therefore, "open" and "closed" indicate the relative degree to which interaction determines evolution. This is the "horizontal" growth of a society.

Societies exhibit a continuum of stages, with simple and closed societies at one end of the continuum and, at the other end, societies open and complex enough to sustain autonomous behavior and demonstrate *emergent* characteristics.[4] As they evolve, societies may progress along the continuum. At some point, although immediate and personal interactions among all its members are still significant, in practice systemic forces may supervene, profoundly influencing the life of each individual. Such open and complex societies inherit *autonomy* and *interactivity* from their constituent individuals and, at a certain level of evolution, become *adaptive*. They thus form *(artificial) agents* by virtue of those three properties (on the ethics of artificial agents see Floridi and Sanders, forthcoming). In such societies, sociopoiesis is no longer reducible to egopoiesis alone. And this is the fundamental limit of virtue ethics. In autonomous, interactive, and adaptive societies, virtue ethics positions acquire an individualistic value, previously inconceivable, and may result in moral escapism. The individual still cares about her own ethical construction and, at most, the construction of the community with which she is more closely involved, like the family, but the rest of the world falls beyond the horizon of her moral concern.

All this was true during the last centuries of the Roman Empire, for example, and applies equally well in our new era of globalization. Phrasing the point in terms of situated action ethics, new problematic hypothetical situations arise from emergent phenomena. Examples include issues of disarmament, the ozone level, pollution, famine and the digital divide. The difficulty becomes apparent in all its pressing urgency as the individual agent tries to reason using "local" ethical principles to tackle a problem with "global" ethical features and consequences.

WHY CYBERETHICS CANNOT
BE BASED ON VIRTUE ETHICS

We are now in a position to distinguish between two phenomena often confused in the literature on cyberethics: the renewed popularity of virtue ethics

(a) in our society (see Slote, 2000, for a sympathetic overview) and (b) in cyberspace (Coleman, 1999, 2001; Grodzinsky, 2001).

In case (a), one is confronted by a context in which an individualistic culture facilitates practically, but does not justify theoretically, the return to a subject-oriented ethics. One should still properly object that (1) the kind of egopoiesis promoted by virtue ethics cannot (indeed, was not meant to) scale to very complex and open social contexts; and (2) virtue ethics presupposes a philosophical anthropology (a theory of what it means to be fully human) that, in a sufficiently evolved social context, cannot be left embedded but that, once it is made fully explicit, requires an ethical justification to become acceptable precisely as a *morally good* anthropology, and hence as ethically preferable.

In case (b), phenomena like the great popularity of "virtual communities" (see the section on virtual communities), which arguably represent the digital reincarnation of the polis, mean that people naturally tend to concentrate on the ethical construction of their "personae" as, at the same time, a contribution to the construction of the agent's self and a substantial contribution to the construction of the local cybercommunity, which is largely characterized by the members constituting and inhabiting it. In this simple and closed context, an egopoietic approach is indeed fruitful, precisely for the same reasons it was in the polis. One is justified in arguing that virtue ethics may be all that is needed for the ethical well-being of the whole community.

The two trends (a) and (b) have merged and currently interact in the information society, but they are better understood separately, lest one should mistakenly argue that because virtue ethics can work in small cybercommunities (comparable to local area networks) and it is popular "IRL" or "OT" (*in real life* or *out there*) it is also all that cyberethics needs as a theoretical foundation. The opposite is true. Because virtue ethics remains limited by its subject-oriented approach and its philosophical anthropology, it cannot provide, by itself, a satisfactory ethics for a globalized world in general and for the information society in particular. If misapplied, it fosters ethical individualism, as the agent is more likely to mind only her own self-construction. If it is uncritically adopted, it can be intolerant, since agents and theorists may forget the culturally overdetermined nature of their foundationalist anthropologies, which often happen to have religious roots. If it fosters tolerance, it may still spread relativism because any self-construction becomes acceptable as long as it takes place in the enclave of one's own private sphere, culture, and cyberniche, without bothering any neighbor.

The inadequacy of virtue ethics is of course historical. The theory has aged well, but it can provide, at most, a local sociopoietic approach as a mere extension of its genuine vocation: egopoiesis. It intrinsically lacks the resources to go beyond the construction of the individual and the indirect role this may play in shaping his or her local community. Theoretically, however, the limits of virtue ethics should not lead to an overall rejection of any *constructionist* approach. On the contrary, the fundamentally constructionist lesson taught by virtue ethics (one of the features that make virtue ethics appealing in the first place) is more important than ever.

In a global information society,[5] the individual agent (often a *multiagent system*[6]) is like a demiurge. Her ontic powers can be variously exercised (in terms of control, creation, or modeling) over herself (e.g., genetically, physiologically, neurologically, and narratively), over human society (e.g., culturally, politically, socially, and economically), and over natural or artificial environments (e.g., physically and informationally). Such an increasingly powerful agent has corresponding moral duties and responsibilities to oversee not only the development of her own character and habits but also the well-being of each of her spheres of influence. Clearly, a constructionist ethics should be retained and reinforced. The mistake (developing cyberethics in terms of virtue ethics) lies not in the stress put on constructionism per se, but in the direction in which constructionism is presupposed to develop—namely, only toward the individual source of the moral action (building the character of a human agent) instead of the receiver of the moral action as well; that is, toward the patient, the object, and more generally the environment affected by the action. The kind of ethical constructionism needed today goes well beyond the education of the self and the political engineering of the simple and closed cyberpolis. It must also address the urgent and pressing question concerning the kind of global realities that are being built.[7] This means decoupling constructionism from subjectivism and reorienting it to the object, applying it *also* to society and the environment, the receivers of the agent's actions.[8]

The term "ecopoiesis" refers to the morally informed construction of the environment based on this object- or ecologically oriented perspective. To move from individual virtues to global values, an *ecopoietic* approach is needed that recognizes the agent's responsibilities toward the environment (including present and future inhabitants) as its enlightened creator, steward, or supervisor, not just as its virtuous user and consumer.

An ecopoietic ethics, like any form of constructionism, raises a fundamental ontological concern. Moral luck aside, the chances of constructing an ethically good x increase the better one knows what an ethically good x is, and vice versa. Constructionism depends on a (satisfactory epistemic access to, or understanding of, the) relevant ontology. In the context of digital environments, an ecopoietic ethics presupposes a substantial answer to the foundationalist question "What is the essential nature of information, computers, and the Internet?" If virtue ethics presupposes a philosophical anthropology, an ecopoietic ethics seems to require a *philosophy of information* (Floridi, 1999,

2002, and 2003a). In the rest of this chapter, we will not pursue this onto-logical foundation of constructionism. Instead of looking at the theoretical roots of constructionism, we concentrate on its branches, and seek to clarify the connection between cyberethics and constructionism by showing how the latter emerges from the Web[9] and how the Web can benefit from a con-structionist approach.

POIESIS ON THE WEB

The Web is changing patterns of moral behavior in many ways, with impor-tant repercussions on the development of ethical discourse. Instances of situ-ated action ethics, primarily with negative consequences, have attracted a large variety of detailed analyses, and account for most of the literature in cyberethics (see, e.g., Spinello and Tavani, 2001, and other chapters in this volume). The Web, however, is not only a source of moral dilemma. As a new social space and digital environment, it has also greatly enhanced the possi-bility of developing egopoietic, sociopoietic, and ecopoietic projects. It has thus contributed to the emergence of a constructionist ethics as a macro-scopic phenomenon. In this section we consider a range of indicative exam-ples that well illustrate the ethics of constructionism.

INTERFACES

Choosing and modeling one's own interface to the digital world represent a first, indicative example of the kind of constructionism promoted by the Web. A user's most immediate interactions with the Web lie with an inter-face, whose features therefore influence her view. By tradition, a well-designed interface offers its user a convenient *mental model* for the actions it supports. For instance, one design principle states that, if an action has dif-ferent effects in different situations, the prevailing *mode* that determines the effect should be intuitively clear to the user. Typical mental models in this context are the "desktop," "folder," and "filing cabinet." As an example of the model clarifying the mode, by adopting the mental model of the text file as a folder, the user is able to appreciate that the depression of a key has different effects when a text file is open or when it is closed. On the other hand, that model is limited because it does not address why the user periodically needs to "save" the results of editing the file.

Laurel (1991) has proposed an alternative view of interfaces as theater, following Aristotle's six elements of drama. In order of increasingly abstract material cause (that one of Aristotle's four causes, operating during the process of creation, that reflects the fabric from which a thing is made), together with their interpretation in human-computer activity, they are (adapted from Laurel, 1991, Table 2.1) as follows.

MATERIAL CAUSE	INTERFACE ACTIVITY
Spectacle/enactment	All sensory components of the action represented
Pattern/melody	The pleasurable perception of pattern in the sensory phenomena
Language/diction	The selection and arrangement of signs, used semiotically
Thought/reasoning	The inferred internal processes leading to choice, of both human and computer
Character/agency	The bundles of predispositions and traits, of both human and computer
Plot/action	The whole action; a collaboration between system and user

This approach places emphasis on designing the action (to be engaged in equally by user and computer) rather, for example, than on the user's mental model. The computer is thought of as an enabling medium instead of a mere tool. Laurel's metaphor, expressed in terms of Aristotle's analysis of theater, highlights the constructionist nature of interface design rather than the ontological properties emphasized in the "mode" metaphor. Indeed, attributes at each level are constructed from those at the lower level. The agent is charged with the responsibility of building her own access to the digital environment. The insights gained by Laurel's approach seem mainly to have been applied to the design of interfaces that are meant to stay in their delivered form.

A more recent, "dynamic" approach has been taken by computer manufacturers who recognize that many users want to configure their interface themselves (with scope ranging from the rather superficial choice of screen saver to more substantial matters of structure and mode of interaction). It seems to be more important to provide the user with a configurable interface than to offer a particularly elegant or efficient one: it is a consequence of the user's constructionist drive that the act of configuring one's own interface makes it preferable.

OPEN SOURCE

The second logical step, after the construction of a personalized interface to the digital world, is the construction of digital entities that populate and interact in cyberspace. What form should these entities take? Along with use of the Internet and subsequently the Web has come demand, from a surprisingly large number of users, for "open source" software. The average computer user interacts with an operating system by clicking on icons, dragging and dropping, and so on. A user-friendly graphical interface (GUI) shields one not only from invoking commands directly (i.e., from typing the command name and whatever parameters it requires) but also, and more interestingly, from the underlying code that implements the operations. Consequently, even the experienced user has no way to access and modify the underlying source code, which executes operating system or applications commands. A system whose code is directly accessible to the user is said to be *open source*.

The high demand for open source code is a reflection of the number of users who prefer, where possible, the option of configuring their own software rather than making do with off-the-shelf packages.[10] This provides further evidence for the strength of constructionism (quite apart from the other factors involved in supporting the open source movement, which include a feeling of 'brotherhood' made possible by the Web and in opposition to being dictated to by a monopolistic software company), but there is also a new factor involved. The major "extraordinary success" of the 1990s was Linux, a free, open source version of Unix, whose remarkable story provides evidence of what may be called *distributed constructionism*. To clarify the point, consider the difference between Richard Stallman and Linus Torvalds's strategies.

On the one hand, Richard Stallman's *Free Software Foundation* (begun October 1985, see Williams, 2002) released the code for components, as they were completed by Stallman himself, of his version GNU (GNU's Not Unix) of the Unix operating system (GNU/Linux). "The overall purpose is to give the users freedom by giving them free software they can use and to extend the boundaries of what you can do with entirely free software as far as possible" (Stallman, quoted in Moody, 2002, p. 28). Stallman's GNU GPL (General Public License) perpetuates, efficiently, the freeness of open source software and any derivatives resulting from modifications by its recipients. "This enormous efficiency acted as one of the main engines in driving the free software projects on to their extraordinary successes during the 1990s" (Moody, 2002, p. 28). Initially, circulation of the original components was by magnetic tape from Stallman or people affiliated to his project, when the Web was not yet a common medium of communication. Controlled by Stallman, the enterprise still exhibited egopoietic values; most notably it was meant to promote a software version of the "freedom of speech" movement.

On the other hand, Linus Torvalds launched his project for the development of Linux by relying entirely on *distributed constructionism*, that is, the unsuspected but evident interest, shared by a growing community, in coordinating efforts to achieve a global product while each realizes only a local specific component of it. The project took full advantage of the Web's *point-to-point* penetration. Human communities tend to be rigidly structured, so that direct communication between individuals is highly constrained. The media can be seen as partially facilitating that tendency, and mobile phones help to implement it to a restricted degree. But the Web removes that constraint almost entirely among its "netizens," and provides a poietic-enabling environment through which the community of users and developers of Linux could interact and communicate easily and efficiently. Linux has clearly developed as an ecopoietic enterprise.

The difference between the two approaches has not passed unnoticed.[11] It has been well summarized by Eric Raymond in *The Cathedral and the Bazaar*:

> Linux overturned most of what I thought I knew. . . . I believed that the most important software . . . [like that of Stallman] . . . needed to be built like cathedrals, carefully crafted by individual wizards or small bands of mages working in splendid isolation, with no beta to be released before its time. Linus Torvalds' style of development—release early and often, dele-gate everything you can, be open to the point of promiscuity—came as a surprise . . . the Linux community seemed to resemble a great babbling bazaar of differing agendas and approaches. (Raymond, 2001, p. 21)

The difference between Stallman and Torvalds's strategies may appear to be partly attributable, historically, to different stages in the development of the Internet. Conceptually, however, it is really the result of two different constructionist ethics. Linux and other similar open source products are built and maintained as an expression of distributed constructionism on the Web. They provide another dimension to Stallman's simple individual construc-tionism, and one supported amply by the Web, which is thereby seen to pro-vide a robust support for *collaboration without attrition*.

DIGITAL ARTS

The availability of Web-based interfaces and software makes possible the con-struction of forms of digital art previously unimaginable. Murray (2000) has identified three characteristic pleasures of digital environments in general:

1. *Immersion:* the participatory immersive medium intensifies the age-old desire to live out fantasy. Rather than Coleridge's "willing suspension of disbelief," she proposes it to be viewed, more realistically, as supporting "the active *creation* of belief" (p. 110, emphasis added).
2. *Agency:* "the satisfying power to make meaningful action and see the results of our decisions and choices" (p. 126).
3. *Transformation:* the shape shifting, morphing possible because of the dig-ital representation of data and the ease with which it can be transformed.

For the purpose of analyzing the future of digital narrative, Murray reflects: "These pleasures are in some ways continuous with the pleasures of traditional media and in some ways unique. Certainly the combination of pleasures, like the combination of properties of the digital medium itself, is completely novel" (Murray, 2000, p. 181). Murray's interest is in digital environments generally, not specifically in those supported by the Web. The Web is *public* in a way that other digital media are not. Nevertheless, if we add to Murray's three pleasures that of *interactivity*, we are led to investigate the wider field of digital art and the impact that constructionism has had on it.

Digital art has shared with cyberethics its first half-century of existence (Reffen Smith, 1997). Over this period, the topic has expanded with the pervasive influence of the digital medium and now includes graphic art, musical composition, poetry, architectural style, and cinema as well as narrative fiction. Despite such variety, it seems that "digital art is novel in two ways, the first deriving from virtual reality techniques and the second deriving from the capacity of computers to support interactivity" (Lopes, 2003). Because the result of some digital art is difficult to distinguish from traditional art, emphasis is placed on the *process* rather than the *product*. (If a computer can solve crosswords faster than I can—albeit by the brute-force method of searching through a dictionary and trying all feasible combinations—then, one reasons, at least the *way* I do it cannot be mimicked by computer. Again, if a computer can produce Picasso-like pictures—albeit routinely by digitizing a photo and then processing an abstraction of it—then, one reasons, at least Picasso's originality is inimitable.) The same emphasis, on process rather than product, is made by Binkley (1998) who identifies the objects being manipulated, or *maculated*, by artists as being digital (data structures rather than paint or cardboard), with the result that the artwork produced lacks physical uniqueness and can in fact be copied electronically indefinitely. His view of process can be interpreted as acknowledging the importance of constructionism. Indeed, Binkley makes the point that, with the Web, the objects of construction may bear little resemblance to those of earlier generations.

HOME PAGES AND THE CONSTRUCTION OF THE SELF

With interfaces, software, and even new forms of art being constructed in cyberspace, the self is next in line. Web sites are certainly popular new objects of creation. The reason lies partly with the recent development of e-commercial models of marketing (if you want to buy a sofa, visit our Web site and simulate how it would appear in your room), partly with human desire or need for communication (from government legislation to photos of a grandchild's first birthday), partly with a new wave of constructionism concerning the self through personal home pages (Chandler, 1998, see also Adamic and Adar, online). Although graduates of computer science who once would have gone into programming jobs now go into Web design, the sale of off-the-shelf software for constructing Web pages is burgeoning.

VIRTUAL COMMUNITIES

With the construction of the self, we have reached the starting point for the construction of virtual communities. What can we learn from sociocyberphenomena like Web-based chat rooms, interest groups, ICQ-like communities, newsgroups, online forum, and so on, which rely for their existence on point-to-point communication offered by the Web? Until recently, it was common to argue, pessimistically, that the Web prompted people to withdraw from social engagement and become isolated, depressed, and even alienated. According to a constructionist view, however, the Web actually provides a poietic-enhancing environment, which should facilitate, rather than hinder, the construction, development, and reinforcement of self-identities, links with local (real and/or virtual) communities, and social interactions. New data confirm this prediction. Virtual communities have become the most popular Web domain category, after search engines and portals (Nielsen//NetRatings, April 26, 2002, http://www.acnielsen.at/at/news/press/ 2002_04_26_110502/FULL-TEXT.PDF). And a report published by the Pew Internet & American Life Project (http://www.pewinternet.org/), entitled *Online Communities: Networks that Nurture Long-distance Relationships and Local Ties* (October 31, 2001), has shown that "the online world is a vibrant social universe where many Internet users enjoy serious and satisfying contact with online communities. These online groups are made up of those who share passions, beliefs, hobbies, or lifestyles. Tens of millions of Americans have joined communities after discovering them online. And many are using the Internet to join and participate in longstanding, traditional groups such as professional and trade associations. All in all, 84% of Internet users have at one time or another contacted an online group." (http://www.pewinternet.org/reports/pdfs/PIP_Communities_Report.pdf). Virtual communities are a flourishing result of the free exercise of the constructionist drive. In them, users reveal personal facts, "flame," and switch personae by endlessly constructing, deconstructing, and reconstructing alternative selves. They collaborate with and participate in a common social project. In general, they behave quite differently from the way they would behave in person. It is as if the normal metric of social distance were expanded by the Web. The Web empowers new categories of users with the possibility of constructing a new self and an e-polis. It makes constructionism an open option for anyone with access to an Internet connection.

CONSTRUCTIONISM ON THE WEB

What is the nature of constructionism as exhibited on the Web? The previous examples show that the characteristic features of the Web that seem particularly relevant to existing instances of constructionism are: interactivity, virtuality, agency, transformationality, process (rather than product) orientation, social publicity, and immediate point-to-point communication, which allows collaboration without attrition due to an apparent increase in social distance. Constructionism emerges as a most significant and intrinsic property of the Web, more fundamental than any policy vacuum or pressing practical problems. The increased social distance means that the ethical consequences of constructionism on the Web are particularly acute. Indeed, the apparent increase in social distance acts as a magnifier for ethical factors.

HOMO POIETICUS

Homo sapiens has primary needs, which relate to survival (like food, shelter, security, and reproduction), and secondary needs (like hedonistic, intellectual, artistic, and physical pursuits), which arise once primary needs are fulfilled. Constructionism seems to be among such secondary needs. It is the drive to build physical and conceptual objects and, more subtly, exercise control and stewardship over them. It manifests itself in the care of existing, and creation of new, realities, whether material or conceptual. Thus, constructionism is ultimately best understood as a struggle against entropy. Existentially, it represents the strongest reaction against the destiny of death. In terms of a philosophical anthropology, constructionism is embodied by what we have termed elsewhere *homo poieticus* (Floridi, 1999). *Homo poieticus* is to be distinguished from *homo faber*, user and "exploitator" of natural resources, from *homo oeconomicus*, producer, distributor, and consumer of wealth, and from *homo ludens* (Huizinga, 1970), who embodies a leisurely playfulness devoid of the ethical care and responsibility characterizing the constructionist attitude.[12] *Homo poieticus* concentrates not merely on the final result, but on the dynamic, ongoing process through which the result is achieved. A punctured bicycle tire may be mended entirely routinely (in primary fashion, for "survival" on a busy day) with little component of construction, or it may be mended in a more deliberate, considered fashion, perhaps with reflection on the process and what it is being achieved. In the case of the Web, the ease with which digital constructs can be created and altered means that cyberspace is an ideal environment for *homo poieticus*. Many influential teachers of constructive disciplines emphasize in their teachings an approach to their art that we can now identify as constructionist, to distinguish it from the ludic, routine, or mundane approach. Often these teachings draw from Eastern philosophy and mysticism to make the point that the process, and the novice's state of mind during it, are of fundamental importance. The end result will "take care of itself," if the process is right.[13]

Given the importance we have attached to *homo poieticus*, it would be surprising if its nature had not been studied in other contexts. Two indicative examples are worth mentioning here, to enable the reader to place our position within a wider context.[14]

Piaget (Gruber and Vonèche, 1995) coined the term *constructivism* for an epistemic model in which children learn while interacting with their environment by manipulating and building objects and developing coherent intellectual structures. Papert (1993) extended Piaget's work from genetic epistemology to the child's construction of *microworlds* and called the result *constructionism*: "My perspective is more interventionist. My goals are education, not just understanding. So, in my own thinking I have placed a greater emphasis on two dimensions implicit but not elaborated in Piaget's own work: an interest in intellectual structures that could develop as opposed to those that actually at present do develop in the child, and the design of learning environments that are resonant with them." Inspired by both, Murray (2000) is interested, as we have seen, in the possibilities for narrative fiction in cyberspace. She uses Piaget's term "to indicate an aesthetic enjoyment in making things within a fictional world" (p. 294). Indeed, she claims that "constructivist pleasure is the highest form of narrative agency the MUD [Multi User Domain] medium allows" (p. 149). While for Piaget and Papert the mental process of construction is autonomous and even subconscious, for Murray (and for us) it is typically explicit. More recently, constructivist methodologies have been applied to digital media. In Eisenstadt and Vincent (2000), for example, we read that: "Our approach to media rich learning experiences derives from constructivist models of education" (p. ix); the aim is "empowering individuals to create their own content" (p. ix). In this case, the difference between the two approaches is that, for our constructionist perspective, the fundamental novelty brought about by computer-based or online learning has got little to do with long-distance courses, virtual classes, and telepresence, for it is rather to be identified in the vindication of the "maker's knowledge" tradition.[15] ICT makes possible hands-on experiences, simulations, collaborations, and interactions with conceptual or information structures that can be built, manipulated, disassembled, and so on, thus completely transforming the learning/teaching experience.

The process-oriented component of our concept of constructionism also has an interesting precedent in literary theory. Genetic criticism (critique genetique)[16] was the name given in the early 1970s to an empirical approach to the literary act "d'expliquer par quels processus d'invention, d'ecriture et de transformation un projet est devenu ce texte auquel l'institution conferera ou non le statut d'oeuvre litteraire" (Gresillon, 1994, p. 206). However, the concept differs from ours in subscribing firmly to written traces:

> Genetic criticism has used the post-structuralist dissolution of the closed text to define its own notion of the fluid, dynamic manuscript text which, since it is not in any published form, is subject to constant revision. At the same time, genetic criticism has abandoned the vague post-structuralist conception of the text as an interactive process. The genetic approach reinstalls the text in its materiality. Its objects of inquiry are the material traces of writing. (Schmid, 1998, p. 12)

CONCLUSION: FROM CYBERETHICS TO INFORMATION ETHICS

For its first half century, cyberethics, the ethics of ICT, and in particular of the Web, has been a situated action ethics. The point becomes clear if one reads Bynum's overview (Bynum, 2001; see also http://plato.stanford.edu/

entries/ethics-computer/), which aims to survey the "historical milestones" of the subject, decade by decade. According to Bynum, "the best way to understand what the field is like is to examine some example sub-areas of current interest." He considers the workplace, security, ownership and professional responsibility. Clearly, the approach to cyberethics (computer ethics) has been predominantly pragmatic and action-oriented.[17] In the absence of any foundational principle, the field is reduced to a collection of case-based analyses.

The battle cry for the 1990s has been James Moor's quote: "A typical problem in computer ethics arises because there is a policy vacuum about how computer technology should be used" (Moor, 1985). In the tailwind of cyberethics's policy vacuum, much of the discussion has concentrated on the extent to which the Web, or Internet more generally, provides only a context of application for standard ethical issues *in silico* (the uniqueness problem of computer ethics). The conclusion has been that, at the very least, the Web magnifies many ethical issues (security, privacy, ownership, and so on).

Yet, not *all* problems of interest arise in this way. For example, Brey's *disclosive (computer) ethics* has more recently provided an alternative approach, which "uncovers and morally evaluates values and norms embedded in the design and application of computer systems" (Brey, 2001, p. 61). Although the resulting study is (by definition) again pragmatic, it acknowledges the importance of emergent ethical phenomena. The future of cyberethics, dictated by this pragmatic outlook, is seen by Bynum (2001, pp. 21–23) as being dominated by the tension between the *conservative view* and the opposing *global view*. According to the former, no issues exist that are unique to cyberethics and so the subject will eventually subside. According to the latter, the information revolution and its issues are causing a reevaluation of traditional ethics and will eventually supervene.

Elsewhere, we have argued for an alternative view (Floridi and Sanders, 2002). Our approach does not undervalue the important contributions provided by technological applications and the ethical questions arising from them. Situated action ethics is important, even when "situated" means "placed in cyberspace." Our approach simply offers an account based more squarely on an appreciation of the artifacts of the new technology. Perhaps this will help to reevaluate Bynum's view (Bynum, 2001) of the future of cyberethics, by suggesting where the originality of this new field lies. In fact, by its lights, a merely situated action cyberethics would necessarily be bound by lack of concepts and hence inevitably suffer criticisms of nonuniqueness. One of the benefits of the current approach is that this issue simply does not arise. From a constructionist perspective, for example, the digital divide (Floridi, 2003b) is not just a matter of denied access to information and recreation, but also a more fundamental problem of anthropological genesis, concerning the prevention of a full epiphany of *homo poieticus* in many cultures and social contexts. The approach promoted by situated action ethics makes it extremely difficult to imagine what a foundation for cyberethics could be. On the contrary, a constructionist view liberates us from that difficulty and makes intellectual progress much easier. By placing value in information, regarded ontologically as the primary, fundamental, and constituent element of our new environment and its artificial agents, it is possible to elaborate a constructionist theory *(information ethics)* that supports an ecopoietic approach to cyberethics (Floridi, 1999, and 2003c; Floridi and Sanders, 1999, 2001). This is a development consistent with a fundamental trend in other ethical fields like environmental ethics. It is encouraging that, at last, it is becoming clearer how cyberethics may be able to feed back and refresh the ethical discourse at large.

NOTES

1. See, e.g., "the trolley problem" (Foot, 1967 and Thomson, 1976); for a very entertaining parody do not miss "the revised trolley problem" in Patton (1988). On "George's job" and "Jim and the Indians" see Smart and Williams (1973). Contrary to the trolley problem, the last two cases are meant to provide counterexamples against purely consequentialist positions.

2. For an entirely "situation-based ethics" approach to the Internet see, e.g., Dreyfus (2001), who seems to ignore entirely any constructionist issue. His "anthropology" includes only single Web users browsing the Internet.

3. We use the term "proactive" technically, to qualify policies, agents, processes, or strategies that (a) implement effective action, in anticipation of expected problems, difficulties, or needs, in order to control and prevent them, at least partially, rather than merely reacting to them as they occur (in this sense an ethically proactive approach can be compared to preventive medicine, which is concerned with reducing the incidence of disease by modifying environmental or behavioral factors that are causally related to illness); or (b) actively initiate good changes, promoting rather than merely waiting for something positive to happen.

4. Communal behaviors that are not immediately or directly so explicable are called emergent. Perhaps the simplest examples come from artificial communities. In Conway's *Game of Life*, e.g., the behavior of an individual is determined by the states of its immediate neighbors. Stable, periodic, or otherwise interesting behavior (e.g. gliders, which retain their collective state but glide across the digital landscape) of subcommunities consisting of several individuals provide examples of emergent behavior. In our own, real, global society, monetary inflation, unemployment, and such phenomena whose dynamics are determined by feedback of data from subcommunities are examples.

5. On the history of the development of the global information society see Mattelart (2001).

6. A multiagent system (MAS) is a conglomeration of interacting components, known as agents, capable of cooperating to solve problems that typically are beyond

the individual capabilities or knowledge of each agent. Thus a MAS exhibits a greater system-level behavior than its constituting agents (Huhns and Singh, 1998).

7. We have addressed the issue of the construction of ethical artificial agents in Floridi and Sanders (forthcoming).

8. In Floridi (1999) and (2003c), we have argued that this is in line with the development of contemporary ethics, which has registered a general shift from the centrality of the agent in standard macroethics such as virtue ethics, deontologism, consequentialism and contractualism, to the centrality of the patient in nonstandard macroethics such as environmental ethics, bioethics, and medical ethics.

9. For current purposes no distinction is drawn between the Internet and the Web.

10. A statistically insignificant presence in 1997, the popularity of Linux and the free/open source software movement has exploded in the last five years. In 2000, the International Data Corporation (www.idc.com) estimated that Linux was the fastest-growing server operating system, with 27 percent (up from 25 percent in 1999) of the server market, second only to Windows NT, which had 41 percent (up from 38 percent in 1999). Moreover, according to a new report from IDC (*Server Operating Environments Market Forecast and Analysis, 2000–2004*), commercial shipments of Linux grew at a compounded annual growth rate of almost 17 percent from 1999 to 2004.

11. Moody (2002) seems to underestimate the "philosophical" contrasts between the two movements, on which see the documents cited in the References under the entries *Free Software Foundation Web Site* and *Open Source Software Web Site*.

12. Evers (2000) has associated the Open Source movement with *homo ludens*.

13. Particularly interesting examples of a constructionist attitude arise in most of the fine arts. To name just two, one may refer to architecture (Alexander, 1970; Liebeskind, online) and cabinetmaking (Krenov, 1976).

14. We do not address here the critical issue of the connections between ethical constructionism and social constructivism. On the interactions between philosophy of technology and social constructivism see Brey (1997).

15. The Maker's Knowledge Tradition goes back to Plato. It is the view that an epistemic agent knows, understands, or otherwise epistemically controls better (or perhaps only) what the agent has made.

16. For a summary of genetic criticism and two case studies (Flaubert and Proust) see Schmid (1998). There is an interesting tension produced by a rigid application of those ideas when text is interpreted as digital art; our notion of constructionism provides one resolution of it.

17. For a conceptual analytic history of information ethics, complementing Bynum's collection of milestones, see Floridi and Sanders (2002) and Tavani (2002).

REFERENCES

Adamic, L. A., and E. Adar E. 2003. You Are What You Link, http://www10.org/program/society/yawyl/YouAreWhatYouLink.htm.

Alexander, C. W. 1970. *Notes on the Synthesis of Form*. Cambridge: Harvard University Press.

Binkley, T. 1998. "Computer Art," in M. Kelly (Ed.), *Encyclopedia of Aesthetics*. Oxford: Oxford University Press, vol. 1, pp. 412–414.

Brey, P. 1997. Philosophy of Technology Meets Social Constructivism, *Society for Philosophy & Technology* 2:3–4. http://scholar.lib.vt.edu/ejournals/SPT/v2_n3n4html/brey.html.

———. 2001. "Disclosive Computer Ethics," in R. A. Spinello and H. T. Tavani (Eds.), *Readings in CyberEthics*. Sudbury, MA: Jones and Bartlett.

Bynum T. W. 2001. "Ethics and the Information Revolution," in R. A. Spinello and H. T. Tavani (Eds.), *Readings in CyberEthics*. Sudbury, MA: Jones and Bartlett.

Chandler, Daniel. 1998. Personal Home Pages and the Construction of Identities on the Web, paper for a conference of the Aberystwyth Post-International Group on the theme of Linking Theory and Practice: Issues in the Politics of Identity, September 9–11, University of Wales, Aberystwyth. http://www.aber.ac.uk/media/Documents/short/webident.html.

Clarke, Roger. 1993–1994. Asimov's Laws of Robotics Implications for Information Technology, *IEEE Computer* 26.12 (1993): 53–61 and 27.1 (1994): 57–66. http://www.anu.edu.au/people/Roger.Clarke/SOS/Asimov.html.

Coleman, Kari Gwen. 1999. "Responsible Computers," in A. D'Atri, A. Marturano, S. Rogerson, and T. W. Bynum (Eds.), Proceedings of the 4th ETHICOMP International Conference on the Social and Ethical Impacts of Information and Communication Technologies, October 6–8, Rome, Italy (Rome: LUISS Guido Carli Centro di Ricerca sui Sistemi Informativi).

———. 2001. Android Arete: Toward a Virtue Ethic for Computational Agents, *Ethics and Information Technology* 3.4: 247–265.

Dreyfus, H. L. 2001. *On the Internet*. New York and London: Routledge.

Eisenstadt, M., and T. Vincent (Eds.). 2000. *The Knowledge Web: Learning and Collaborating on the Net*. London: Kogan Page.

Evers, S. 2000. *An Introduction to Open Source Software Development*, thesis, Technische Universität Berlin, http://user.cs.tu-berlin.de/~tron/opensource/opensource.html.

Floridi L. 1999. Information Ethics: On the Theoretical Foundations of Computer Ethics, *Ethics and Information Technology* 1.1: 37–56. Preprint available at http://www.wolfson.ox.ac.uk/~floridi/.

———. 1999. *Philosophy and Computing—An Introduction*. New York and London: Routledge.

———. 2002. What Is the Philosophy of Information?, *Metaphilosophy* 33.1/2: 123–145. Preprint available at http://www.wolfson.ox.ac.uk/~floridi/.

———. (Ed.). 2003a. *The Blackwell Guide to the Philosophy of Computing and Information*. New York and Oxford: Blackwell.

————. 2003b. Information Ethics: An Environmental Approach to the Digital Divide, *Philosophy in the Contemporary World* (9.1): 39–45. Preprint available at http://www.wolfson.ox.ac.uk/~floridi/.

————. 2003c. On the Intrinsic Value of Information Objects and the Infosphere, *Ethics and Information Technology* (4.4): 287–304. Preprint available at http://www.wolfson.ox.ac.uk/~floridi/.

————, and J. W. Sanders. 1999. Entropy as Evil in Information Ethics, *Etica & Politica*, special issue on *Computer Ethics*, 1.2. http://www.univ.trieste.it/~dipfilo/etica_e_politica/1999_2/homepage.html.

————. 2001. Artificial Evil and the Foundation of Computer Ethics, *Ethics and Information Technology* 3.1: 55–66. Preprint available at http://www.wolfson.ox.ac.uk/~floridi/.

————. 2001b. On the Morality of Artificial Agents, *CEPE 2001, Computer Ethics: Philosophical Enquiry*, Lancaster University, December 14–16, forthcoming in *Minds and Machines*. Preprint available at http://www.wolfson.ox.ac.uk/~floridi/.

————. Forthcoming. Computer Ethics: Mapping the Foundationalist Debate, *Ethics and Information Technology* 4.1: 1–9. Preprint available at http://www.wolfson.ox.ac. uk/~floridi/.

Foot, Philippa. 1967. The Problem of Abortion and the Doctrine of the Double Effect, *Oxford Review*, 5. Reprinted in B. Steinbock and A. Norcross (Eds.), *Killing and Letting Die*. New York: Fordham University Press, 1994, pp. 266–279.

Free Software Foundation Website. "Why 'Free Software' Is Better than 'Open Source.'" http://www.gnu.org/philosophy/free-software-for-freedom.html.

Gresillon, A. 1994. *Elements de Critique Genetique*. Paris: Presses Universitaires de Frances.

Grodzinsky, F. 2001. "Revisiting the Virtues: The Practitioner from Within," in R. A. Spinello and H. T. Tavani (Eds.), *Readings in CyberEthics*. Sudbury, MA: Jones and Bartlett.

Gruber, H. E., and J. J. Vonëche. (Eds.). 1995. *The Essential Piaget: An Interpretive Reference and Guide*, 2nd ed. Northvale, NJ: Jason Aronson.

Huhns, M. N., and M. P. Singh. 1998. "Agents and Multi-agent Systems: Themes, Approaches, and Challenges," in M. N. Huhns and M. P. Singh (Eds.), *Readings in Agents*. San Francisco: Morgan Kaufmann, pp. 1–23.

Huizinga, J. 1970. *Homo Ludens: A Study of the Play Element in Culture*. London: Paladin. (First published in 1938.)

Krenov, J. 1976. *A Cabinetmaker's Notebook*. Fresno: Linden Press.

Laurel, B. 1991. *Computers as Theatre*. Reading: Addison-Wesley.

Liebeskind, D. online. http://www.solearth.com/pages/art10.htm and http://library.thinkquest.org/26499/db-architect.php3?browser=3&architectIndexd=69.

Lopes, D. M. M. 2003. "Digital Art," in L. Floridi (Ed.), *The Blackwell Guide to the Philosophy of Computing and Information*. New York and Oxford: Blackwell.

214 LUCIANO FLORIDI AND J. W. SANDERS

Mattelart, A. 2001. *Histoire de la Société de l'Information*. Paris: Éditions La Découverie.

Moody, G. 2002. *Rebel Code: Linux and the Open Source Revolution*. London: Penguin. (The 2001 edition had a slightly different title: *Rebel Code: How Linus Torvalds, Linux and the Open Source Movement Are Outmastering Microsoft.*)

Moor, James H. 1985. What Is Computer Ethics?, *Metaphilosophy* 16, 4:266–275.

Murray, J. H. 2000. *Hamlet on the Holodeck: The Future of Narrative in Cyberspace*. Cambridge: MIT Press.

Open Source Software Website. "Why 'Free' Software Is too Ambiguous," http://www.opensource.org/advocacy/free-notfree.php.

Papert, S. A. 1993. *Mindstorms: Children, Computers and Powerful Ideas*, 2nd ed. New York: Basic Books.

Patton, M. F. Jr. 1988. Tissues in the Profession: Can Bad Men Make Good Brains Do Bad Things?, Proceedings and Addresses of the American Philosophical Association, 61–63, http://www.mindspring.com/~mfpatton/Tissues.htm.

Raymond, E. S. 2001. *The Cathedral and the Bazaar: Musings on Linux and Open Source by an Accidental Rrevolutionary*, rev. ed. Sebastopol, CA: O'Reilly & Associates.

Reffen Smith, B. 1997. "Post-modern Art, or: Virtual Reality as Trojan Donkey, or: Horsetail Tartan Literature Groin Art," in S. Mealing (Ed.), *Computers and Art*. Exeter: Intellect.

Schmid, M. 1998. *Processes of Literary Creation: Flaubert and Proust*. Oxford: Legenda.

Slote, M. 2000. "Virtue Ethics," in H. La Follette (Ed.), *The Blackwell Guide to Ethical Theory*. Oxford and New York: Blackwell, pp. 325–347.

Smart, J. J. C., and B. A. O. Williams. 1973. *Utilitarianism: For and Against*. Cambridge: Cambridge University Press, 1973.

Spinello, R. A., and H. T. Tavani. (Eds.). 2001. *Readings in CyberEthics*. Sudbury, MA: Jones and Bartlett.

Tavani, H. T. 2002. The Uniqueness Debate in Computer Ethics: What Exactly Is at Issue, and Why Does It Matter?, *Ethics and Information Technology* 4.1: 37–54.

Thomson, J. J. 1976. Killing, Letting Die, and the Trolley Problem, *The Monist* 59: 204–217. Reprinted in W. Parent (Ed.), *Rights, Restitution, and Risk*. Cambridge: Harvard University Press, 1986.

Williams, S. 2002. *Free as in Freedom: Richard Stallman's Crusade for Free Software*. Farnham: O'Reilly & Associates.

TEN

The Impact of the Internet on Our Moral Condition

Do We Need a New Framework of Ethics?

HERMAN T. TAVANI

IN *THE IMPERATIVE OF RESPONSIBILITY*, an influential text in ethics and technology, Hans Jonas argues that "[m]odern technology has introduced actions of such novel scale . . . that the former framework of ethics can no longer contain them."[1] He goes on to claim that the "novel powers to act" made possible by modern technology require "novel ethical rules and perhaps even a *new ethics*."[2] Although Jonas put forth his thesis in the pre-Internet era,[3] some recent remarks on the part of authors in the field of computer ethics[4] suggest that Jonas's claims involving the impact of modern technology for our moral condition could be extended to cybertechnology as well.[5] Has the advent of the cybertechnology in general, and the Internet in particular, radically altered our moral condition? And, if so, does it follow that we need a new framework of ethics? The purpose of this chapter is to gain a clearer sense of what is meant by each of these questions.[6]

We begin with an analysis of what Jonas means by the expressions "moral condition" and "framework of ethics." We then consider a case illustrating the use of cybertechnology to determine whether our moral condition has been so severely altered because of the kinds of actions made possible by this technology that a new ethical framework is required. We next examine some specific arguments on both sides of this debate. One group of philosophers, whom we will call *traditionalists*, suggests that our existing framework of ethics is adequate to account for the kinds of actions made possible by cybertechnology. Other philosophers, whom we will label *expansionists,* argue that either a new or revised ethical framework is required. Although both expansionists and traditionalists have contributed some important insights to this ongoing debate, it will be argued that each side ultimately fails to see what exactly is needed. Finally, a case is made for the view that what is required for the Internet era is not a new framework of ethics but rather a revised methodological scheme, which expands slightly on the "standard method" of applied ethics and helps us to identify and analyze certain kinds of ethical issues that arise out of the use of cybertechnology.

HOW HAS MODERN TECHNOLOGY
ALTERED OUR MORAL CONDITION?

Jonas points out that in our traditional framework of ethics, the "human condition" was viewed as something "determined by the nature of man and the nature of things" and thus fixed or "given once for all."[7] Such a conception of our human (and, by extension, our moral) condition as "readily determinable" is, according to Jonas, no longer accurate in the era of modern technology.[8] Jonas's thesis includes two distinct, but related, claims: (a) the nature of human action has changed in fundamental ways; and (b) a fundamental change in the nature of human action requires a change in ethics.[9] With regard to (a), Jonas goes on to say that the change is not merely one in which "new objects of action have been added." Rather, it is a more radical change in the sense that "the qualitatively novel nature of certain of our actions has opened up a whole new dimension of ethical relevance."[10]

How exactly has the nature of human action changed? And how has this change affected our moral condition? Jonas believed that the nature of human action has changed dramatically because our actions (1) now have a global reach and (2) can affect future generations of humans. It is essentially for these reasons that Jonas suggested that the novel powers to act made possible by modern technology have created for us a new "moral condition."[11] Diane Michelfelder interprets Jonas's sense of a new moral condition as one in which we face "novel threats," such as those posed by atomic energy, the "innovations of bioengineering," and (technologically driven) "overconsumption of natural resources."[12] Because of the impact on nature itself, our new powers to act have implications not only for future generations of humans, but for the future of the planet as well. Furthermore, we find ourselves in the precarious position of being responsible for the future; yet, as Michelfelder correctly notes, we are simultaneously unable to predict the effects of our new powers to act for those who will inhabit the planet in the future.[13]

To illustrate Jonas's concern about our new powers to act with respect to issues of global reach and future impact, consider the example of nuclear warfare. Although it had been possible in previous eras to annihilate entire civilizations in conventional warfare, doing so required considerable time, effort, and sacrifice of human life on the part of the aggressors. With nuclear weapons, however, a single act or set of actions can accomplish this same task in a matter of minutes. Consider that by pressing a button, one can launch missiles that will deliver nuclear warheads to geographically remote regions of the world, thus killing millions of people in a single blow. Jonas believes that it is not simply that greater numbers of humans can be killed as a result of nuclear warfare; rather it is the qualitatively different nature of the effects of such warfare—both for humans and the planet—that have changed radically.[14] Thus, Jonas inferred that our new moral condition is one in which ethical significance can no longer be limited to the "direct dealing of man with man" in the here and now.[15]

Jonas noted that in our former scheme of ethics, we took for granted the view that human beings alone are worthy of moral consideration. This assumption was rejected by Jonas, however, who believed that we must now extend the sphere of moral consideration to include additional "objects" such as future generations of human beings as well as (the whole of) nature itself.[16] In the final section of this chapter, we consider more closely the claim that new moral objects have been generated by modern technology. There, we focus more specifically on the question whether any new moral objects have been introduced by cybertechnology. The primary objective of this chapter, however, is to determine whether cybertechnology has introduced any qualitatively novel kinds of human actions, which in turn have altered our moral condition to the point where either a new or revised ethical framework is required.

Jonas believed that the new moral condition created by the "altered nature of human action" has raised some important issues of responsibility for which our previous ethics "has left us unprepared."[17] For example, he suggested that our traditional conception of "neighbor ethics"—that is, an ethical system consisting of (Aristotelian) moral virtues[18] such as justice, courage, honesty, and so on—is no longer adequate in the era of modern technology. Such an ethical system, according to Jonas, has been "overshadowed," requiring a "new dimension of responsibility" for ethics.[19] In effect, Jonas believed that we need a new framework of ethics. But what exactly does he mean by this claim?

WHAT IS AN ETHICAL FRAMEWORK?

An ethical framework can be conceived of as a *system* that is composed of normative principles, rules, and theories. We can distinguish between a complete "ethical system" and the various components that constitute such a system. Although Jonas put forth neither a precise nor an explicit definition of an ethical system, he briefly differentiates among three notions that give us an insight into his conception of a framework of ethics: (1) *enjoinders* to do and not to do certain things, (2) *principles* for defining such enjoinders, and (3) and the *grounds of obligation* for establishing such principles.[20] Consider an example of each. First, specific enjoinders, in the form of imperatives such as "Respect a person's property" or "Don't steal," direct individuals either to do or refrain from certain courses of action. Second, various principles, including those of utility and impartiality, are typically appealed to in the process of defining and issuing enjoinders. Third, the ethical principles themselves must ultimately be grounded in either a legal, religious, or philosophical system of ethics.[21]

Consider a brief example of how the elements that compose a framework of ethics function together in a philosophical system versus a religious system. In a philosophical system such as that of Aristotle's, an enjoinder might be: "Don't spend too much time engaged in online activities." The principle grounding this enjoinder would be: "Act so as to comply with the mean and avoid the extremes." And the grounds for that principle would be the Aristotelian theory of the soul and the connection (moral virtue) between reason and desire (Aristotle's theory of human happiness). Contrast this scheme with one in which the component elements of an ethical framework are grounded in a religious system. An enjoinder might be the following: "Do not steal (copy) this piece of proprietary computer software." This enjoinder could be grounded in the principle: "Stealing violates one of God's Ten Commandments." And the grounding for that principle could be based on the notion of absolute obedience to divine command.[22]

We now have at least some sense of what Jonas means by a "framework" of ethics. But what does he mean when he says that our former framework of ethics is no longer adequate to contain the kinds of actions made possible by modern technology? Does he mean that the entire ethical framework, consisting of enjoinders, principles, and grounds of obligations, is inadequate and thus must be jettisoned in favor of an entirely new, and perhaps radically different, framework? Or does he mean that one or more of the individual components that constitute such a framework must be replaced or perhaps revised?[23] In examining the arguments advanced by expansionists, we will consider both interpretations. First, however, we consider whether cybertechnology has introduced any "novel powers to act" and, if so, whether such actions have altered our moral condition.

If we limit our analysis to actions made possible by those modern technologies pertaining to nuclear warfare, we might be inclined to agree with Jonas that our moral condition has been significantly altered. Can the kind of argument used by Jonas also be applied to cybertechnology? Has this particular form of technology also introduced certain "novel powers to act"? And are the kinds of actions made possible by cybertechnology such that they alter our moral condition so severely that they cannot be handled by our traditional framework of ethics? We consider this range of questions by examining a recent case of cyberstalking to see whether certain kinds of activities made possible by Internet technology pose any special challenge to our traditional framework of ethics.

CASE ILLUSTRATION: STALKING ON THE INTERNET

In October 1999, Amy Boyer, a twenty-year-old resident of Nashua, New Hampshire, was murdered by a young man who had stalked her via the Internet. The stalker, Liam Youens, was able to carry out most of the stalking activities that eventually led to Boyer's death by using a variety of tools available on the Internet. Through the use of standard Internet search facilities, Youens gathered information about Boyer that was readily accessible from databases available to online search requests. Simply by taking advantage of online tools available to any Internet user, he was able to find out where Boyer lived, where she worked, what kind of vehicle she drove, and so on. Youens was also able to use tools provided by Internet Service Providers (ISPs) to set up two Web sites about Amy Boyer. On one site, he posted personal information about Boyer, including a photograph of her. On another Web site, Youens described, in explicit detail, his plans to murder Boyer.

The Amy Boyer case raises a number of controversial questions, many of which would seem to have significant ethical implications. Among the ethical concerns raised are issues involving personal privacy in public space, security, anonymity, free speech, and the flow of information. Also raised are questions about moral responsibility, both at the individual and collective levels. For example, do individuals in online forums have an obligation to notify and assist others in danger? And do Internet Service Providers (ISPs) that host electronic forums have an obligation to monitor the content of the forums that reside in their Internet "space" to protect against harm caused to individuals?[24] So it would seem that the Amy Boyer stalking incident can be viewed as a paradigm case in which the issues raised are representative, if not exhaustive, of the wide range of ethical concerns associated with the use of cybertechnology. But is there anything morally peculiar or special about the ethical problems involving the Boyer case such that they have profoundly altered our moral condition?

Traditionalists suggest that ethical issues generated by cybertechnology such as those raised in the Boyer case of Internet stalking can be understood and analyzed in terms of our existing ethical categories. From the traditionalists' perspective, the use of Internet technology could be seen as simply the latest in a series of techniques that have been made available to stalkers to assist them in carrying out certain immoral and illegal activities. Traditionalists reject the claim that the ethical issues generated in the Boyer case are such that they cannot be evaluated by our traditional framework of ethics.

Expansionists, on the other hand, see the matter quite differently. They suggest that cybertechnology has made possible certain kinds of activities that cannot be analyzed satisfactorily via our traditional framework of ethics. To support their position, expansionists consider factors having to do with *scope* and *scale*. With respect to scope, expansionists citing the Amy Boyer case of cyberstalking would point to the fact that someone using the Internet for stalking purposes can stalk multiple victims simultaneously via the use of multiple "windows" on his or her computer. The stalker can also stalk victims who happen to live in communities that are geographically distant from the stalker. Expansionists also suggest that cybertechnology has made it possible for stalking activities to occur on a scale or order of magnitude that could not have been realized in the pre-Internet era. For one thing, more individuals can engage in stalking behavior because cybertechnology has made it so easy to do; as a result, significantly more people can now become the victims of stalkers. These and other factors[25] lead expansionists to conclude that our traditional framework of ethics is not sufficiently robust to handle the kinds of actions made possible by cybertechnology.

TWO INTERPRETATIONS OF THE
EXPANSIONISTS' ARGUMENT

Following Jonas's line of reasoning, we can approach the issue of whether a new framework of ethics is required to handle Internet-related ethical issues by first inquiring into whether cybertechnology has provided us with any "new powers to act." At the very least, it would appear that this technology has introduced certain "novel modes" for human action. Consider, for example, that in the cyberstalking case involving Amy Boyer, Liam Youens was able to stalk his victim without ever having to leave his house. He was also able to locate the home and work addresses of his victim via online search facilities that required only a few keystrokes and mouse clicks. And he was even able to disseminate personal information about Boyer, as well as explicit details of his plans to murder her, to a potentially global audience. These activities, which arguably are novel modes of action, might also seem to qualify as instances of what Jonas calls "novel powers to act."

Certain expansionists suggest that because of these novel modes of action, an entirely new system of ethics is required for the Internet age; other expansionists, however, imply that our traditional system of ethics need not be replaced in its entirety. Instead, they argue, it should be expanded or revised so as to include what Jonas referred to as "novel rules," that is, a new ethical theory (as opposed to an entirely new ethical framework). Both interpretations of Jonas's thesis can be found in the kinds of arguments that have been advanced by expansionists with respect to claims about what is needed to evaluate the kinds of actions made possible by cybertechnology. Henceforth, we refer to these two views as the *strong thesis* and the *weak thesis*.

THE STRONG THESIS

Assuming that Internet technology has provided us with novel modes for action, does it necessarily follow that our moral condition has been so radically altered that our traditional framework of ethics must be replaced by an entirely new ethical system? At least two philosophers have suggested that the answer to this question is "yes." Carl Mitcham claims that "because cybertechnology has transformed information and human communication in unanticipated ways . . . it is not clear that ethics in any traditional sense is possible."[26] And Walter Maner has argued that the impact of computing technology is such that it has forced us to "discover new moral values."[27] But neither Mitcham nor Maner offers specific examples to support the claim that an entirely new framework of ethics is required.

Consider once again the Amy Boyer cyberstalking case. Are the ethical issues raised in this case such that they cannot be understood and analyzed in terms of our traditional ethical framework? We can concede that the Boyer case demonstrates some ways in which Internet technology has made possible "novel modes" for human action whose scope and scale appear to challenge our traditional categories of ethical analysis. However, it is by no means evident that our traditional framework of ethics must be jettisoned in favor of a brand new ethical system.

Perhaps what at least some expansionists who hold the strong thesis really mean to assert is that we need to revise or expand specific elements in our existing moral framework.[28] Of course, this is a very different position than that advocated in the strong thesis. Let us next consider the weaker thesis of the expansionists' view.

THE WEAK THESIS

Instead of replacing our entire ethical framework with a radically new one, the weak expansionist position suggests that we simply need novel ethical rules.[29] Those ethical rules could be conceived of in terms of one or more ethical theories; or they might possibly be thought of more broadly to include certain moral principles or perhaps even moral virtues, such as honesty, courage, temperance, and so forth. First, consider the claim for novel moral rules in terms of a need for novel moral virtues. Do the kinds of issues raised by cybertechnology require the introduction of certain kinds of moral virtues (i.e., virtues in addition to the standard set introduced by Aristotle)? Although expansionists believe that novel ethical rules of some sort are required for cyberspace, there do not appear to be any convincing arguments to show that new virtues are needed.

Other philosophers have suggested that novel ethical rules in the form of one or more new ethical theories are required. For example, Krystyna Gorniak-Kocikowska has recently argued that a new ethical theory is needed for the computer era. She argues that just as the "revolution" brought on by the printing press affected our social institutions and ethical values in profound and fundamental ways, so, too, has the computer revolution.[30] And because the computer revolution is global in its impact, Gorniak-Kocikowska claims that we need a new global ethical theory. A new ethical theory that can respond to problems generated globally by computer technology is needed, she further claims, in the same way as new ethical theories were required to respond to social issues triggered by the printing-press revolution. She notes that in the period following the impact of the printing press, new ethical theories, which have since become classic or standard theories, were introduced by modern philosophers and ethicists such as Bentham, Kant, and Mill. What is needed, Gorniak-Kocikowska argues, is a new ethical theory for cyberspace that would have to be accepted by all cultures in the global community, and not merely by those in the West.

Why is a new universal ethical theory required? Is it because new kinds of human actions have been made possible by computing technology? Gorniak-Kocikowska's central argument would seem to turn on what she refers to as the "global aspect of computing." Clearly, the use of computer technology has had a global impact, as Gorniak-Kocikowska correctly points out. But does it follow that a new ethical theory is needed *because of* this global impact? Surely other technologies raise concerns that have a global impact. Consider the case of transportation technologies and reproductive technologies, both of which are truly global in terms of the scope of their impact. Does it follow that we also need new, universal ethical theories to account for the global impact of these technologies? On Gorniak-Kocikowska's logic, it would seem that we would. But clearly such a position would be difficult to defend.

From the arguments we have considered thus far, it would seem that there is no compelling reason to accept the expansionist position, in either its strong or weak formulations. So, by default, one might infer that we should ipso facto accept the traditionalists' position. We can ask, however, whether such an inference is justified.

THE TRADITIONALIST'S POSITION: MUST WE ACCEPT IT BY DEFAULT?

As we saw earlier, traditionalists believe that we can apply our ordinary scheme of ethical analysis to issues involving cybertechnology. Thus, we would need no new ethical theories; nor would we need any new ethical principles or enjoinders. Traditionalists assume that after we have identified a particular ethical issue involving cybertechnology, we can simply apply one or more standard ethical theories to that problem.

Is it the case that traditionalists essentially deny what expansionists assert, and vice versa? If so, it would seem to follow that if one thesis is false, the other must be true. In other words, if the expansionists' position is incorrect, then the traditionalists' position would be correct by default. But should we necessarily accept the traditionalists' view simply because we can reject the expansionists' thesis? I believe that we can still ask whether the traditionalists are correct in maintaining that ordinary ethics has remained altogether unaffected by the advent of the Internet and the use of cybertechnology.[31]

If we can show that the arguments used by both expansionists and traditionalists proceed from a commonly shared assumption that is erroneous, then we could also demonstrate that both views are inadequate. Traditionalists and expansionists both seem to assume the truth of a premise, which can be expressed in the form of the following conditional statement:

> If ethical problems involving Internet technology pose special challenges to our ordinary conception of ethics, then either an entirely new ethical system or a new ethical theory is required.

Expansionists correctly affirm the antecedent of this conditional statement. They point out that ethical problems involving cybertechnology pose some special challenges to ordinary ethics, as suggested in our analysis of the Amy Boyer cyberstalking case. However, expansionists then go on to infer the consequent of this conditional statement, insisting that either a new ethical theory or a new system of ethics is needed.

Traditionalists, on the other hand, correctly deny the consequent of the conditional statement by pointing out that neither a new ethical system nor a new ethical theory is required. However, traditionalists then go on to infer that cybertechnology poses no special challenges to our ordinary scheme of ethical analysis. We will see why this inference is difficult to defend.

How is it possible to hold a coherent position that rejects both the traditionalists and expansionists views overall, while still accepting the insights of each position? We can do this by accepting the traditionalists' thesis that neither a new ethical theory nor a new ethical system is required for cybertechnology, and at the same time acknowledge the expansionists' insight that our ordinary mode of ethical analysis is significantly challenged by that technology. In order to do this, however, we must shift the focus of our analysis somewhat. Instead of concentrating our attention solely on questions having to do with our ethical framework per se, and the elements that compose that framework, it will be useful to look more closely at the methodology that is typically used in analyzing ethical issues. In doing this, we will see that what cybertechnology requires is not a new or revised ethical framework but rather a modified and slightly expanded *methodology*—that is, a new methodological approach for both identifying and analyzing moral issues from within our existing ethical framework.

AN ALTERNATIVE SCHEME FOR ANALYZING THE TRADITIONALIST-EXPANSIONIST DISPUTE

Because we have discovered no compelling evidence for the expansionists' claim that we need either a new framework of ethics or a new ethical theory, and because our traditional framework would still appear to be adequate, one might be inclined to infer that our standard methodological approach for identifying and analyzing ethical issues can automatically be extended to cyberspace. However, we will see that some important distinctions can and should be drawn between an ethical framework (or system that is composed of ethical theories, principles, and enjoinders) and the methodological scheme used to analyze ethical issues. We will also see that when the traditional or standard methodological approach[32] used in the various fields of applied ethics is extended to ethical issues involving cybertechnology, it falls short for at least two different reasons. For one thing, Philip Brey has pointed out that many ethical issues surrounding computing technology, when compared to issues in other fields of applied ethics, are not always easy to identify. He believes that in applying the standard methodological approach to ethical issues involving computer technology, we tend to limit our analysis to those kinds of issues that are already known or "transparent." So in using the standard method, we fail to recognize some morally controversial features of computer technology that are "nontransparent."[33] Also, James Moor has pointed out that the use of computing technology has made possible certain kinds of actions that have generated "policy vacuums" and sometimes also raise "conceptual muddles," both of which can pose a significant challenge for our standard methodology for ethical analysis.[34] We examine both Brey's and Moor's insights involving the need for a revised methodological scheme in more detail in the two following sections.

BREY'S "DISCLOSIVE" METHOD

Brey describes the traditional or standard methodological approach for analyzing applied ethics issues as consisting of three stages: (1) identify a moral problem, (2) analyze the problem by clarifying concepts and examining the factual data associated with that problem, and (3) deliberate on the problem via the application of one or more ethical theories. Consider how this methodology would be applied to an examination of ethical issues involving computer technology. First, a practice involving computer technology, such as software piracy, is *identified* as morally controversial. At the second stage, the problem is *analyzed* in descriptive and contextual terms to clarify the practice and situate it in a context. In the case of software piracy, for example, the concept of theft can be analyzed in terms of intellectual property theory. At the third and final stage, the problem is *deliberated* over in terms of moral principles and arguments. Brey describes this stage in the method as the "deliberative process," in which various arguments are used to justify the application of particular moral principles to the issue under consideration. For example, software piracy issues can be deliberated on in terms of aretaic (virtue ethics), deontological, and utilitarian theories. Brey believes that in the case of cybertechnology, however, the standard or what he calls "mainstream" methodological approach used to identify ethical issues is not always adequate.

Brey suggests that a central problem with the mainstream methodology when applied to ethical issues in computing is that it limits itself to an analysis of controversial issues and practices that are already known to exist.[35] Because of this limitation, Brey is concerned that we might fail to pay attention to certain practices involving computer technology that have "moral import" but are not yet known.[36] He refers to such practices as having *morally nontransparent* or *morally opaque* features. Brey further notes that these features can be morally opaque for one of two reasons: either they are *unknown* or they are *known*, but are perceived to be "morally neutral."[37]

Consider an example of each type of morally opaque feature. Computerized practices involving data mining would be "unknown" to those who have never heard of the concept of data mining and are unfamiliar with data-mining technology. However, we should not necessarily assume that this technology is "morally neutral," merely because data-mining techniques are unknown to nontechnical people, including many ethicists. It turns out that data-mining practices have raised moral issues pertaining to personal privacy, even if techniques used in those practices have been morally nontransparent to many ethicists.[38]

Next consider that Internet users might be very familiar with a technology such as search-engine programs. What those users might fail to recognize, however, is that certain uses of search-engine technology can raise moral issues involving personal privacy. In this case, a morally controversial feature or practice involving search-engine technology might not be obvious or transparent to many people, including those who are very familiar with that particular technology. So while a well-known technology, such as search engines, might have the appearance of "moral neutrality," a closer analysis can "disclose" that certain aspects of that technology also have moral implications.[39]

Brey concludes that an adequate methodology for computer ethics must first disclose issues that, without proper probing and analysis, would go unnoticed *as* ethical issues. He calls his methodological scheme "disclosive computer ethics."[40] Once all the ethical issues have been disclosed, Brey suggests that we can then apply our standard ethical theories in the deliberative process.

MOOR'S METHODOLOGICAL SCHEME

James Moor provides a different kind of critique of what we have referred to as the standard methodological approach to ethical issues involving computing technology. At the core of his methodological scheme are two important notions: *logical malleability* and *policy vacuums*.[41] Moor has argued that computer technology, unlike other technologies, is "logically malleable" because it can be shaped and molded to perform a variety of functions.[42] He notes that noncomputer technologies, which are typically designed to perform some particular function or task, lack the universal or general-purpose characteristics that computing technologies possess. For example, microwave ovens and videocassette recorders are technological devices that have been designed to perform specific tasks. As such, microwave ovens cannot be used to view videotapes; videocassette recorders cannot be used to cook or warm food. However, a computer, depending on the software used, can perform a range of diverse tasks. That is, the same computer can be instructed to behave as a video game, a word processor, a spreadsheet, a medium to send and receive e-mail messages, an interface to Web sites, and so forth.

Moor points out that because of a computer's general-purpose nature, which is due to its logical malleability, this particular technology can generate new possibilities for human action. Some of these actions, in turn, generate what Moor calls "policy vacuums."[43] That is, sometimes we have no normative rules and policies to guide the new choices made possible by computer technology. A seemingly simple solution to this problem would be to identify the vacuums that have been generated and then to fill them by framing new policies. However, the solution to this problem is not always as simple as it might initially appear. Moor notes that sometimes the new possibilities for human action generated by computing technology also introduce "conceptual muddles." In these cases, we must first clear up the muddles before we can fill one or more voids in which there is either no policy or no adequate policy to guide our actions.

A policy vacuum that emerged in the period following the introduction of personal computers is apparent in the debate over whether it was permissible to make a copy of a software program for personal use. Shortly after personal computers became commercially available, PC users discovered that they could easily duplicate proprietary computer programs such as word processing programs, spreadsheets, and video games. Many users made copies of these and similar programs for their friends. Furthermore, many users assumed that in making these copies they were doing nothing wrong. At that time,

there were no explicit laws, or even informal policies, that regulated the subsequent use and distribution of software programs after they had been pur-
chased by an individual or an institution. Although it might be difficult for
some to imagine today, at one time proprietary software was not clearly protected by either copyright law or the patent process.

Of course, clear laws and policies regarding the theft of physical property were already in existence. Such laws and policies protected against the
theft of personal computers themselves, as well as the theft of a disk drive
residing in a PC on which the proprietary software programs could easily be
duplicated. Because certain conceptual muddles or confusions regarding the
nature of software still needed to be resolved, it was not easy to frame a
coherent policy or legal statute for the protection of proprietary software.
Thus, a policy vacuum arose with respect to whether proprietary software
could be freely duplicated. Eventually, however, the policy vacuum was filled
with explicit laws.

A more recent illustration of a policy vacuum involving the copying of
proprietary information can be seen in the controversy involving Napster.
Currently, there is a debate in the courts over whether the unauthorized sharing of proprietary information (contained in MP3 files) across the Internet
should be viewed as a form of software piracy. The problem, of course, is that,
until recently, we had no clear and explicit policies governing the activities
that occurred on Napster and similar Web sites. Even though the courts have
ruled against Napster, other Web sites that facilitate the sharing of music via
MP3 files, such as Gnutella, Morhpeus, and KaZaA are still allowed to operate. Why these sites are legally permitted to operate while Napster is not is a
point of contention that still is not clear. So, it would seem that certain conceptual muddles or confusions still surround the original Napster controversy;
these confusions will need to be resolved before we can frame a coherent set
of laws and policies involving the sharing of proprietary information on the
Internet. Unfortunately, applying the standard methodological approach that
has been used in most areas involving applied-ethics issues will not help us in
resolving this particular controversy.

EXTENDING BREY'S AND MOOR'S INSIGHTS TO AN
ANALYSIS OF THE AMY BOYER CYBERSTALKING CASE

We next examine the Amy Boyer case in light of the proposed alternative
methodological approaches to determine whether there are any nontransparent or opaque moral features in the technology (Brey), or whether any policy
vacuums (Moor) have been generated in online activities such as cyberstalking. Earlier in this chapter, we saw that the cyberstalking incident involving
Amy Boyer raised a number of ethical concerns, one of which involved personal privacy. Was Boyer's privacy violated, as some have suggested?[44] Or

should the personal information about Boyer that Youens was able to retrieve be considered public information because that information was publicly available on the Internet? It would seem that, once again, we have a policy vacuum—this time, a vacuum involving the protection of personal privacy in public space.

Does the fact that vast amounts of personal information currently residing in computer databases can now be accessed with relative ease by ordinary Internet users via online search facilities pose any special challenges for our existing laws and policies regarding personal privacy? Have any policy vacuums or conceptual muddles been introduced with respect to our traditional criteria for distinguishing between personal information that is essentially public in character versus what is essentially private? Consider that in stalking Amy Boyer, Liam Youens was able to gather personal information about her from various Internet resources, including online search facilities. It would seem that we might need some new or revised privacy laws and policies because of a current vacuum of policies involving search engines and online public records.

INTERNET SEARCH ENGINES AND
SOME IMPLICATIONS FOR PERSONAL PRIVACY

Few would dispute the value that search engines have provided Internet users. Consider the useful, and arguably important, function that Internet search engines offer in directing us to online resources involving research, commerce, recreation, and so forth. Hence, some might be surprised by the suggestion that search-engine technology itself could be controversial in some way. Recall, however, what Brey had said about morally nontransparent features of computing and Internet technology. We have already noted that search engines can be used to locate personal information about individuals, even though the persons on whom searches are conducted might have no idea that such personal information can be easily retrieved from online search facilities. Furthermore, those individuals have little, if any, control over how information about them is entered into databases that are accessible to Internet search engines.[45] For example, Amy Boyer had no knowledge about or control over the fact that certain kinds of personal information about her were accessible to the public through various Internet resources. Consider also that Boyer placed no personal information about herself on the Internet.

Some might argue that all information currently available on the Internet, including information about individual persons such as Amy Boyer, is *public information*, by virtue of the fact that it resides on the Internet. We can, of course, question whether all the information about persons that is currently available online *should* be accessible to the public, without some kind of restrictions. For example, should online public records that contain personal information be treated merely as public data that deserve no legal protection? Or do these records deserve more normative protection because of the ways in which they can be so easily accessed and then potentially abused?

DO WE NEED NEW PRIVACY POLICIES IN THE INTERNET ERA?

Currently, we have explicit laws that protect the transfer and exchange of personal information between and across databases in instances where the information has been determined to be *confidential* or *intimate* in nature. For example, we have explicit laws and policies that protect an individual's financial and medical records. Helen Nissenbaum has pointed out that such protection does not apply to personal information in what she calls "spheres other than the intimate."[46] Unfortunately for Amy Boyer, the kind of information that was gathered about her by Youens would be considered nonintimate and nonconfidential in nature and thus would likely be viewed, by default, as "public" in nature. Is this presumption about how personal information contained in public records tends to be viewed by some still one that is reasonable in the Internet era?

It would seem that, currently, we have a policy vacuum regarding the access of personal information included in online public records. Unfortunately, standard methodological approaches to ethical issues involving computing and Internet technologies do not always reveal such vacuums, at least not in a straightforward way. Using the methodological schemes provided by Brey and Moor, we can disclose certain kinds of morally controversial features and practices involving cybertechnology and then identify policy vacuums that otherwise might go unrecognized. For example, Brey's scheme can help us to isolate certain morally nontransparent features in cybertechnology, including those embedded in data-mining and search-engine technologies. And Moor's methodological scheme enables us to identify certain policy vacuums surrounding our current privacy laws and norms, such as those involving online public records.

SOME PRELIMINARY CONCLUSIONS

We began this chapter by asking whether our moral condition has been radically altered because of the kinds of actions made possible by cybertechnology, and, if it has, whether a new framework of ethics is required. An ethical framework was then defined as a system composed of ethical enjoinders, principles, and theories. We argued that there is no convincing evidence to show that the kinds of actions made possible by cybertechnology are such that they require a new ethical framework to contain them.[47] We also saw that whereas expansionists tend to exaggerate the need for either a new or expanded moral framework, traditionalists significantly underestimate the problems that must be faced in attempting to apply ordinary modes of ethical analysis to issues involving cyberspace. It was argued that what is needed is a revised methodological scheme—one that expands slightly on the traditional or standard model that has been used in applied ethics. This expanded methodological scheme helps us to disclose certain normative features embedded in cybertechnology, which are not always obvious or transparent. It also helps us to identify certain vacuums regarding our normative policies.

We have seen that some of our ethical concepts, such as those associated with privacy and property, have been stretched and strained because of certain uses of cybertechnology. In particular, we saw how our concept of privacy needs to be reexamined in light of currently available techniques for accessing personal information online, including certain kinds of personal information contained in online public records. (For example, we observed how that kind of information can be abused by cyberstalkers.) We should note, however, that while normative concepts such as privacy and property may need to be revised because of cybertechnology, we have not seen any evidence to show that our core moral notions—that is, agency, autonomy, respect for persons, responsibility, and so on—have been affected. Nor have we encountered any evidence to suggest that our core moral virtues, such as those initially articulated by Aristotle, have changed in the Internet era. We have argued that by proceeding along the lines of the alternative, that is, slightly expanded, methodology that incorporates the insights of Brey and Moor, we are well prepared to meet many of the challenges that cybertechnology poses to our existing ethical framework.

We should also acknowledge, however, that it is possible that in the future our moral condition may become so radically altered by developments in cybertechnology that a new framework of ethics may be needed. For example, if "autonomous electronic agents" emerge with certain morally relevant characteristics, then it might be necessary to grant at least some degree of moral status to these agents. In this case, we may need to revise, and possibly even expand, our existing ethical framework.

Earlier in this chapter, we briefly considered the claim that modern technology has generated new "objects of moral consideration." Recall that Jonas believed that our "novel powers to act" significantly affected our moral condition, not only because of the global reach of our actions but also because of the new moral objects that those actions generated. We saw that Jonas closely linked the introduction of new moral objects with novel human actions, suggesting that the former resulted from the latter. We already have seen that there are good reasons to be skeptical of the claim that cybertechnology has introduced qualitatively novel powers to act. However, we can still ask if it is possible for new moral objects to emerge from the use of cybertechnology, even if cybertechnology has not provided us with any genuinely novel kinds of human actions.[48]

FUTURE CONSIDERATIONS: WILL CYBERTECHNOLOGY
GENERATE NEW ETHICAL OBJECTS?

We saw that Jonas believed that ethical consideration, which had tradition-ally been accorded to human beings alone, must now be extended to include eligible nonhuman entities such as "nature as a whole." Today, many envi-ronmentalists would agree with Jonas that we should extend the domain of ethical consideration to include objects such as trees, land, and the ecosys-tem itself. Should ethical consideration also be extended to any objects, or "entities," in the cyberrealm? Recently, Luciano Floridi has argued that the domain of ethical consideration should be expanded to include entities in addition to the (biologic) life forms in our "ecosphere." He believes that moral consideration should also be granted to a certain kind of inanimate object—namely, to information itself (or what Floridi refers to as "data enti-ties")—that resides in the "infosphere."[49]

Floridi and J. W. Sanders suggest that if we explore the infosphere, we will find several interesting analogies with the ecosphere,[50] some of which have moral relevance.[51] An interesting aspect of the model put forth by Floridi and Sanders is that it causes us to consider the ontological status of information (i.e., data entities). Reflecting on this question might also help us to determine whether at least certain kinds of electronic agents are worthy of moral consideration. In their discussion of "artificial evil," Floridi and Sanders draw an interesting distinction between what they call "autonomous electronic agents" and "heteronomous electronic agents."[52] Such a distinction could potentially help us to sort out some important questions having to do with whether we should grant moral status to certain kinds of electronic agents, but not to others.

I believe that we should take into consideration the *possibility* that cer-tain kinds of electronic agents (e.g., "softbots") might eventually qualify as "objects" that warrant moral consideration. For example, it has already been suggested that some of these sophisticated "agents" have characteristics that enable them to qualify as both rational and autonomous "beings." Such vir-tual beings might be objects of moral consideration on Kantian grounds, at least, where criteria involving rationality and autonomy are paramount. However, those beings would likely have far more difficulties in qualifying on Aristotelian grounds, where the criterion of having a biological substrate would seem to be an essential one for an agent to be granted moral consider-ation. For example, it has been argued that because such virtual beings lack either "sentience" or "interests," it would be difficult to make the case that these agents should could command any ethical consideration,[53] even if they have some "cognitive capacity." As Michelfelder correctly notes, beings with-out "volume, mass, orientation, embodiment, or capacity for suffering" would hardly seem to quality as the kinds of creatures that could be understood as capable of developing and exhibiting any virtues in the Aristotelian sense.[54] However, Floridi and Sanders believe that moral good and evil can be "determined even in the absence of biologically sentient participants."[55] And Kari Coleman has recently suggested that a framework of virtue ethics could be extended to include "computational agents."[56]

Note that I merely wish to raise the possibility that at some point in the near future, electronic agents might evolve in such a way that it would be plausible to grant them moral status.[57] If such agents should emerge, then we may need to modify or revise altogether the conclusions reached in this chapter. In that case, Hans Jonas's claims regarding our moral condition and the corresponding requirement for a new ethical framework would perhaps apply to cybertechnology as well.

NOTES

1. H. Jonas, *The Imperative of Responsibility: In Search of an Ethics for the Technological Age* (Chicago: University of Chicago Press, 1984), p. 6.

2. Ibid., p. 23 (italics added).

3. Jonas first published his ideas about the impact of modern technology on our moral condition in the early 1950s. His discussions of this topic often focused on aspects of modern technology involving atomic power.

4. See, e.g., K. Gorniak-Kocikowska, "The Computer Revolution and the Problem of Global Ethics," *Science and Engineering Ethics* (Vol. 2, No. 2, 1996): 177–190; W. Maner, "Unique Ethical Problems in Information Technology," *Science and Engineering Ethics* (Vol. 2, No. 2, 1996): 137–154; and C. Mitcham, *Thinking Ethics and Technology: Hennebach Lectures and Papers 1995–1996* (Golden, CO, Colorado School of Mines, 1997).

5. For purposes of this chapter, "cybertechnology" is understood to include a wide range of computing and network technologies, from stand-alone computers to privately owned computer networks to the Internet and World Wide Web.

6. I am grateful to Lloyd Carr for his helpful suggestions on an earlier draft of this chapter. I am also grateful for comments received from participants at two conferences in which earlier versions were presented: "The Impact of Multimedia Technology on Languages and Literatures," Graduate Center, City University of New York, February 28, 2002; and at a session on Ethics and Technology at the Eastern Division Meeting of the American Philosophical Association, Philadelphia, December 28, 2002. In composing this chapter, I have drawn from material in my book *Ethics and Technology: Ethical Issues in an Age of Information and Communication Technology* (New York: John Wiley & Sons, 2004) and from two previously published articles: "The Uniqueness Debate in Computer Ethics: What Exactly Is at Issue, and Why Does it Matter?" *Ethics and Information Technology* (Vol. 4, No. 1, 2002): 37–54; and "Some Ethical Reflections on Cyberstalking," *Computers and Society* (Vol. 32, No. 1, 2002): 22–32 (coauthored with Frances Grodzinsky).

7. H. Jonas, op. cit., p. 1.

8. Ibid.

9. Ibid. According to Jonas, "the *nature of human action* has changed, and since ethics is concerned with action, it should follow that the changed nature of human action calls for a change in ethics as well" (italics in original).

10. Ibid.

11. Ibid.

12. D. Michelfelder, "Our Moral Condition in Cyberspace," *Ethics and Information Technology* (Vol. 2, No. 3, 2000): 148.

13. Ibid.

14. It has been argued that more people died in the fire bombings of Tokyo in 1945 than as a result of the atomic bomb that exploded in Hiroshima that year. However, if a fraction of the number of conventional bombs used in Tokyo had been nuclear bombs delivered to a broad range of targets, the ensuing destruction (both to humans and to the planet) would have been qualitatively different from that caused by previous technologies used in conventional warfare.

15. H. Jonas, op. cit., p. 8.

16. Ibid.

17. Ibid., pp. ix–x.

18. See Aristotle, *Nicomachean Ethics*.

19. H. Jonas, op. cit., p. 6.

20. Ibid., p. 1.

21. A philosophical grounding for ethics, which is based on logical argumentation and ethical theory, can be distinguished from schemes that ground morality in religious and legal authority. I discuss these distinctions in more detail in my book *Ethics and Technology: Ethical Issues in an Age of Information and Communication Technology* (New York: John Wiley & Sons, 2004).

22. I wish to thank Lloyd Carr for suggesting the use of examples similar to the two included here.

23. Jonas's remarks about our framework of ethics might be interpreted to represent an antifoundationalist or anti-essentialist position. However, we will not pursue such an interpretation of Jonas here, since doing so would take us beyond the scope of the present study.

24. For a detailed discussion of these ethical issues vis-à-vis cyberstalking in general, and the Amy Boyer case in particular, see F. Grodznsky and H. Tavani, 2002, op. cit.

25. On a somewhat different, but perhaps related, note, consider that because stalkers can navigate the Internet either anonymously or pseudonymously, individuals who never would have considered stalking individuals in physical space might now be tempted to do so in cyberspace.

26. C. Mitcham, op. cit., p. 90. This passage is cited in D. Michelfelder, op. cit.

27. W. Maner, 1996, op. cit., p. 137.

28. For example, Maner (op. cit.) says ethical issues generated by computing technology sometimes force us to "formulate new moral principles" and to "find new ways to think about the issues presented to us."

29. For example, H. Jonas (op. cit., p. x.) suggests that new rules are needed when he calls for "a new reflection of ethical principles."

30. K. Gorniak-Kocikowska, 1996, op. cit., p. 177.

31. D. Michelfelder (op. cit.) has also suggested that this interpretation is possible. For example, she argues that even if we do not need a brand new cyberspace ethics, it doesn't follow that cyberspace has posed no philosophically interesting and challenging ethical issues.

32. L. Floridi has suggested that an essential difficulty in developing computer ethics as a legitimate philosophical field has to do with a problem that is fundamentally methodological in nature. As a solution to this problem, however, Floridi puts forth a new theory called "information ethics." An examination of that theory would take beyond the scope of the present chapter. See L. Floridi, "Information Ethics: On the Philosophical Foundation of Computer Ethics," *Ethics and Information Technology* (Vol. 1, No. 1, 1999): 37–56. Another account of the importance of the role of a methodological scheme for computer ethics can be found in J. van den Hoven, "Computer Ethics and Moral Methodology," *Metaphilosophy* (Vol. 28, No. 1, 1998): 14–21.

33. See P. Brey, "Disclosive Computer Ethics," *Readings in CyberEthics*. Eds. R. Spinello and H. Tavani (Sudbury, MA: Jones and Bartlett, 2001), pp. 51–62.

34. See J. Moor, "What Is Computer Ethics?" *Metaphilosophy* (Vol. 16, No. 4, 1985): 266–275; and "Reason, Relativity, and Responsibility in Computer Ethics," *Computers and Society* (Vol. 28, No. 1, 1998): 14–21.

35. P. Brey, op. cit., p. 52.

36. Ibid.

37. Ibid.

38. See, e.g., my account of this problem in H. Tavani, "KDD, Data Mining and the Challenge for Normative Privacy," *Ethics and Information Technology* (Vol. 1, No. 4, 1999): 265–273.

39. See H. Tavani, "Internet Search Engines and Personal Privacy," *Proceedings of the First Conference on Computer Ethics—Philosophical Enquiry: CEPE '97*. Ed. J. van den Hoven (Rotterdam, The Netherlands: University of Rotterdam Press, 1998), pp. 214–223.

40. P. Brey (op. cit.) also points out that that the mainstream methodological approach tends to focus on the *use* of computing technology, thus overlooking many ethical issues having to do with the design of that technology.

41. Because Moor (1998, op. cit.) claims that "routine ethics" is inadequate to handle moral issues generated by computing technology, some might interpret his

remarks as supporting a variation of the expansionist argument. However, I believe that Moor's methodological approach cuts across the traditionalist-expansionist divide.

42. J. Moor, 1985, op. cit.

43. Ibid. Elsewhere, Moor has pointed out that policy vacuums are not unique to computing technology. For example, he notes that policy vacuums have been generated in genomic and genetic research as well as in the use of reproductive technologies. See J. Moor, "Using Genetic Information While Protecting the Privacy of the Soul," *Ethics and Information Technology* (Vol. 1, No. 4, 1999): 65–69.

44. For example, Amy Boyer's stepfather, Tim Rensberg, has filed a lawsuit in which it is alleged that his stepdaughter's privacy was violated because of information about Boyer that Youens acquired via Docusearch.com.

45. For a more detailed discussion of this issue, see H. Tavani, 1998, op. cit.

46. See H. Nissenbaum, "Protecting Privacy in an Information Age," *Law and Philosophy* (Vol. 17, 1998): 559–596.

47. It might be objected that I have drawn this conclusion prematurely since I examined only one case of cybertechnology in detail, viz., the Amy Boyer cyberstalking incident. For example, Selmer Bringsjord has raised this objection. I have replied by noting that I selected the Boyer case because the ethical issues it raises—issues that include privacy, free speech, security, anonymity, and moral responsibility at both the individual and collective levels—are representative, if not exhaustive, of the field of computer ethics (see my discussion in the section on stalking). I have also noted in my reply that issues involving intellectual property (i.e., the Napster controversy) and "privacy in public" (in my discussions of online public records and Internet search engines) are also examined in this chapter. So while additional examples and cases could be used to strengthen my preliminary conclusions, I believe that the specific cases examined are sufficiently representative of the kinds of morally controversial behavior made possible by cybertechnology.

48. Here I wish to separate or delink the two notions that some of Jonas's commentators, such a D. Michelfelder (op. cit.), interpret to be strongly connected.

49. See L. Floridi, 1999, op. cit.

50. See L. Floridi, "Does Information Have Moral Worth?" *Proceedings of the Second Conference on Computer Ethics—Philosophical Enquiry: CEPE 98* (London School of Economics, 1998), pp. 144–158. See also the two following essays by L. Floridi and J. W. Sanders: "Artificial Evil and the Foundations of Computer Ethics," *Proceedings of the Third Conference on Computer Ethics—Philosophical Enquiry: CEPE 2000* (Dartmouth College, Hanover, New Hampshire, 2000), pp. 55–66; and "On the Morality of Artificial Agents," *Proceedings of the Fourth Conference on Computer Ethics—Philosophical Enquiry: CEPE 2001* (Lancaster University, United Kingdom, 1998), pp. 84–107.

51. Whereas environmental ethics is "biocentric" with respect to which objects it is willing to extend the status of moral consideration, Floridi and Sanders point out that information ethics (or IE) is "ontocentric." IE is ontocentric because it grants moral status to inanimate objects—i.e., to nonbiologic objects or entities—as well as

to entities that can be regarded as standard life forms. See L. Floridi and J. W. Sanders, "Computer Ethics: Mapping the Foundationalist Debate," *Ethics and Information Technology* (Vol. 4, No. 1, 2002): 1–9.

52. Ibid.

53. See, for example, D. Michelfelder, op. cit., p. 148.

54. Ibid.

55. See L. Floridi and J. W. Sanders, 2000, op. cit. I will not pursue this interesting debate any further here. For a detailed discussion of this question, see H. Tavani, 2002, op. cit.

56. K. Coleman, "Android Arete: Toward a Virtue Ethic for Computational Agents," *Ethics and Information Technology* Vol. 3, No. 4, 2001: 247–265. Coleman suggests that we might consider computers not as tools, but rather as "participants in human-computer interaction." She believes that such an analysis might also "open up the possibility" that humans have obligations and responsibilities to computers as well as to other humans.

57. For example, in the science fiction movie *AI* (Steven Spielberg, 2000) a futuristic situation is portrayed in which human-like artificial agents are capable of experiencing certain forms of human emotion (such as a child's need to be loved by its mother). If future technology provides us with the means to create such beings, we would need to debate what kind of moral obligations humans have to them. And if such beings are sufficiently autonomous and rational, we may need to debate whether these agents have any moral obligations to humans.

REFERENCES

Aristotle. 1969. *Nicomachean Ethics*. Trans. David Ross. Oxford: Oxford University Press.

Brey, Philip. 2001. "Disclosive Computer Ethics," in R. A. Spinello and H. T. Tavani (Eds.), *Readings in CyberEthics*. Sudbury, MA: Jones and Bartlett, pp. 51–62.

Coleman, Kari Gwen. 2001. Android Arete: Toward a Virtue Ethic for Computational Agents, *Ethics and Information Technology* 3, 4: 247–265.

Floridi, Luciano. 1998. "Does Information Have a Moral Worth in Itself?," in L. D. Introna (Ed.), *Proceedings of the Second Conference on Computer Ethics—Philosophical Enquiry: CEPE98*. London School of Economics, pp. 144–158.

———. 1999. Information Ethics: On the Philosophical Foundation of Computer Ethics, *Ethics and Information Technology* 1, 1: 37–56.

———, and J. W. Sanders. 2000. "Artificial Evil and the Foundations of Computer Ethics," in D. G. Johnson, J. H. Moor, and H. T. Tavani (Eds.), *Proceedings of the Third Conference on Computer Ethics—Philosophical Enquiry: CEPE 2000*, Dartmouth College, pp. 142–156.

———. 2001. "On the Morality of Artificial Agents," in R. Chadwick, L. Introna, and A. Marturano (Eds.), *Proceedings of the Fourth Conference on Computer*

Ethics—Philosophical Enquiry: CEPE 2001, Lancaster University, UK, pp. 84–107.

———. 2002. Computer Ethics: Mapping the Foundationalist Debate, *Ethics and Information Technology* 4, 1: 1–9.

Gorniak-Kocikowska, Krystyna. 1996. The Computer Revolution and the Problem of Global Ethics, *Science and Engineering Ethics* 2, 2: 177–190.

Grodzinsky, Frances S., and Herman T. Tavani. 2002. Some Ethical Reflections on Cyberstalking, *Computers and Society* 32, 1: 22–32.

Jonas, Hans. 1984. *The Imperative of Responsibility: In Search of an Ethics for the Technological Age.* Chicago: University of Chicago Press.

Maner, Walter. 1996. Unique Ethical Problems in Information Technology, *Science and Engineering Ethics* 2, 2, 1996: 137–154.

Michelfelder, Diane. 2000. Our Moral Condition in Cyberspace, *Ethics and Information Technology* 2, 3: 147–152.

Mitcham, Carl. 1997. *Thinking Ethics in Technology: The Hennebach Lectures and Papers 1995–1996.* Golden, CO: Colorado School of Mines.

Moor, James H. 1985. What Is Computer Ethics?, *Metaphilosophy* 16, 4: 266–275.

———. 1998. Reason, Relativity, and Responsibility in Computer Ethics, *Computers and Society* 28, 1: 14–21.

———. 1999. Using Genetic Information While Protecting the Privacy of the Soul, *Ethics and Information Technology* 1, 4, 1999: 257–263.

———. 2001. The Future of Computer Ethics: You Ain't Seen Nothing Yet, *Ethics and Information Technology* 3, 2, 2001: 89–91.

Nissenbaum, Helen. 1998. Protecting Privacy in an Information Age, *Law and Philosophy* 17: 559–596.

Tavani, Herman T. 1998. Internet Search Engines and Personal Privacy, in J. van den Hoven (Ed.), *Proceedings of the First Conference on Computer Ethics—Philosophical Enquiry: CEPE97.* Rotterdam: University of Erasmus Press, pp. 214–223.

———. 1999. KDD, Data Mining, and the Challenge to Normative Privacy, *Ethics and Information Technology* 1, 4: 265–273.

———. 2002. The Uniqueness Debate in Computer Ethics: What Exactly Is at Issue, and Why Does it Matter?, *Ethics and Information Technology* 4, 1, 2002: 37–54.

———. 2004. *Ethics and Technology: Ethical Issues in an Age of Information and Communication Technology.* New York: John Wiley & Sons.

van den Hoven, Jeroen. 1997. Computer Ethics and Moral Methodology, *Metaphilosophy* 28, 3: 234–248.

Contributors

TERRELL WARD BYNUM is Professor of Philosophy at Southern Connecticut State University, Director of the Research Center on Computing and Society there, and Visiting Professor at De Montfort University in Leicester, England. He is a lifetime member of Computer Professionals for Social Responsibility, Past Chair of the Committee on Professional Ethics of the Association for Computing Machinery, and Past Chair of the Committee on Philosophy and Computers of the American Philosophical Association. For twenty-five years Dr. Bynum was Editor-in-Chief of Metaphilosophy, an international scholarly journal published by Basil Blackwell of Oxford, England. Dr. Bynum also edited Computers and Ethics, Blackwell, 1985; and co-edited Computer Ethics and Professional Responsibility, published by Blackwell in 2002.

ROBERT J. CAVALIER is Associate Teaching Professor of Philosophy at Carnegie Mellon. A member of the Department's Center for the Advancement of Applied Ethics, he directs the Digital Media Lab for Applied Ethics and Political Philosophy. Dr. Cavalier has been past President of the International Association for Computing and Philosophy as well as past Chair of the APA Committee on Philosophy and Computers (2000-2003). He has co-authored several award-winning interactive media applications, including A Right to Die? The Dax Cowart Case (Routledge, 1996).

SUSAN DWYER is Associate Professor of Philosophy and Director of the Masters Program in Applied and Professional Ethics at the University of Maryland Baltimore County. She is editor (with Joel Feinberg) of The Problem of Abortion, 3rd edition (Wadsworth, 1997) as well as Editor of The Problem of Pornography (Wadsworth 1994). Dr. Dwyer is currently working on Pornography: Freedom, Fantasy, and Moral Risk and Knowing Good and Evil: Psychopaths and Moral Responsibility.

CHARLES ESS is Distinguished Professor of Interdisciplinary Studies, Drury University. He has edited two volumes for SUNY Press, *Philosophical Perspectives on Computer-Mediated Communication* (1996) and (with Fay Sudweeks) *Culture, Technology, Communication: Towards an Intercultural Global Village* (2001). He also serves on the editorial board of *New Media and Society* and *Arts and Humanities in Higher Education*. With Fay Sudweeks (Murdoch University, Western Australia), Ess co-founded and co-chairs the biennial conferences on "Cultural Attitudes towards Technology and Communication."

LAWRENCE M. HINMAN is a Professor of Philosophy and Director of the Values Institute at the University of San Diego. He is author of *Ethics: A Pluralistic Approach to Moral Theory*, 3rd. ed. (Wadsworth, 2003) and *Contemporary Moral Issues*, 3rd ed. (Prentice-Hall 2004). In 1994, Dr. Hinman founded Ethics Updates and five years later began Ethics Videos, which provides free streaming video of ethics-related lectures, discussions and interviews.

JAMES H. MOOR is professor of philosophy at Dartmouth College. He developed early computer programs to teach symbolic logic and is co-author of *The Logic Book*, now in its fourth edition (McGraw-Hill, 2004). Along with Terry Bynum, Dr. Moor is co-editor of *The Digital Phoenix: How Computers Are Changing Philosophy* (Blackwell, 1998) and *Cyberphilosophy: The Intersection of Philosophy and Computing* (Blackwell, 2002). He is also editor of the philosophical journal *Minds and Machines* and of the recent book *The Turing Test: The Elusive Standard of Artificial Intelligence* (Kluwer, 2004).

HELEN NISSENBAUM is in the Department of Culture and Communication at New York University. Her research interests include ethical, social, and political dimensions of information and communications technology (privacy, security, accountability, intellectual property rights, computing in education); information and communications policy; and applied and professional ethics. She is author of *Ethical Values in an Information Society* (in progress) and of numerous compendia, articles, and policy reports.

LUCIANO FLORIDI was Lecturer in Philosophy at the University of Warwick (1990- 1) and joined the Oxford Faculty of Philosophy in 1990 and the Faculty of Computation in 1999. He is currently Associate Professor of Logic and Epistemology, a research position funded by the Università degli Studi di Bari, and in Oxford Senior Markle Fellow in Information Policy at the Programme in Comparative Media Law and Policy, and Coordinator of the Information Ethics research Group, Faculty of Computation. He has published over fifty papers in the areas are computer ethics and the philosophy of computing and information. His articles have appeared in such journals as

Ethics and Information Technology, International Journal of Human-Computer Studies, Metaphilosophy, Minds and Machines, Social Epistemology, Synthese, and *Zeitschrift für Allgemeine Wissenschaftstheorie.*

J. W. SANDERS is a Fellow of Lady Margaret Hall and a University Lecturer in Computation at the University of Oxford. He is primarily interested in mathematical aspects of computation but also in the philosophical foundations of computation.

RICHARD A. SPINELLO is Associate Research Professor in the Carroll School of Management at Boston College where he teaches courses on information technology ethics, social issues in management, and corporate strategy. He has written and edited five books on information technology ethics, including *CyberEthics: Morality and Law in Cyberspace* and *Regulating Cyberspace: The Policies and Technologies of Control.* He has also written numerous articles and scholarly papers on ethics and management that have appeared in journal such as *Business Ethics Quarterly* and *Ethics and Information Technology.*

HERMAN T. TAVANI is Chair of the Philosophy Department and Director of the Liberal Studies Program at Rivier College in Nashua, NH. He also holds an appointment as an ethicist in the Visiting Scholars Program at Harvard University's School of Public Health. The author of numerous publications in applied ethics, his published works have appeared in scholarly journals and periodicals as well as in textbooks, anthologies, proceedings, and encyclopedias. His recent books include *Ethics and Technology: Ethical Issues in Information and Communication Technology* (John Wiley & Sons, 2004) and *Readings in CyberEthics* (Jones and Bartlett Publishers, 2001), which he co-edited with Richard Spinello. He has guest edited special issues of two quarterly journals: *Ethics and Information Technology* (Kluwer Academic Publishers), for which he is also the book review editor; and *Computers and Society* (ACM Press), for which he is currently Associate Editor. He currently serves as Editor of the *INSEIT Newsletter*, a quarterly electronic publication.

JOHN WECKERT is a Senior Lecturer in Information Technology in the School of Information Studies at Charles Sturt University, Australia. He teaches mainly in the areas of Artificial Intelligence and Knowledge-based Systems, at both undergraduate and postgraduate levels, in both the internal and external education modes, and is involved in the organization of conferences and workshops in these areas.

Index